THE PRACTICE OF
FACILITATION

THE PRACTICE OF FACILITATION

Managing Group Process and Solving Problems

HARRY WEBNE-BEHRMAN

QUORUM BOOKS

Westport, Connecticut • London

Library of Congress Cataloging-in-Publication Data

Webne-Behrman, Harry.
    The practice of facilitation : managing group process and solving
problems / Harry Webne-Behrman.
       p. cm.
    Includes bibliographical references and index.
    ISBN 1–56720–067–2 (alk. paper)
    1. Group problem solving. 2. Group facilitation. I. Title.
HD30.29.W43   1998
658.4′036—dc21   97–32989

British Library Cataloguing in Publication Data is available.

Library of Congress Catalog Card Number: 97–32989
ISBN: 1–56720–067–2

First published in 1998

Quorum Books, 88 Post Road West, Westport, CT 06881
An imprint of Greenwood Publishing Group, Inc.

Printed in the United States of America

The paper used in this book complies with the
Permanent Paper Standard issued by the National
Information Standards Organization (Z39.48–1984).

10 9 8 7 6 5 4 3

To Michael, Geremy and Maya

what really matters

Contents

Figures   ix
Preface   xi

1. Introduction: Definitions and Challenges   1
2. Communication Skills   11
3. The Facilitated Meeting Process   21
4. Problem Solving in Facilitated Groups   49
5. Facilitation and Conflict Resolution   71
6. Facilitating Consensus   109
7. Facilitating Team Development   125
8. Stages of Group Development: Impacts Upon the Facilitator   145
9. Facilitation and Its Philosophical Traditions: 167
   Personal Reflections

Appendix A: Situational Conflict Styles Assessment Exercise   175
Appendix B: Role Plays   187
Appendix C: Sample Set of Meeting Notes from the Facilitator   197
Glossary of Terms   201
Bibliography   207
Index   211

Figures

1.1	Six Responsibilities of the Facilitator	5
2.1	Active Listening Techniques: Statements That Help the Other Person Talk	13
3.1	Functions of the Opening Statement	28
3.2	Considerations in Formulating an Agenda	31
3.3	Strategies for Managing Impasse	36
3.4	Key Issues of Closure	38
4.1	Preconditions for Effective Problem Solving	52
4.2	Mind Map	56
4.3	Age Breakdown of Riverside, USA	63
4.4	Racial/Ethnic Diversity of Riverside, USA	63
4.5	Food Service Unit Mind Map	68
5.1	The Conflict Cycle	75
5.2	The Conflict Budget	77
5.3	Conflict Management Styles	77
5.4	Payoffs for the Prisoner's Dilemma	79
5.5	Triangle of Needs in Negotiation	81
5.6	PEACE/6: A Six-Part Model for Conflict Resolution	85
5.7	Strategies for Managing Impasse	90
5.8	Special Concerns When Facilitating Multi-Party Disputes	92
7.1	Ten Factors Contributing to Team Effectiveness	127
7.2	Characteristics of a Healthy Organization	129
7.3	Strategies for Achieving Healthy Teams	131
7.4	Team Building Blocks	132

Preface

Several years ago, I outlined a book on facilitation that I hoped would fill a void in the field. It was based largely upon my continued teaching and training of work group facilitators, and it seemed to be timely as a resource for facilitators and others concerned with fostering effective group process. That book, *Guardian of the Process* (published by Collaborative Initiative in December 1994), was quite successful within that limited audience. But there are many others whose questions still require a thoughtful response: As a manager, how do I organize work teams so their meetings are more successful? As a team leader, how do I help my team build a consensus that all members accept and enthusiastically endorse? As a consultant, how do I help my clients solve problems and resolve conflicts so they can improve the quality of their organizations? As a facilitator, how do I improve my own skills as I encounter new types of clients and situations?

This book is intended as a field guide for all of these practitioners. It seeks to answer many of the pertinent questions about the facilitator role within a deeper understanding of the issues facing work groups. Using case studies, exercises, and strategies taken from nearly twenty years experience as a facilitator, mediator, educator, and consultant, I have attempted to share in a cogent, practical manner the model we use at Collaborative Initiative. There are specific suggestions regarding what to do and how to do it. But there are also sections that discuss why these things are important and opportunities to reflect upon the broader meaning of the approach.

The true test of success with a book of this type is in the "eating." I want you to read this book as a complete guide, stopping from time to time to practice strategies developed along the way. Then, it may be worthwhile to return and linger on certain sections that prove more relevant to your specific work. Finally, I hope you find this book to be a reference source in times of need. When you are stuck and require a process for getting going again with a work group, I hope you'll be able to turn a few pages here and find some help.

As in any enterprise of this nature, there are many people who deserve mention. First, there are professional colleagues who have been important models of how to do this work through the years. Members of the Center for Conflict Resolution in the early 1980s, provided a crucial foundation for my work in facilitation. From this group, I wish to especially thank Roger Volkema, who has continued to provide critical insights into effective group process in business throughout the years. Other colleagues from various organizations have been especially supportive through the years, including Sue Bronson, David Pilati, Zena Zumeta, Michael Lang, Ann Milne, Peter Salem, Gail Gumness, and Maggi Cage. Their insights and encouragement have clarified the need for this type of book.

This manuscript is the direct product of painstaking typing and editing by Patricia Salem, who has dedicated herself to the quality of the final product in a highly professional manner. She has continually sought ways to refine coarse material and to define ambiguous concepts. This book would never have made it to publication without her support. As well, Eric Valentine of Quorum Books has been a firm yet patient champion of the process. Since his initial commitment to the project nearly three years ago, Eric has remained a voice of reason and practicality. Finally, and most importantly, I wish to thank my partner and wife, Lisa Webne-Behrman. Her insights regarding the work we share are woven throughout the text. Her knowledge of facilitation and the integrity of her work keep me aware of the central focus of the role.

Chapter 1

Introduction: Definitions and Challenges

The term facilitator means, literally, "one who makes the process easy," and it is a concept that has gained in popularity in recent years. As businesses seek to increase staff participation in decision making and to develop democratic work places, the managerial role is undergoing profound transition. Managers and others are becoming de facto facilitators, as they are called upon to expedite communication among staff members from an impartial stance. But what does it take to be a successful facilitator? What guidelines are available to aid facilitators in their role as "guardian of the process," and how does the facilitator role change in varying circumstances? What are the underlying principles they follow?

This book seeks to answer these questions with some practical strategies for the facilitation of meetings, whether problem-oriented or conflictive, the formal meeting of an ongoing work group, or the informal efforts of a neighborhood wrestling with immediate crises. This book is offered because such a resource is now timely. We hope these ideas remain close at hand in times of urgency; if you come to rely on this handbook, we will know we have accomplished our purpose.

When we use the term facilitator in this book, we are speaking of a person (or persons, known as "co-facilitators") who has been openly designated by group members to be the caretaker of the meeting process. It may be an outsider who has been retained to provide this function. It may be the head of the group by title or ownership, or it may be a group member who has been designated on a temporary or long-term basis for this purpose. But the facilitator, in any event, is a person empowered by the group whose primary function is to guide the meeting process.

Facilitation, therefore, should not be confused with instruction, counseling, consulting, or other third-party functions. The facilitator is *neutral* with respect to the solutions of the problems being brought before the group, *objective* regarding the meaning of the alternative issues and resources relating to the problem, and *committed* ethically to collaboration and democratic decision making in problem solving. The facilitator is a negotiator for the process in this context, primarily concerned with apprizing participants of their own opinions through reflection, summarization, and clarification. This truly empowers them to participate effectively with one another to the best degree possible. In conflictive situations, the facilitator's role is very much like a mediator, a neutral third party committed to helping bring about consensual negotiation. However, some of the conditions under which facilitators and mediators operate may differ significantly (see Chapter Five, "Facilitation and Conflict Resolution").

In their path-breaking work *A Manual for Group Facilitators* (Auvine et al. 1977), the Center for Conflict Resolution defines the work of a facilitator:

A facilitator's job is to focus on how well people work together. The purpose of this focus is to insure that members of the group can accomplish their goals for the meeting. The facilitator trusts that each member of the group can share responsibility for what happens. The effect of this sharing can be to equalize the responsibility for the success or failure of the group (in whatever way that group has defined its goals and function) and to allow more people to have control in determining what happens within the group and what decisions are made.

This description remains timely today broadened far beyond its initial audience of cooperatives and progressive political activists. Today's facilitator brings together work teams to manage corporate change efficiently, diffuses tensions that arise from shifting social policies, and helps solve complex problems through collaboration among conflicting interest groups. These contexts cross all sizes and types of organizations and encompass diverse procedural challenges. Therefore, the role must be grounded in a clear understanding of the facilitator's responsibilities.

RESPONSIBILITIES OF THE FACILITATOR

Encouraging Full Participation

One of the facilitator's major responsibilities is to ensure that all members of the group have an equal opportunity to speak. This is a critical component of democratic process (Gastil 1993), and it is fundamental to groups using facilitation. Full participation must be perceived as open and accessible to all members, and it is the facilitator's responsibility to protect this privilege. This comes through turn taking, timing of discussion and debate, simplification of complex tasks into manageable problems, use of small group work, and other strategies. It is important to improve the participation of the reticent while channeling the energies of the engaged.

Fostering Effective Listening

It is also the facilitator's job to encourage group members to listen effectively to one another. It is one thing to speak, another to be heard. The facilitator promotes a safe listening environment, where people demonstrate their commitment to understanding one another, especially in the face of disagreement. This is accomplished through the establishment of ground rules, whether informal or parliamentary (including Robert's Rules, if properly applied), for clarity of decision-making procedures. Explicit attention is paid to participants' demonstration of their understanding conflictive positions (through restating, for example.) Most importantly, the facilitator models active listening, setting a tone of respectful leadership for the group. (Active listening, including restating, is discussed in detail in Chapter Two.)

Clarifying Goals and Agendas

Helping the group clarify its goals and the agenda that follows from those goals is another challenge that faces the facilitator. Whatever the configuration of the group that is meeting, it is a group with work at hand. The facilitator helps members clarify the nature of that work, helps them set realistic objectives and parameters for achieving it, and organizes a process that improves their chances of success in their endeavor. If this is a problem-solving group, the facilitator helps to clarify the problem, to analyze the steps required to solve it, and to keep the group on task. The facilitator helps track time, resources, and other agenda-sensitive concerns, while supporting full and meaningful participation.

Balancing Individual Needs with Group Tasks

All groups face the challenge of balancing the personal and collective needs of their participants. The facilitator's role is to help people remain sensitive to these inevitably conflicting challenges. He or she checks with members through regular evaluations of the process, both within the context of regular meetings and through separate communications with members between meetings. As groups evolve, the facilitator must remain sensitive to group members' differing perceptions of success and be vigilant regarding strategies available to the group to resolve conflicts. As group culture evolves, the facilitator helps orient new members to the norms of the group. Links between personal and group agendas are fostered. Veteran group members learn to cope with issues and concerns brought by new faces.

Encouraging Shared Leadership

A facilitated group is not one whose process is owned by a few; the meeting belongs to all. Therefore, the facilitator must help all members develop a sense of pride and purpose, build interdependent relationships that emerge from the strengths and abilities of all members, and transcend formal role relationships that may exist beyond the meeting. The facilitator accomplishes this by fostering an open and affirming environment, encouraging people to share skills and tasks, delegating responsibilities to interdepartmental subgroups between meetings, and other strategies designed to promote effective participation. The facilitator encourages members to take risks (rather than stay within traditional bounds), to play new roles, and to learn how to accept constructive criticism from one another.

Sharing the Role of Facilitator

Finally, and perhaps most importantly, the facilitator is committed to sharing this role with all other members. Even if someone has been formally designated, the truly empowering philosophy of this process encourages all to take responsibility for its perpetuation. We are frequently asked, "What are we going to do when you aren't here?" Our response is simple: "You will do what we have done, and you will learn how to do it well together." The greatest compliment to someone who has served as facilitator is to no longer be needed because the group's members now possess the skills to manage the meetings effectively.

In summary, the facilitator is the guardian of the process, the group member whose explicit role is to help all other members attend to the tasks at hand (see Figure 1.1). This is accomplished through attention to the issues set before you in this handbook, through practice and experience, and through a commitment to the values of facilitation. It is also accomplished through a continued willingness to learn about ourselves, our biases, our strengths, and our weaknesses in this work together. Through such reflection, we become far more able to support others in their work.

THE VALUES OF FACILITATION

The facilitated approach to group process is derived specifically from the belief that people are capable of solving the problems they encounter, and that they need to be empowered to do so. In short, they are *competent*. This belief challenges traditional approaches to management that control interactions of employees and limit access to key information to designated decision makers. It also runs counter to patronizing management styles that, while well intentioned, limit growth, investment, and participation by subordinates. In such organizations, the facilitation model lacks credibility: it is confusing and frustrating to participate in a process that appears democratic, only to have power removed at the discretion of the boss.

Figure 1.1
Six Responsibilities of the Facilitator

1. To ensure that all members of the group have an equal opportunity to speak.
2. To ensure that all members listen effectively to one another.
3. To help the group clarify its goals and the agenda that follows from those goals.
4. To help the group accomplish its tasks while maintaining the individual needs of its members.
5. To help all members exercise leadership functions in the accomplishment of group tasks.
6. To encourage all group members to facilitate the process of the group.

A second key value is democracy, a dedication to people participating effectively in the decisions that are meaningful in their lives. Democracy presumes competency, but it also requires further commitment. Participants are entitled to education and support if they are to have legitimate access to the power they have been given. In his excellent book, *Democracy in Small Groups* (1993), John Gastil presents a definition of democracy, with special emphasis on its application to small groups. He argues that an effective definition of democracy must include reference to: (1) group power; (2) inclusiveness; (3) commitment to democratic process; (4) relationships among individuals, including an affirmation of competence; and (5) deliberative procedures. As we examine the role of the facilitator and affirm the value of democracy within the facilitated process, we intend it to reflect the components Gastil has emphasized.

Clearly, this conception of democracy goes far beyond voting. The options for decision making transcend the traditionally limited alternatives of majority rule versus consensus. It is a deliberative opportunity for meaningful participation in the identification of problems, the development of alternative responses and strategies, and the application of meaningful criteria to decision making. It is an attempt to integrate the concerns of all stakeholders in the process and to engage in true collaboration.

A third important value is *equality*: equal access to information, equal participation in decision making, equal opportunity to exercise power within the group. Facilitators create group conditions that support assertive confrontation, the safe expression of dissent, and consensus building. Facilitation is a model of inclusion, not exclusion. We seek to embrace differences so they are understood and negotiated rather than turned into barriers. This also means coming to grips with the true parameters of the process facing a particular group. This group does not exist in utopia. The degree to which its members are not actually equal must be genuinely understood and resolved.

A fourth important value is *respect*, the sincere regard for the competency and rights of other members of the group. It has become clear from our work over the years that all members need not like one another or necessarily share the same concerns. However, they must be capable of extending fundamental respect to one another if they are to participate in a democratic group. This value is often represented by a commitment to effective listening, a desire to be concise and not dominate the discussion, and the use of assertive communication styles. It also means that, although I may not share your concern, I am willing to work with you to find an effective solution to a problem that is important to you. In so many relationships, the value of respect can be extremely powerful, and the specific strategies that groups adopt to demonstrate respect can be crucial to their success.

A fifth value of facilitation is *forgiveness*, the willingness to allow people to be the imperfect beings they are, to make mistakes out of their best efforts, and to move forward. This value is especially important in conflictive situations, where the willingness to forgive is so often in short supply. Participants must be willing to entertain the possibility that they can resolve the issues confronting them and go into the future with whatever relationship they now define together. If we truly believe that all participants are deserving of respect, it necessarily follows that they are deserving of forgiveness; if I am to engage in nonviolent conflict resolution with another person, this value is crucial to my ability to engage in the process.

There are likely other values that underpin the collaborative ethic promoted by facilitation. Those who assume this role must examine their own values and beliefs and understand the assumptions and prejudices brought to the process. Biases must be understood for their effects on the tasks before the group. These values of the competency of all people, the democratic process in our decision making, equality of participation in the deliberations of the group, respect for one another in our dealings together, and forgiveness for mistakes made along the way are vital to the facilitation model and its integrity.

EXAMPLES OF FACILITATION

In our work at Collaborative Initiative, we have consulted with numerous organizations, businesses, and public agencies in an attempt to establish internal facilitation systems. These experiences may shed light on the true opportunities and challenges faced when integrating the values and responsibilities of facilitation into the workplace.

A Shift to Team-Based Management in an Industrial Setting

A large manufacturing corporation with multiple sites and several thousand employees was making a transition from a traditional hierarchical model to a more decentralized, team-based management system. We initially determined together that a major cultural shift was occurring within the company, causing: (a) resistance to changes in roles and relationships; (b) fears regarding the consequences of such changes; and (c) powerlessness in resolving disputes effectively. Starting with leadership from both union and management, we provided training in facilitation and conflict resolution skills. While encouraging the informal application of these skills and modeling them in appropriate situations, we established a cadre of staff facilitators who could respond more formally, as needed.

Initially, while there remained a general distrust and concern among most workers, successes led to increased acceptance. Internal champions of the process encouraged broad experimentation, resulting in an extensive pilot project in a single plant. Following an overview of key concepts to all workers and managers, training in communication and conflict resolution skills was offered to small groups, on a voluntary (with incentives) basis. This effort reached 70% of the workforce. While perceived structural barriers remained significant challenges, the opportunity to discuss sources of resistance, fear, and powerlessness constructively resulted in a broad sense of ownership for the change process. From such a vantage point, establishing diverse opportunities for internally facilitated problem-solving groups, task forces, team meetings, and the like, became a natural next step.

A New Vision for an Established School District

A medium-sized school district had a long history of closed, hierarchical decision making, labor negotiation impasse, and distrust between staff and administration. A new superintendent brought a vision of participation and consensus into this environment, but he lacked the infrastructure to make site-based management a reality. He began by articulating the vision to his board and staff, modeling the process in his daily interactions. He created specific, meaningful opportunities for staff and administration to interact and problem solve together. We then became involved by: (a) training hundreds of staff in conflict resolution, mediation, facilitation, and consensus-building skills, both for themselves and for their students; (b) designing a peer-mediation/ conflict-resolution education system that extended from elementary through high school; and (c) training internal trainers who could replicate the training and monitor implementation throughout the district. The district simultaneously adopted site-based decision making in each building, created opportunities for staff to take the time needed in order to meet effectively, and facilitated genuine involvement in key planning decisions. As a result, there was a significant cultural transformation from which there is little likelihood of retreat. We played a relatively minor role in this shift, but we had the opportunity to witness its benefits.

Dealing with Bureaucratic Conflict within a Government Agency

A large government agency had evolved to a point where numerous divisions and bureaus were beset by conflict and distrust. As we approached this situation initially, it was through training in communication skills and interventions in specific disputes arising within the agency. But over a period of years an evolving ethic has emerged: rather than continuing to allow such problems and poor relationships to fester for ten years or longer, there is now an attitude that encourages intervention. With this shift, from management and staff alike, has come an increased desire to: (a) train individuals in mediation and facilitation skills; (b) design a problem-solving system that encourages site-based resolutions, using peer facilitators to help area bureaus; and (c) apply these strategies and skills to client interactions and services.

Increasing Productivity and Satisfaction within a University Department

A mid-sized university department had developed an atmosphere of distrust and dysfunction, resulting in low productivity and high levels of fear among faculty and staff. After externally facilitating small and large group problem-solving sessions, we provided training in facilitation skills and effective meeting management. We helped develop a management group for the department, in which group members rotated through the facilitator role. This resulted in both an increased sense of empathy and ownership for the process. We continued to monitor their development, through both routine observation of meetings and specific consultations on issues. Within two years, this became a more democratic organization with greatly increased participation and effectiveness.

From these examples, we may identify several factors that contribute to the establishment of a facilitated model of management within an organization. First, an affirming environment must be fostered through the timely establishment of ground rules for positive interaction. This process requires both internal organizational courage and strong facilitation skills. Also, communication channels must be established that provide safe avenues to demonstrate this new commitment. Externally facilitated meetings are useful strategies, but they should give way to internally directed approaches. Internal monitoring of new collaborative problem-solving approaches is needed to mentor people in their newfound skills. This helps staff make the transition from old patterns of interaction to new ones. A cadre of internal facilitators must be trained to fill a clearly defined place within the problem-solving and dispute resolution systems of the organization. This group forms the core of a new leadership model that helps all staff fulfill an emerging vision of participatory management. The formal leadership of the company (including labor and management) must then monitor the results of innovation carefully, honestly assessing their impacts on the organization. They must use the newly established communication channels to keep everyone informed. As leaders of learning organizations, managers must respond to new difficulties with integrity.

Chapter 2

Communication Skills

THE FACILITATOR AS COMMUNICATOR

There is a Native American tradition known as council for which we should be deeply grateful. When meeting in council, participants are concerned with being together and developing a clear, respectful understanding of each other, rather than dealing solely with issues (Zimmerman and Coyle 1991). This is a vital model for those of us who serve as facilitators, for it reinforces that communication is the underpinning of the democratic meeting.

The facilitator, as discussed in Chapter One, has several key functions within the meeting. The primary one is that of communicator, modeling effective communication and helping participants understand one another. The facilitator fulfills this role through the practice of several skills: active listening, practicing neutrality, and assertively negotiating for the process.

Active Listening

In active listening the goal of the listener is to understand, rather than to defend or judge. One communicates the commitment to understanding through both verbal and nonverbal behaviors. Contrary to many people's behaviors in conversations or meetings, it involves full participation by the listener. Instead of taking a critical or investigative stance, the active listener assumes a tolerant and respectful position. While this may appear to be common sense, for many of us it is hard work that requires patience, energy, and discipline. Active listening is the basis of the facilitator's credibility, and through its modeling, it serves as the foundation of trust, respect, and honest disclosure within democratic groups.

Active listeners demonstrate their commitment to listening through nonverbal behaviors, such as:

1. Staying focused on the speaker, with appropriate eye contact
2. Sitting upright or leaning forward, showing interest
3. Using a soothing, supportive tone of voice
4. Removing distractions, such as other work or telephone calls

Active listening requires empathy, the ability to put oneself in another person's position and understand that point of view. By withholding judgment, listeners are freed to support the speaker in his or her efforts to be understood. By not interrupting, listeners model behaviors that should be used by others in the meeting. By staying calm and focused, all are encouraged to participate with respect, not allowing emotions to overwhelm their desire to solve problems together.

Figure 2.1 summarizes active listening techniques and gives examples of how they might be applied. It should be reviewed by the facilitator and used as a reference by participants in the two activities outlined at the end of this chapter.

Practicing Neutrality

When we discuss facilitator neutrality, we are speaking specifically of the role of the facilitator in solution seeking. The facilitator should always remain neutral and objective with regard to subject matter being discussed. The facilitator is not neutral regarding process, and this is important to reiterate. The facilitator is clearly a stakeholder in regard to process and advocate passionately for democratic process. But the facilitator is impartial regarding solutions and must remain personally open to the possibility that either no solution will be found or that the group may decide to implement solutions that are different from those the facilitator prefers.

In taking a neutral stance, the facilitator must refrain from labeling certain solutions as preferable. Some ideas may appear to be inappropriate, but from the perspective of the participants they may be viable, legitimate options. Even if these options are not chosen, the respect demonstrated by the facilitator for them keeps everyone engaged in the process and encourages new ideas. Thus, even those who offered ideas that were ultimately rejected feel heard and understood in the decision-making process.

Refraining from labeling feelings is another important demonstration of facilitator neutrality. Instead of asking people, "Don't you feel badly about having argued this way?" or "How would you feel if you were treated the way you are treating her?" it may be more appropriate to ask people more generally, "How are you feeling, given the things that have been said here today?" The ability of the facilitator to resist judgments or opinions about substance is crucial to his or her legitimacy in the role.

Among the ways a facilitator demonstrates impartiality and encourages full participation is through the use of open-ended questions. Open-ended questions are

Figure 2.1
Active Listening Techniques: Statements That Help the Other Person Talk

Statement	Purpose	Do This	Examples
Encouraging	* To convey interest * To encourage the other person to keep talking	* Don't agree or disagree * Use neutral words * Use varying voice intonations	* Can you tell me more?
Clarifying	* To help clarify what is said * To get more information * To help speaker see other points of view	* Ask questions * Restate wrong interpretation to force speaker to explain further	* When did this happen?
Restating	* To show you are listening and understand what is being said * To check your meaning and interpretation	* Restate basic facts, ideas	* So you would like for your supervisor to trust you more. Is that right?
Reflecting	* To show that you understand how the person feels * To help the person evaluate his/her own feelings after hearing them expressed by someone else	* Reflect the speaker's basic feelings	* You seem very upset.
Summarizing	* To review progress * To pull important ideas, facts, and feelings together * To establish a basis for further discussion	* Restate major ideas expressed, including feelings	* These seem to be the key ideas you have expressed.
Validating	* To acknowledge the worthiness of the other person	* Acknowledge the value of the speaker's issues and feelings * Show appreciation of the speaker's efforts and actions	* I appreciate your willingness to resolve this matter.

those that: (a) cannot be answered through a simple "yes" or "no" response; (b) may be interpreted creatively to suggest a variety of possible responses; and (c) encourage brainstorming or other approaches to problem solving that create options and optimal solutions. Open-ended questions stimulate discussion in ways that may prove quite important, for group members are freed to explore possible solutions in new ways.

For example, a teaching staff was struggling with the implementation of team teaching approaches in their school. They had fallen into impasse, where every idea was rebutted by reasons why the idea wouldn't work. The facilitator posed the following question: "In what ways might we effectively implement team teaching at our school?"   This question led to a brainstorm of possible responses:

1. Eliminate it until next year.
2. Hire additional staff.
3. Include only staff who wish to participate, rather than mandating it for all.
4. Provide team planning times in order to have effective classes.
5. Involve staff who are in sixth grade this year, then expand to seventh grade next year.
6. Identify team "captains" for each cluster in the school.
7. Renovate the old wing so that combined classes have enough space.
8. Improve the heating in the old wing; too many kids are hot right now.

The facilitator's role at this point was to ask open-ended questions about these ideas, clarify their meaning, and lead the group into the important discussion about the criteria for evaluation of options.   By involving the staff in this type of discussion, alternating between large- and small-group contexts, the facilitator shifted the focus away from areas of disagreement and onto areas of potential agreement. When group members realized that there were many possible ways of interpreting the problem, they became less rigid and positional. Eventually, this process yielded solutions, not only to the problem initially identified, but to new issues that were now recognized as important to the group.

Assertively Negotiating for the Process

Assertively negotiating for the process may entail confronting possible abuses of the group's ground rules, allowing others equal air time in the face of domination by a few, or taking risks to check the general undercurrent of the group when others might be reluctant to do so. The facilitator has not only the responsibility to model effective listening, she or he must also demonstrate the skills required to make listening meaningful. This is demonstrated through the use of assertive communication, the sharing of one's needs and concerns while respecting the needs of the other persons involved. Our watchwords in this area are "bring them to their senses, not their knees," or, as a colleague has put it, "be hard on the issues and soft on the people." The courage to confront others in the meeting requires ongoing reinforcement and empowerment from other group members. By modeling this approach, the facilitator helps build risk-taking behavior and a willingness to apply the skills that exist among group members.

Several steps to follow in assertive confrontation are shared below. These should be kept in mind in any context in which assertive communication is desired. Although we have stressed the importance of the facilitator as a listener, it is also crucial to practice and model assertive confrontation as a tool of this process:

1. Clarify your rights, what you want, what you need, and your feelings about the situation. Try to let go of blame. Define your desired outcome and keep it in mind when you negotiate for change.
2. Arrange a time and place to discuss your problem that is appropriate for you and the other person. This may be outside the normal meeting context, but it may be appropriate within the group.
3. Use an "I"-message (see below) to define the situation and describe your feelings specifically and accurately.
4. Many of the situations requiring assertion are difficult areas for us and are likely to cause us some discomfort. One way to help get started is to admit to the difficulty and then follow with assertion. Examples: "This is really tough for me to say . . ." or "I'm feeling uncomfortable, but this is important to me . . ."
5. Don't feel like you have to respond immediately. It's okay to five yourself a moment to think about how you want to respond and what you want to say. You may even want to say something like "I'd like to think about that for a moment before I respond."
6. Let your body posture be as assertive as your words. Remember eye contact, firm stance, and assertive tone of voice.
7. Avoid using apologies when they are not appropriate. Prefacing your message with "I'm sorry, but . . ." often takes away from the effectiveness of the message and gives the other person the impression you don't feel you have the right to say what you are saying.
8. Assertive behavior aims at equalizing the balance of power, not in winning the battle by putting down the other person or rendering him/her helpless. (Davis et al. 1988)

Remember: Bring them to their senses, not their knees.

"I"-Messages

Among the strategies commonly employed in assertive communication is the use of "I"-messages. Use "I"-messages that express your feelings without evaluating or blaming others. Rather than saying "You are inconsiderate," or "You hurt me," the first part of the "I"-message would be, "I feel hurt." "I"-messages then connect the feeling statement with specific behaviors of the other person. For example, "I feel hurt when you ignore my wishes about where we meet." Contrast the clarity of this message with the vague blame statement, "I feel hurt because you are inconsiderate." The following is a suggested "I"-message formula:

I feel _____

when you _____ (specific behavior)

because _____ (personal consequences).

This leads to the example: "I feel hurt when you ignore my wishes about where we meet, because it indicates you don't care about whether we have a good meeting together."

The response to assertive confrontation may well be defensive, hostile, or confused. It is important, therefore, to follow up by actively listening to this response. Restate what you have heard, then follow it with an assertive statement. You may reasonably expect two people to go back and forth four times before they understand the problem clearly (Bolton 1978). Once the problem is identified, both people may proceed to generate possible solutions together. For example, here is an imaginary dialogue between two women:

Bonnie: I feel hurt when you ignore my wishes about where we should meet, because it indicates you don't care whether we have a good meeting together.

Ruth: What do you mean? I care that the meeting goes well. But I just don't want to spend a lot of time figuring out a location. We could meet right here for all I care.

Bonnie: So you are committed to an effective meeting. You just don't feel location matters very much. Is that right?

Ruth: Yes, that's right. And I didn't mean to seem inconsiderate. But what's the big deal?

Bonnie: Well, there are two things. First of all, if we stay in the office, we'll be distracted by calls and interruptions. Second, I'd like some privacy for this discussion.

Ruth: You are right about the distractions. They are unavoidable around here. And I didn't realize that privacy was a concern for you. Okay, where should we meet?

Bonnie: Thanks for listening to me and respecting my needs here. It was difficult to bring this up. How about using one of the conference rooms on the fourth floor?

Ruth: Fine, or if you like, we can just take a corner of the coffee shop. It's not busy at this time of day.

Bonnie: Sure, that will work well.

Often the handling of small concerns festers for some people. As a result, lessons about how to manage differences are lost. Of course, in a group context, these discussions are more complex and time consuming.

ACTIVITIES IN LISTENING AND COMMUNICATION

Active Listening Triads

This activity provides a format for practicing active listening, an important skill in communication and conflict resolution. Allow thirty to forty minutes for this activity.

Set up. Have participants brainstorm a list of possible topics for discussion. Ask them, "If you had a chance to talk about anything, what would you like to discuss?" Generate a list of eight to ten topics of interest to them, encouraging controversial subjects. Divide participants into groups of three. Within these triads, the following roles should be assigned:

1. Speaker: Pick any topic from the list on the board. You will have the chance to talk about subject for four minutes.
2. Listener: Your job is to use active listening to try to understand the Speaker's point of view, without sharing your own opinion. Use the range of techniques outlined earlier in the chapter, not merely sitting attentively and nodding, "uh huh."
3. Observer: Your role is to watch the Listener to see how well she or he practices active listening techniques to understand the Speaker. After the round is over, the Observer will give feedback to the Listener based on his or her observations. However, before giving your critique, seek feedback from the Speaker and Listener. This ensures their honesty in critiquing one another. Share positive feedback as well as negative criticism. Be as specific as possible, and be supportive!

Exercise. Conduct three rounds, with roles rotating among the participants after each round. Generally, it makes sense to discuss their experiences after each round, rather than to wait for the end of the exercise. Processing is very important to this activity. Take time to do so properly. If necessary, demonstrate good and bad listening styles to underscore key points.

Processing. The following points are important in evaluating the participants' experiences in this exercise:

1. Active listening is more than mere restating, which can sound patronizing; it is an empathic search for meaning by the Listener. Take the various strategies and use them to find what is important to the Speaker. Discuss differences between open and closed responses and their role in promoting or discouraging dialogue. An open response acknowledges the speaker's right to his or her feelings by demonstrating that the listener accepts the speaker's feelings, as well as his or her words. An open response indicates that the listener is empathic or understands. Conversely, a closed response denies the speaker a right to his or her feelings by demonstrating the listener's unwillingness to accept and understand.
2. Certain techniques are more or less useful, depending on the Speaker. For example, if the Speaker is comfortable telling a lot about the situation, restating, reflecting, and summarizing are most helpful. If the Speaker is reticent, the Listener may help by encouraging, clarifying, and validating.
3. The Observer has an important role, providing feedback to the Listener. However, Observers are often challenged to pay attention to the Listener, rather than the Speaker

and to resist the urge to join the discussion and express an opinion. In this way, the Observer is similar to a mediator who must simply check to be sure that disputants are listening to one another. In giving feedback, it is important that Observers wait until others have shared perspectives and to then give honest input. These active listening triads are useful in a variety of conflict resolution and communication skills workshops and form the basis for the conflictive activity described below.

Spend a Buck

This activity, which is adapted from a similar activity from the Community Board of San Francisco Elementary Conflict Manager Program, promotes active listening while solving a challenging problem. Small work groups of four to six participants work best for this activity:

Instructions. Your group has been given $25,000 by an anonymous donor. The donor wants you to decide how best to spend the money by choosing among the following options:

1. Hire additional staff in a key area where we have been short of people.
2. Do necessary repairs and renovations in a key area of the physical plant.
3. Hold an employee recognition event that supports the outstanding efforts of staff.
4. Provide staff development in a key training area.
5. Establish an innovative fund to encourage the development of new ideas within the company.
6. Provide an across-the-board salary increase, or an increase to a segment of staff that has been neglected in the past.

The donor insists that you must choose from among these options. Furthermore, your group must reach consensus regarding your choice (i.e., all group members find the decision to be acceptable). In reaching your decision, please follow the following ground rules:

1. One person speaks at a time, with no interruption.
2. Before stating your own opinion, you must use active listening to be sure you have understood the previous person's point of view to that person's satisfaction.
3. Work to find a solution that meets all members' concerns, is perceived to be fair, and considers the future.

Allow twenty to thirty minutes for groups to reach consensus. Then allow five minutes for them to process the experience in small groups before discussing it with the larger group. If they reach consensus very easily, you might have them try to decide on a second choice, but this is quite unusual, in our experience.

In summary, these activities help groups develop and master communication skills that will be applied to their work together. As they improve their collective ability to communicate, problem solving is more likely to occur within a positive, creative environment. As they experience conflict together, these communication skills will be tools for successfully negotiating and managing their differences.

Chapter 3

The Facilitated
Meeting Process

There is a deliberate order to the facilitated meeting that often eludes the casual observer. The phases of the process are outlined below. They demonstrate that as the process unfolds, the successful meeting evolves in a manner that is likely to meet participants' needs. These are phases; they are not intended to be as discretely mechanical as steps. This chapter offers a guide to your organization of the process, recognizing that different phases will be more or less emphasized in various situations. There is value in viewing each stage as a puzzle piece, rather than as a linear assembly line: by remaining flexible to understand how each piece contributes to our learning of the entire process, we remain open to discovering new tools that emerge from the experience itself.

PHASE 1: PRE-NEGOTIATION

The willingness of all parties to participate in a facilitated meeting is an often overlooked, yet critical, phase of the meeting process. Especially in conflictive situations, where it is natural for people to approach the possibility of a meeting with great reluctance and skepticism, the facilitator may need to engage in pre-negotiation with each participant. We define pre-negotiation as the intervention of a concerned third party to encourage participation in the negotiation process. The third party may be a stakeholder, that is, someone with a vested interest in the situation, or it may be a neutral player, a person whose primary concern is in the parties attempting to resolve their differences, solve problems, and so on.

The facilitator approaches pre-negotiation from a position of authenticity, attempting to encourage participation in the process, while respecting other options available to each person. Pre-negotiation requires the same skills as the facilitated meeting: The facilitator asks open-ended questions, seeks the perspective of each potential participant, and gets the lay of the land being entered. He or she also attempts to build rapport with each party by answering any concerns and addressing potential sources of resistance to participating in the next steps of the process. As appropriate, the facilitator gains insights into the history of the group and the issues to be addressed, including previous efforts to resolve concerns. Finally, the facilitator seeks to pull together the results of this fact-finding by offering a proposed agenda for next steps; in certain cases, the person or persons with power to approve the agenda may prove significant. In summary, the purpose of the pre-negotiation process is to gain the willingness of participants to engage in a facilitated meeting process together and to gain credibility for the facilitator as the organizer of that process.

The time required for pre-negotiation varies widely: In some circumstances we meet individually for 20 to 30 minutes with each participant, using the time to determine best future courses of action. On other occasions, brief telephone conversations with key players may be more appropriate. Levels of formality also vary: in official situations, certain protocol may be important, while in work groups a more relaxed approach may be most helpful. Certain ground rules, such as confidentiality, may need to be established in these discussions in order to gain a willingness to participate. In any event, pre-negotiation is an important initial phase that helps establish the foundation for the facilitated meeting process.

PHASE 2: MEETING AND GREETING

The "meeting" has begun before anybody arrives. The pre-negotiation phase has initiated the process, and the willingness of participants to attend the meeting has now been established. The facilitator takes care, therefore, with the details that precede the formal start of the meeting. Identifying an appropriate location, arranging furniture to ensure appropriate communication, providing refreshments, and checking the availability of flip charts and other equipment that may be needed are all important aspects of this preparation. Sending reading materials and an initial agenda is also an important way of focusing the participants' energy on the purpose of the meeting. The considered process of meeting and greeting flows from this attention to detail.

The facilitator uses the opportunity to greet people for specific purposes that are intentional and consistent with the needs of the group at that time. In an ongoing group, new participants begin to understand the operation of the group through informal discussion, and there is a chance to learn what they see as their roles in the meeting. Experienced members may wish to express satisfaction or reservations they bring from last time. For a new group, greeting provides an opportunity to relieve anxieties among some who arrive with them. Rarely, we have found, do people come to a meeting with equal perceptions of the experience about to begin, and it is with sensitivity to such diversity that we approach this phase.

Prior to an initial meeting, the facilitator may have only interacted with participants in another role, if at all. For example, a manager may normally be seen as an authority figure or decision maker; today, she or he is a facilitator, and this needs to be clearly understood by all. An outside facilitator may only have interacted through pre-negotiation. Taking a moment to validate and affirm each participant, especially those who may have been reluctant, can be important. There may also be introductions among participants that may prove important: an *ad hoc* task force may include people who have never met or people who only know each other by reputation (they may well be historic adversaries). Taking the initiative to help these people break the ice is a form of leadership offered by the facilitator.

Finally, the facilitator should consider where people will be seated and, if appropriate, direct people to sit at particular places (having name plates at specific locations simplifies this process). In certain types of meetings, it may be important that people from opposing sides sit near one another, while at other times there is value in seating allies together. The position of the company head or other person with higher authority may prove supportive or inhibit participation. Whatever one's approach, a facilitator should consider seating arrangements during this phase.

PHASE 3: SETTING THE TONE—OPENING STATEMENT AND GROUND RULES

Once all participants have settled into their seats, you are ready to formally begin the meeting. The meeting should begin with some form of introduction, an opening statement by the facilitator. Occasionally, the facilitator's remarks may be preceded by those of a sponsor, a person who has brought this group together for a particular purpose. For example, it has been important in our experience to have the process introduced when a task force has come together to establish particular policies or when mediating disputes among several organizations. If the sponsor's credibility is important, the ritual of introduction may underscore the integrity of the process.

An opening statement serves three major functions: it (a) sets the tone for the meeting, (b) establishes ground rules for the process, and (c) clarifies the process to be followed. The opening statement clarifies the role of the facilitator, not as a judge, counselor, or advocate for a particular viewpoint, but as guardian of the process. It is often helpful to lay out some history of how this meeting came to be and to state the purpose of the meeting as clearly as possible. The facilitator should offer initial ground rules for the operation of the group, followed by any changes or additions by the members, and gain consensual agreement to the ground rules.

There are many variations of ground rules, from the formal order of Robert's Rules to the gentle prodding of the Quaker meeting. Ground rules may be characterized by informality, with people saying to each other, "Well, let's go one person at a time with no interrupting. Let's focus on the problem at hand, not on other incidents that have bogged us down in the past. And we'll meet for one hour to start and schedule a second meeting if necessary." Or they may be a formal statement from the facilitator, establishing a tone of seriousness or re-establishing civilities that have been lost in a conflict. A group that is agreeing to a facilitated process, buttressed by the values discussed earlier, commits to follow certain ground rules together. They also commit to evaluating their abilities to honor these rules and to support the facilitator (and each member) in expressing concern when they are not being followed. Ground rules are not etched in stone; they are a point of departure for the process, to be revisited and revised as needs change. To become a prisoner of antiquated ground rules defeats the purpose of having them.

Establishing Ground Rules: A Case Study

A case study illustrates the importance of setting ground rules within a group. A university department was characterized by extensive conflict and dysfunction among the faculty. They had resolved that it was crucial to become a more cohesive team but they lacked insights into how that may best be accomplished. As we facilitated their problem-solving process, it became clear they had never clarified expectations regarding how they should communicate with one another. This had resulted in many misunderstandings, hurt feelings, and turf battles that threatened the future viability of their program.

Initially, they spent several hours talking about the results of these prior experiences. From this discussion, they identified ground rules that would ease their meeting new expectations of one another (examples of such rules are shared below.) After they had agreed to these ground rules, a new sense of hope and confidence filled the group. They built upon this confidence and began problem solving on substantive issues, always referencing the ground rules (now posted in the front of the room) whenever process problems arose. As facilitators, we may easily use the presence of such ground rules to bring people back to task or as leverage for encouraging democratic participation. They also serve as a means of validation for groups as they successfully struggle with difficult issues. In future meetings, this group routinely referred to the ground rules, occasionally revised them, and incorporated them into their self-facilitated meetings. These process changes resulted in great improvements in teamwork and productivity.

This group did not eliminate conflict through the establishment of ground rules, but they developed an important tool for managing conflict within a respectful group process. In subsequent months beyond our involvement, they were able to establish a new culture of honesty and trust that replaced their previous expectations. As new faculty joined the group, this new set of expectations allowed the group to accept new ideas. They made changes to adjust to common pressures and affirmed a course of action that reflected a common vision for the department. The ground rules were the foundation of a successful transformation in this case, and we have witnessed similar experiences in other groups.

Examples of Ground Rules

We are occasionally asked for examples of the ground rules that groups require in order to encourage a safe, affirming environment. The following list represents some of the more common, and important, rules to consider for your group.

1. *One person speaks at a time.* This piece of common sense is often at the foundation of safe, effective communication. Knowing that one will not be interrupted helps promote good listening.

2. *We will make a sincere commitment to listen to one another and to try to understand the other person's point of view before responding.* The use of active listening skills is an important tool for conflict resolution. The explicit commitment to try to understand conveys good will within the group.

3. *What we discuss together will be kept in confidence, unless there is explicit agreement regarding who needs to know further information.* The confidentiality of communications can be crucial to progress. It is important to be honest and clear in this area, as there is no common-sense understanding of confidentiality.

4. *We agree to talk directly to the person with whom there are concerns and not seek to involve others in gossip or alliance building.* The group's commitment to honest, direct communication regarding problematic areas is often a major shift in style. It requires hard work and diligent support from all members.

5. *We agree to try our hardest and trust that others are doing the same within the group.* The ability to say "no" is often elusive within work teams, especially within environments that are under pressure to satisfy all customer demands. To trust that your colleagues are as committed to success as you are, including the right to admit that certain deadlines cannot be met, is important to creating an affirming environment.

6. *We will support the expression of dissent in a harassment-free workplace.* The expression of disagreement is fundamental to honest communication and effective problem solving. The explicit support of this concept is important in groups where members perceive that new ideas are put down or where ownership of group meetings has been limited.

7. *We agree to attack the issues, not the people with whom we disagree.* This idea flows naturally from the rule that precedes it. Put-downs are out of line.

This list forms a starting point for further discussion about group ground rules. A typical list contains 5–7 of these rules; too many become difficult to monitor and cumbersome to enforce. As facilitator, you might share any others you feel are important in your group, but the adoption of ground rules must clearly be done by the group. This will become the first problem they solve together.

Activity: Setting Ground Rules

Ground rules, whether formal or informal, need the acceptance and commitment of the participants. Depending on the purpose of the meeting, the facilitator may offer initial ideas or seek them from group members. In the approach that follows, small groups are used as a means to elicit ideas from participants. First, the facilitator clarifies the purpose of having ground rules.

1. *The facilitator introduces the concept of ground rules to the group.* Ground rules are initially defined as, "rules of conduct that will govern the process of interaction among group members in the meeting." The purpose of ground rules is to support an effective, democratic, respectful, inclusive group process, through which all members may be encouraged to express ideas safely and effectively, negotiate through areas of difference, and reach consensual agreements.

2. *The facilitator divides the group into subgroups of 3–5 members.* Occasionally, there is value in "intentional subgroups," where membership is assigned in order to promote certain types of communication. Generally, however, this initial formation is more random. The facilitator then asks each group to consider:

> What are some ground rules you feel would be helpful to the work of this group? Please take five minutes to brainstorm possible ground rules that may be helpful.

3. *The facilitator then records the reports of each subgroup, identifying ideas for ground rules and criteria that are emerging as significant to group members.* These reports are recorded without judgment, using discussion only to clarify ideas as they are shared.

4. *The facilitator then seeks to build consensus among group members regarding the ground rules they will use for their deliberations.* Generally, several key ideas have emerged from various subgroups. These form a confidence-building consensus and a foundation upon which to build. Often, there are differing interpretations and understandings of the ground rules that have been offered. For example, the term "confidential" has varying meanings to participants. The facilitator helps people navigate this problem-solving process. Be patient with this process, for it takes much longer than most members would have anticipated. Some may even get frustrated that the group is delaying its real business, spending time on small details. But if there has been any history of conflict that has prevented the group from operating effectively, this activity may prove to elicit deeply held fears and concerns that must be respected.

5. *The facilitator then posts the ground rules in a prominent place.* The facilitator posts rules where they may be viewed by all. In some cases, members sign this sheet in a small ceremony. In most cases, copies are made for all members. It is important

at this stage to be supportive of the group. Encourage the group to revisit the ground rules from time to time. Often it is appropriate to designate a specific time in the future at which this evaluation will occur. Participants should also be encouraged to take personal responsibility for enforcement and monitoring, as the facilitator is only one member with a stake in the group's success.

More on Opening Statements

In addition to clarifying ground rules and the facilitator's role, the opening statement is used to educate participants about the organization of the meeting. We are not yet delving into specifics of the agenda but are bridging participants' experiences from the world outside the meeting into the focused needs of the session. Psychologically, this transition is crucial if we are to commit our energies to the present, rather than remain mired in the past. Specifically, the facilitator is speaking about substantive needs of the group. For example: "In this meeting, we will address several issues, but we will tend to use a similar procedure for examining each one. First, we will give each person an opportunity to express initial positions—that is, the desired outcome they'd prefer on that issue. Then, after clarification and sharing needed background information, we will generate several possible options for solving the problem, without judgment. Third, we will discuss criteria that may be appropriate for selecting the best solutions, and eliminate those options that are clearly unacceptable."

As you can see in the example above, the facilitator's discussion gives participants a window into the process that they share together. They are making a psychological transition into a common experience through the opening statement. This phase sets the tone for all that follows. While it is presumptuous to give the facilitator more credit and power than is deserved vis-à-vis the outcomes of the meeting, it is naive to overlook the power, both actual and potential, exercised in negotiating for the process in the opening statement. (See Figure 3.1 for a summary of these functions.)

The facilitator's opening statement may be followed by statements from each participant. This is often called, check-in, for it affords each group member an opportunity to share how he or she is feeling as this meeting begins. Check-in may be focused; for example, a continuing group may start with a statement from each person about the last meeting. For other groups, check-in may meet important social needs by sharing personal items at the start of the meeting, allowing the group to focus on its business with the rest of the time (some groups actually set aside an hour for check-in, because it is so important to the members). However accomplished, check-in can be an important meeting phase that gives members a sense of the group that may otherwise be overlooked. If omitted, members may have distractions that serve as unknown barriers to effective participation.

Figure 3.1
Functions of the Opening Statement

1. Sets the tone for the meeting.
2. Establishes ground rules for the process.
3. Clarifies the process.
4. Clarifies the role of the facilitator as the guardian of the process.

PHASE 4: AGENDA SETTING

It is now time to focus on the formal agenda for the meeting. The agenda is an intentional ordering of items for discussion, related to the purpose of the meeting. Items on the agenda should reflect the investment of the participants. The facilitator's role is to create an initial agenda that can assist the group in determining that purpose and accomplishing its work for the day. In formulating an agenda, the facilitator should consider: (a) types of items to be discussed; (b) the sequencing of items; (c) the amount of time required for each item individually; and (d) the timing of items collectively. There are numerous philosophies regarding each of these concerns; we present our current wisdom on the subject and encourage the reader to experiment, share insights from prior experiences, and continue improving on these ideas.

Types of Agenda Items

1. *Information items are brief, timely, and relevant types of information that group members need to know.* These may include announcements of changes, notices of resources being made available for later discussion, or other one-way communications that certain members feel should be shared with other members. The only discussion involved in information items is clarifying discussion; any further conversation goes beyond the purpose of this item. Often, members will present an information item that warrants further discussion; if so, it should be added to the appropriate part of the agenda or reserved for discussion at a future meeting.

For example, the announcement of the company picnic might appear to be an information item, even if it involves sign-up for picnic foods to bring. But when people start raising concerns about the date and location of the event, it becomes a discussion item. The facilitator's role is to help the group focus on the item at the level desired by the group, in order to achieve its meeting purpose.

2. *Discussion items are issues that warrant the full attention and participation of the group.* These items generally run a bit longer than information items; under some circumstances, a single discussion item may be

the entire agenda for the meeting. Participants are encouraged to share their perspectives and concerns honestly with one another, as well as to listen with understanding to differing perspectives. The facilitator models this approach to communication. He or she may actively engage those who are reluctant or channel communication of those who are dominant. The purpose of discussion items is to illuminate, not to reach decisions regarding the issues at hand. Differences are expressed with deep passion and respect. Fear, anger, and upset are all understandable feelings that need to be expressed within discussion; their articulation need not preclude others from viewing matters differently. The facilitator seeks to understand and be empathic. Through this model, all group members are engaged in the discussion. For many, this is the most challenging aspect of facilitation.

3. *Decision items are issues that require judgments and action decisions during the meeting.* Decisions may be reached by consensus, majority rule, or other decision-making processes (see Chapter Six, "Facilitating Consensus," especially "Other Decision-Making Options Within Democratic Groups"). The group must participate effectively both in determining the decision-making procedure and, ultimately, in making the decision itself. The role of the facilitator in this process is to ensure that all members have an opportunity to participate effectively. This includes the right to pass without comment. The group operates within its adopted decision-making rules in a timely manner. This last concern of timeliness should not be overlooked. Most meetings have several agenda items, and it is the facilitator's responsibility to help participants stay attuned to the variety of issues facing them.

A rushed consensus will often be perceived as undemocratic, and it will undermine the integrity of the decision and the willingness of group members to participate in future discussion. The facilitator must seek a balance between being and doing in the process of the group, helping them be together (cohesion) while gaining a necessary sense of accomplishment (effectiveness); both are necessary components if a group is to achieve its purpose.

These three types of items are archetypes, blended in various hybrids throughout the meeting process. The facilitator should help members clarify their expectations of each item honestly so they may realistically accomplish their goals within the parameters of the meeting.

Sequencing Meeting Items

Sequencing of items is another important consideration of agenda planning, contributing to the rhythm and flow of the meeting. Often, people find it most satisfying to gain a quick sense of accomplishment by working through easy items. Scheduling information items or easy decision items, which require little time, at the start of the meeting helps people feel that they are getting things accomplished. However, it may prove useful to save such items for later in a difficult meeting, as they can break the seriousness and tension that follow a challenging discussion.

It is our general practice to begin with information items and then move into an important, but medium-length, issue. It should be an issue that all agree is worth discussing. It may be a discussion item that people recognize as such (preferably it should not be an item that may easily stretch into a drawn-out decision item). It could be an issue that will build confidence and encourage people to continue. This item should be followed by a key issue requiring action (decision) today, one that is commonly perceived to be an important issue. Such discussion, after a brief break, may be followed by an item that is fun and easy for people to enjoy. On occasion, the facilitator may even prepare an activity that meets this need (we call these "light and livelies"). This helps energize the group and gives participants a renewed willingness to participate thoroughly in the process. It is also helpful to group related items together on the agenda. This way, the group uses information from solving one problem to address a similar issue. As a result, momentum develops, and the group is more efficient.

Timing the Meeting

Time allotments for individual items should be considered by the facilitator and then decided upon by the group. These should be analyzed as realistically as possible, considering the type of item (i.e., information, discussion, decision) and the skills of the group in addressing such items. Insights gained from pre-negotiation should be taken into account. If there are conflictive perspectives on an item, appropriate time must be allocated for their honest expression, clarification, and negotiation. Generally speaking, information items require only a few minutes; if longer, the presenter might consider an alternative form of presentation, such as a memorandum. Discussion items may range from five to fifty minutes or longer, depending upon complexity and interest. Participants should clarify the amount of time they wish to devote, and the facilitator should help them make that time meaningful. Decision items vary with complexity, degree of consensus prior to the meeting, decision-making procedure being used (for example, majority rule is often less time-consuming than consensus), and whether or not further discussion is required prior to making the decision. Again, it is the facilitator's role to help the group achieve its purpose as reasonably as possible, balancing their task and maintenance needs.

Timing the collective meeting is the final agenda setting function of the facilitator. When the total agenda of old business (or carry-over items), anticipated new business, and unforeseen business is taken into account, it will appear to take x minutes. The facilitator should check with group members to see if this time total is acceptable, or if there are any concerns (that arise from people needing to leave early, for example). If there are concerns, these must be resolved satisfactorily, under the group's ground rules, before proceeding. (See

Figure 3.2 for a summary of the foregoing considerations.) A significant source of frustration for many people comes from staff meetings that are filled with too many items and too little time. Another comes from board meetings that go on indefinitely, until the agenda is completed. Most groups find it far more satisfying to have clearly agreed upon starting and ending times, including an understanding of how non-present members will be considered by the group (for example, the group may agree to refrain from decision items once anyone has left). The facilitator helps the group start and end as scheduled or helps the members express feelings and concerns about the schedule not being honored. It is often considered a sign of respect to attempt to start and end on time. It is problematic when meetings routinely start and end late. It is symptomatic of other problems when people come to accept this as a fact of life over which they have little influence.

Figure 3.2
Considerations in Formulating an Agenda

1. Types of items to be discussed:
   Informational items
   Discussion items
   Decision items
2. Sequencing of items
3. Time allotments
4. Timing the collective meeting

PHASE 5: SHARING IDEAS AND CONCERNS—PROMOTING ACTIVE LISTENING

The major portion of any facilitated meeting is the time spent sharing ideas and concerns among members. This may seem obvious, but when compared to many typical meetings, this goal is more easily set than achieved. In many meetings, the manager (or other designated leader) will commonly report his or her perspective on issues facing the group, followed by questions, comments, and answers. Perhaps there are technical reports offered by individuals perceived as knowledgeable on a particular subject. The meeting might then include agenda items from other members, perhaps shared by going around the table, until either the time or the agenda have been completed. Although it is hoped that such meetings produce an opportunity for meaningful dialogue, in reality many of these meetings are characterized by one-way or two-way communications. Frequently, many members of the group are silent for significant portions of the meeting.

A facilitated meeting is characterized by multi-party, multi-directional communication, where numerous group members initiate discussion and respond across the table to one another. There should be little differentiation among leaders and followers in the direction of ideas. This markedly different flow of information is due, in part, to the active role of the facilitator in fostering effective communication among members of the group. This is achieved through the use of active listening, assertive responses, open-ended questioning and leadership in problem solving.

As discussed earlier, active listening is the process of seeking to understand another person's point of view, demonstrating a desire to understand the meaning of that person's communication without judgment. Active listening involves both verbal and nonverbal responses. In this phase of the meeting, the facilitator routinely encourages participants to share their perspectives with one another, seeks clarification of ideas and feelings, restates and summarizes those concerns, and helps members validate one another, especially at points of difficulty or impasse.

The facilitator also assists members in assertive confrontation with one another. In this process, people clearly and specifically state their needs in a respectful manner. The facilitator enforces the ground rules established by the group, assists in the clarification of confusing issues as they arise, and helps members listen to one another. Participants evaluate the meaning of their differences and negotiate solutions together.

Finally, the facilitator fosters effective communication by encouraging open-ended responses to the issues that are raised. There is frequently great reluctance, even in groups where members are quite comfortable together, to express dissent. By encouraging positive responses that support the expression of differences, key ideas are more likely to be fully expressed.

As the facilitator works to support the process, a number of concerns and difficulties arise in practice. How does the facilitator resist offering suggestions? How are judgments and biases managed? How do you address your own ideas of valuable solutions being missed by the group? There are differing philosophies regarding how best to respond to these questions. From our experience, we assume a posture that is actively supporting the process. This means that ideas or suggestions that help participants be at their best in developing solutions are appropriate and encouraged of the facilitator. But the facilitator should resist temptations to offer substantive suggestions whenever possible. As judgments creep into your consciousness, be aware of their existence as much as possible. *Why are they present? Are they appropriately my concern in this role? Are these biases affecting my focus on the process? Is there anything I can do to manage these biases?*

Occasionally, a facilitator needs to step away from a situation if such concerns become too great. If one is also a group member, there is value in passing the clipboard to another for the discussion of a particular item, if greater objectivity is required. This is not a flaw but a sign of honesty; you have recognized the need for the process to be supported.

In summary, the facilitator's primary role in the major portion of the meeting is to help people communicate effectively with one another. This includes a commitment to fostering active listening and assertive communication, affirming the ground rules of the group, and following the agenda previously developed. These considerations are paramount if a willingness to problem-solve is to be present. The problem-solving process will probably fail if communication channels are viewed as closed or clogged.

PHASE 6: PROBLEM SOLVING

Problem solving is the process by which people seek effective responses to important situations. In such approaches, people take deliberate actions; these actions form the essential outcomes of decision-making procedures. There are many issues facing groups that are not perceived to be problematic. At certain times, many groups find scheduling, budgeting, and other issues to be fairly routine. Even if these are complex situations, they recognize effective strategies through which they may find decent solutions. At other times, these same issues can be extremely problematic: old solutions no longer work; previously satisfactory approaches now face resistance; or new people join the group who have different values and experiences bringing new concerns. It is not a matter of fault or blame that groups have problems. It is a natural consequence of being a group that problems will arise. In a democratic group, the honest expression of these issues is at the heart of its process.

The facilitator's responsibility is to help the group devise problem-solving approaches that maximize their chances of achieving optimal solutions. This is achieved through leadership in problem identification and analysis. By deferring judgment of alternative solutions and clarifying criteria by which the group will choose the best solutions, the group then utilizes a decision-making procedure that suits the problem and is consistent with the group's ground rules. Group members can then evaluate the problem-solving process and learn from it. Problem solving is addressed in greater depth in Chapter Four and is discussed here only as it relates to the other steps of the meeting process.

Within the meeting agenda, the group has identified the items it will address. The need to problem-solve might arise for any type of item. For informational items, a problem may arise if unanticipated discussion and/ or decisions need to be made, perhaps taking time that has been otherwise allocated within the meeting. For discussion items, problems frequently arise over the scope and definition of the topic being discussed: Some people may feel that the group should only discuss "the current scheduling dilemma," for example, while others may see the issue as "arising from ongoing labor shortages in the department." Finally, decision items most commonly present problems. As issues appear to be complex, patience is lost, and people tire, solutions to some appear obvious while they remain elusive to others. In all of these cases, the facilitator bears a special responsibility within the group to help devise a process by which people simultaneously reach efficient decisions for effective solutions and uphold the values of competency, democracy, equality, respect, and forgiveness that form the foundation of the facilitated meeting.

Some groups become overwhelmed with minutiae, the little decisions that eat away at time, energy, and resources. The facilitator may help the group categorize such issues and devise a process, such as delegation to a subgroup, by which such problems get solved. Occasionally, there are aspects of the discussion that, while worthwhile, prevent effective focus on the problem at hand. The facilitator needs to ask for clarification when such pathways are taken, helping the group recognize where they have gone and decide together where they would prefer to be. Other groups are stalled by the complexity of the issues they face. In such cases, the facilitator helps them make the problem manageable and use the skills they have to navigate difficult terrain together. Finally, other groups reach impasse and become personally stuck with one another. Here, the facilitator helps members understand their underlying concerns, supports them on working through difficult issues, and helps them find new energy.

The facilitator does not need to be an effective problem solver. The facilitator helps the group become effective at solving its own problems, meeting its own needs, and defining its own terms. Ownership of both problem and solution must belong to the group, not to its facilitator. Creating a climate that fosters effective communication for responding to the right problems is an important responsibility of the facilitator.

PHASE 7: NEGOTIATING THROUGH IMPASSE

Impasse is a point during negotiations at which parties perceive that they are no longer able to find effective solutions. It is characterized by inflexible attitudes, emotional fatigue, and a lack of creativity in problem solving: a stalemate. It is important to recognize that impasse is a normal phase of any conflict resolution process. It offers significant opportunities for new insights and collaborative solutions. Therefore, rather than viewing this phase as reflecting failure, it should be perceived as an opportunity for significant, meaningful learning that would never occur in a more superficial treatment of the negotiation process. One of the primary challenges facing the facilitated group is the chance to make such progress. The facilitator's role in negotiating through impasse is to help the group accept this phase as a normal aspect of the process, honestly confront the emotional elements it presents, and seek insights into whether or not they wish to continue.

Strategies for Dealing with Impasse

Identify underlying concerns. As discussed in greater detail in Chapter Five, disputants take a positional stance into the negotiation. They express certain ideas as wants, rather than in terms of underlying needs or interests. We must help them express themselves in terms of substantive, emotional, or procedural needs, rather than remaining entrenched in initial positions.

Respect the variety of needs. This is often difficult for group members, who only view the issues in terms of their own values and beliefs. Clarifying these differences with respect and tolerance may be important to generating a renewed willingness to negotiate. This may be especially important in value-based disputes, where parties typically perceive their core beliefs to be at risk. The group must renew its commitment to ground rules that allow the variety of beliefs to exist, and focus instead on interest-based concerns that may be negotiable.

Explore alternatives to a negotiated agreement. This strategy may provide an important moment of truth for group members in impasse who may no longer feel able to problem solve. By helping them look at their alternatives, they may gain renewed energy to seek solutions through negotiation. Of course, they may also clarify their lack of interest in finding such a solution, resulting in a clearer understanding of the reasons to adjourn.

Experiment with active listening variations. Experimentation can present creative opportunities to break impasse. Have group members reformulate in different subgroups, have them intentionally restate and summarize to one another, and have them role play each other's perspectives. By giving group members intentional opportunities to listen to one another, rather than forging ahead with problem solving (it can even take the form of an exercise, setting aside the issue at hand), empathy may be restored and we can return to problem solving.

Respect silence. Like diversity, silence must also be honored. There are times when the quiet allows group members to reflect on their current situation. It may be accompanied by a break, a reflective walk outside, or similar activities. Occasionally, a silent time may be combined with a focused written exercise or caucus.

Talk about feelings. Talking about feelings in impasse can be a powerful strategy for transcending it. Participants benefit from acknowledging their frustrations, remembering other successes, and discussing fears that come with lack of resolution. Supportive validation and reflection from the facilitator can be extremely valuable.

Caucus. Caucus allows the facilitator the opportunity to meet with each individual (or with defined subgroups or parties) separately. It is especially useful during impasse, for caucus allows the facilitator to: (a) explore possible sources of resistance, some of which may have gone unstated; (b) serve as "agent of reality" while not embarrassing individuals or betraying neutrality; and (c) break the pattern of gridlock that has emerged, helping people gain a needed emotional release from one another. It should be noted that whatever is said in caucus is confidential, unless permission is given by all involved to share it in open session.

In approaching any of these strategies, as summarized in Figure 3.3, it must be remembered that a natural conflict will exist between the being (maintenance) and doing (task) needs of any group. At times, facilitators may fall prey to the task needs and issues that present themselves, focusing on substantive outcomes as the only true measures of success. But, in many situations, group members also have a strong need for affiliation and support, for respect of process while going slow on outcomes. The facilitator must remain flexible and respectful of this variety and not become overly responsible for pushing the agenda before the group is ready to assume it. (See Chapter Five for a more thorough discussion on strategies for managing impasse.)

Figure 3.3
Strategies for Managing Impasse

1. Identify underlying concerns.
2. Respect a variety of needs.
3. Explore alternatives to a negotiated agreement.
4. Try active listening variations.
5. Respect silence.
6. Talk about feelings.
7. Caucus.

PHASE 8: BUILDING CONSENSUS

The process previously outlined generally results in the emergence of consensus on the various issues facing the group. Consensus is defined here as a situation in which all members of the group find the outcomes to be acceptable. A consensual process is also one in which members perceive the environment of problem solving to be safe and where dissent may be expressed with integrity. Consensus is most effectively reached through a process of clear ground rules, effective listening on the part of all members, and a sense of legitimate empowerment within the group. It is the facilitator's responsibility to help the group achieve a level of consensus that is appropriate to the issues and consistent with the ground rules of the group. It is also his or her role to provide for evaluation of the process and to clarify the degree to which the consensus reflects honest, satisfied agreement versus a sense of coercion or exhaustion.

This goal is achieved through effective structuring of the problem-solving process and the assertive management of conflict, both discussed earlier.

Building consensus relies upon: (a) a commitment of participants to use consensus as a decision-making option; (b) an attitude of respect for the contributions of all members; (c) sufficient freedom from external hierarchies to independently reach decisions; (d) a commitment to evaluating process within the group, and to learning from such evaluation; and (e) sufficient knowledge, information, and skills available to make an informed decision.

The facilitator works with the group to establish and enhance the presence of such conditions for decision making. Note that I am not suggesting the need for trust in order to be successful. While trust may certainly enhance consensus, it is not prerequisite. In fact, since most groups tend to be characterized by an absence of trust, this point is essential. Participants are driven to consensual agreements by self-interest, and the evaluation component of a good agreement reduces the need for trust, per se. (See Chapter Six for a more thorough discussion of these strategies.)

PHASE 9: CLOSING AND EVALUATION

The concluding phase of the facilitated meeting is an important, though often overlooked, aspect of the process. It sets the stage for future interactions, with several possible results. There may be an agreement that resolves outstanding issues, or there may be decisions regarding future actions to be undertaken by all or some members. There may be needs for further research or other communication, possibly involving parties not present at the meeting. Or there may be varied perceptions of how the process is going thus far.

Key Issues of Closure

Identifying the importance of evaluation within the agenda. By explicitly presenting the evaluation process as a phase of the meeting, group members improve the likelihood of it being given appropriate time. The facilitator may even offer a structured evaluation process to help the group and, in multi-session situations, provide for written feedback between meetings.

Reviewing agreements before adjournment. This is an important way to improve understanding of the issues resolved. Yet it is frequently assumed to be clear without formal restatement. However, agreement review is a critical need, especially in conflictive issues; indeed, the ritual of signing an agreement is often appropriate to symbolize resolution of the issue.

Delegation and assignment of responsibilities between meetings. This plays an important role in the continued investment and involvement of the group. The true work of the group usually occurs between meetings. The facilitator's leadership in acknowledging this fact and helping members assume realistic, balanced responsibilities commensurate with their needs can be vitally important.

Separating process from product. This is another important component of the closing phase. The group should take a moment to reflect on its meeting process and have members recognize and support one another. It is also imperative to acknowledge areas that require improvement in the future. (See Figure 3.4.) This is part of the ongoing learning of the group, and it provides insights that may prove especially useful in the future.

Figure 3.4
Key Issues of Closure

1. Identifying the importance of evaluation within the agenda.
2. Reviewing agreements before adjournment.
3. Delegation and assignment of responsibilities between meetings.
4. Separating process from product.

PHASE 10: BETWEEN MEETINGS

There is great variation in the needs of groups between meetings, depending upon the mission of the group, the needs of members, and the role of the facilitator as a resource in accomplishing tasks between meetings. As noted earlier, the facilitated group must explicitly regard that time between meetings as a meeting phase. The facilitator may have special responsibilities for sending information to members, implementing decisions of the group, organizing the agenda for the next meeting, checking with people who were absent, scheduling resource people to come to a future meeting, organizing facilities, and so on.

In conflictive situations, the facilitator may need to communicate with each group member (or caucus, for that matter) in order to clarify the needs for the next meeting. This may be especially pertinent after the group has concluded a discrete phase of its work and may be groping for clarity of mission. Caucus may be helpful if the meeting adjourned in impasse, or if there were varying perceptions of success of the process. In a very real sense, the pre-negotiation phase recurs between meetings.

By treating the time between meetings as a legitimate phase of the process, the facilitator is able to consider the value of other negotiations that may need to occur, such as discussions by representatives with constituents or conversations within subgroups, that could not occur at the meeting itself. In this manner, a systematic approach to organizing the meeting process may be undertaken, truly facilitating the process of the group toward achieving its mission.

As a related concern, the facilitator may also evaluate the merit of participants engaging in direct negotiations with one another between meetings. This may be especially worthwhile if the goal of the meeting process is to have members of two or three separate groups work more effectively together or if theirs is a problem-solving goal that relies upon long-term structural changes, such as a merger. There may be resistance to this idea among participants, however, as they are used to dealing poorly with one another, and trust of their abilities to address issues together may be low. Also, they may be more comfortable in the structured setting of the facilitated meeting, depending upon a third party to express concerns on their behalf. The facilitator's response to such opportunities must be judicious, for the momentum gained in any given phase or meeting may be fragile.

CASE STUDIES IN THE FACILITATED MEETING PROCESS

Board Retreat

A nonprofit human services agency decided to utilize an external facilitator for their board of directors' meeting. The agency director had historically run these meetings, but he now felt there were some challenging issues facing the group. As the agency had grown, it had become unclear where priorities should be placed, what role the board should play in meeting those priorities, and what process should be used to recruit new board members to fulfill the emerging needs of the agency. In addition, the board had little history of effective group process; their meetings had always been sessions dominated by the agency director and one or two senior members, where most staff would passively receive information from their superiors.

The facilitator discussed the meeting at length with the director, to gain his perspective on the purpose of the meeting and its priorities. The facilitator then sought written input from each of the eight board members regarding the meeting, their hopes for it, and any hesitations or concerns they might be bringing to the session (Phase 1: Pre-negotiation). From these ideas, the facilitator drafted a tentative agenda for the meeting that was shared with the director and approved:

TENTATIVE AGENDA
1. Introductions/Ground rules/"Check-in" (twenty minutes)
2. Outcomes Identification Exercise: What are our expectations of one another in our work together on this board? (sixty minutes)
    a. Small group sharing of ideas
    b. Large group affirmation of priorities
3. Mission Review and Clarification (ninety minutes)
    a. What strategies might be useful for achieving this mission?
    b. In what ways might Board members contribute to these strategies?
> Lunch
4. Problem Solving (ninety minutes)
    a. What barriers need to be overcome in order to accomplish our goals?
    b. Who needs to be involved in these actions? How might we recruit them?
5. Synthesis/Next Steps: Where do we go with these ideas? (forty-five minutes)
    a. Assignments, review of tasks
    b. Target dates for completion of tasks, report dates
6. Evaluation of the meeting/Check-out (twenty minutes)

As people arrived, the facilitator made a point of meeting each participant (Phase 2: Meeting and Greeting). He also privately affirmed the value of their initial written responses to his questions and underscored their importance in developing the meeting agenda. Board members took the initiative to introduce themselves to one another; although an ongoing group, their contact was infrequent. In addition, a few had not attended the previous meeting, and there were two new members of the group.

As the meeting began, the director introduced the facilitator, who then explained his role in the meeting. He also clarified expectations and ground rules for the retreat (Phase 3: Opening Statement and Ground Rules). From there, members introduced themselves and checked in. These initial comments also focused on hopes for the meeting. The facilitator then presented the tentative agenda for approval by the group. Members raised concerns about whether some initial group building activities were necessary, hoping instead to move directly to what they considered substantive issues. They also asked not to break into small groups for any of this work; in their minds, eight members plus the director already constituted a small group. After some discussion, all agreed to follow the tentative agenda, but not to use small groups at all (Phase 4: Agenda Setting).

The morning session was quite successful, as members articulated anxieties and honestly expressed hopes and fears for the agency. It became clear that they truly cared about the agency and respected the staff immensely (Phase 5: Sharing Ideas and Concerns—Promoting Active Listening). They efficiently developed strategies that flowed from the mission they had previously developed (Phase 6: Problem Solving). Little conflict was experienced during the meeting, although the director voiced a fear that the ambitious plan now emerging might not be attainable without significant board involvement.

This concern led to discussion of the relationship between the board and the director, who on the one hand expressed the desire for partnership, while on the other hand minimized board involvement in the day-to-day knowledge required for success. This issue forced the group to temporarily set aside some of the later agenda items in order to address some heartfelt concerns that had accumulated over the years (conflict resolution). Within an hour, a new commitment emerged between board and director, from which confidence in the strategies could be built. After a break, the group returned to the agenda, agreed to postpone decisions on item 4 (problem solving and board recruitment), and moved to clarify needs for the next meeting.

At check out, members commented on the quality of the discussion, their sense of effective problem solving through the agenda, and their confidence in their capability to work as a group. They decided to use the external facilitator to help conclude their work, but they set up subcommittees to be led by internal facilitators to accomplish various tasks required in the coming year.

In understanding this meeting process, the reader should notice several key points. First, the facilitator received input from all participants, if only through pen and paper, prior to the meeting. This helped them "own" the meeting and built rapport with the facilitator. Second, the agenda was truly open to review and, as a result, somewhat modified. Even at that point, an important item came along that further shifted the agenda. While some might call this derailing the agenda and regard it negatively, I see this as necessary flexibility for meeting the true needs of the group. However, the group must agree to take on any new agenda items and examine their impact on the remaining items. In this way, power remains with the group to determine its own direction and sense of accomplishment. Finally, there is value in explicitly identifying impressions at the close of the meeting. These include agreements about subcommittee tasks, staff duties, facilitator responsibilities, and other substantive items. They also include feelings about the meeting shared through check-out that help the group improve its future meeting process.

Staff Retreat: Significant Changes in Organizational Decision Making

A small service company had operated by consensus for many years. Originally a group of five people, they were now fifteen. As their staff had grown, they had come to view the consensus process as cumbersome and inefficient. Their meetings were routinely characterized by a lack of closure, so items were automatically carried over, burdening the next agenda. A sense of frustration and low morale had settled on the group. The group had always utilized an internal facilitator, with the role rotated among members. They decided to utilize an external facilitator to do two things: (1) to educate them about options in meeting organization, decision making, and problem solving that might help improve their efficiency, and (2) to facilitate a specific discussion and decision-making process through which they would determine whether to continue to operate by consensus.

The facilitator received pen and paper input about needs of the group through a brief survey of staff members and more extensive discussion with the director (Phase 1: Pre-negotiation). The agenda was quite clear. In the first ninety minutes, training in organized meeting processes would be provided. In the next ninety minutes, the group would attempt to resolve, by consensus, how it would make future staff decisions.

The training and discussion uncovered a number of issues that had not been expressed in the earlier needs assessment. There were fears of domination by the director if consensus were compromised. There were also philosophical differences regarding future company direction that had not been resolved, and there were cumbersome traditions in their meeting approach (minutes review and committee reports) that slowed their discussions. Among the knowledge shared by the facilitator were the distinctions between various democratic decision-making forms (discussed in Chapter Six) and the possibility that a group could seek broad areas of agreement by most members, while not making all of its decisions by consensus.

This information bridged naturally into the group's next discussion, in which it attempted to develop decision-making protocols for different types of situations. They contrived an elaborate scheme and matrix in which they clarified these options. For example, they agreed that personnel decisions would require two-thirds majority, while small expenditures could be decided by subgroups that were directly involved. Policy and mission decisions would continue to be decided by consensus of the entire staff.

However, beneath this collaborative exterior, the facilitator remembered the earlier divisions that were now going unexpressed. As the group "efficiently" addressed its issues, the underlying concerns and fears were not being addressed. He identified this worry to the group. Most were silent in response. A few, however, said that it was more important to resolve these issues and try them out, rather than delay closure to address underlying fears within the group. "We have to trust one another enough to try this new approach," they said. The director, without speaking, nonverbally affirmed this need for closure within the allotted time. As noon approached, lunch was getting set up in an adjoining room, signaling the end of the meeting. The facilitator led a brief check-out, which merely affirmed people's satisfaction with what they had learned and their desire to try the new system.

In reflecting upon this meeting, one can identify competing values within the process. Should a group slow its problem-solving process in order to address underlying concerns, or is it more helpful to reach tentative conclusions of burdensome issues and hope the other concerns can be addressed at a later time? What is the power and responsibility of the facilitator in such situations, especially as an external resource hired to work with the group on a temporary basis?

Generally, we find that groups need smaller issues to jump start the process. This is especially true if they fear the discussion of emotional issues. The best choice, initially, may be to take a safe topic. However, once this issue is addressed, people need to be encouraged to deal with more meaningful concerns. If we naively assume that they will now get along, an important opportunity may be lost. Furthermore, people will now view this process as ineffective.

The facilitator is responsible for providing leadership to the group, so the group's capacity to solve problems is brought to the table. He or she must resist the uncomfortable desire to avoid hard discussions. However, great care must be taken to respect the timeliness or "ripeness" of certain topics. We understand the facilitator brings significant power to the group, and has an ethical obligation to use this power wisely (Mayer 1987).

As a footnote to this story, the facilitator checked with the company a few months later. The director reported that the new system was working well, and that she appreciated the work that had occurred at their staff retreat. There were some staff changes as well, resulting in some new people who lacked the "baggage" associated with the old system. However, the facilitator happened to meet three of the staff members a short time later. They reported that the company had now become more autocratic and that the fears about abandoning consensus had been realized under the new system. They were all in the process of seeking new employment and reported that others had left already. They appreciated what the facilitator had done at the meeting, they said, but they now realized that they should have addressed the underlying concerns in that context before allowing the new system to be adopted.

Organizations often vacillate among decision-making and management approaches. As a normal part of this process, some staff members will become dissatisfied and leave. It is also reasonable that managers will assemble new staffs that reflect their philosophies and vision. The facilitator's role is not to judge such changes, but to help group members evaluate them. If the group can openly and democratically come to terms with the conflictive feelings of its members, it can manage these transitions effectively. The facilitated meeting is a forum for the expression of such concerns. So long as it remains a safe place, supported by the assertive management of the process by the facilitator, many possible outcomes can emerge that benefit the organization and its members.

Learning How to Walk the Walk: Building an Internal Capacity to Manage Meetings

A publishing company had operated successfully for many years, growing from a small staff to employ dozens of people in a variety of roles. A management system had evolved that was highly reliant upon the president, as she was involved in running or approving virtually all aspects of the company. Over time, feelings of exclusion had emerged among the staff and were brought to the boiling point by a particularly harsh supervisor. The president, always disinclined to address conflict, reluctantly contacted a consultant to address issues within the company.

Fortunately, the consultant was able to mediate specific interpersonal conflicts and help identify strategies for improving relationships. The president embraced the situation as an opportunity for growth and established a management team to help run the company. She also agreed to allow various group members to take turns facilitating meetings. The consultant provided training to the group and agreed to mentor facilitators and observe occasional meetings for the first year.

At first, meetings retained a traditional format. They had an agenda of twelve to fifteen items for a three-hour meeting, without regard to time, order, or level of discussion required. There was no opportunity for check-in or review of ground rules (although they were established). The president brought seventy percent of the agenda and dominated discussion. Most group members sat back and listened, and the facilitator simply took inventory of the agenda items as they were covered and called the next item on the list.

After critique and mentoring from the consultant, including help with several difficult issues, the group began to change. Increasingly other members brought items to the meeting. Facilitators became more actively involved in constructing agendas and negotiating with individuals between meetings to gain commitment to new tasks. The management of conflictive discussion was still uncomfortable, but dissenting ideas were expressed and understood. The group also tackled larger concerns within the company, a role not imagined by the president in previous years. Challenges included the growing perception that the management team was a new clique. Team members addressed this misconception by facilitating their own departmental meetings in a more democratic manner, transferring their learning from the management team to other settings. This had the added benefit of giving them more experience in the new approach. They also created additional vehicles for soliciting genuine input within the company, which directly addressed employee concerns. Over time, staff came to trust that management was actually learning to "walk the walk" of participation. With the addition of a few new managers with previous experience in participatory team-based organizations, the capacity of the management team was greatly enhanced. To her credit, the company president accepted new people in positions of power and worked diligently to change long-standing patterns of behavior. The result was great improvement in the company's efficiency and its ability to respond flexibly to changing conditions in a dynamic industry.

This case study illustrates some of the real challenges in adopting a democratic approach within a company. If there is a history of distrust and dysfunction among staff members, but the company is able to meet its expectations for output and productivity, there is little incentive to change behaviors and confront such difficulties directly. However, if there is a precipitating event, such as a supervisor/subordinate conflict or shift in financial health, it may serve as springboard for a thorough evaluation of the structural contributions to the problem and, perhaps, to changes in management styles. Even so, the actual implementation of the facilitated meeting requires care, support, and vigilance. In this case, the consultant was required to: a) provide training; b) model the new approach; c) offer specific critique of meetings, based upon actual observation; and d) mentor new facilitators who had to construct agendas and run the meetings. After a year of occasional, yet regular, participation in such activities, the consultant was able to withdraw completely and allow the company to demonstrate its new internal capacity to manage its affairs. This type of facilitative consulting underscores the importance of the values outlined earlier. [1]

Facilitating an Ongoing Project Team

A few years ago, a mid-sized service company decided to utilize a team approach to all projects. This company provided technical consulting on the organization of medical conferences: how to host them; best sites for various types of events; costs of alternatives; expert resources and speakers; and the like. Internally, the company had the usual departments with sales, marketing, production, accounting, and other traditional functions. They formed interdepartmental project teams, covering all aspects of their operation, so that all units felt included and informed in every aspect of the organization. They also created opportunities for cross-training and involvement in new areas, fostering professional growth.

As a component of this reform, the company provided two important types of training. First, they offered education in team management and development, through which a clearer appreciation of the opportunities and challenges of this approach was reached (see Chapter Seven on teams for more information). Second, they offered training in facilitating effective meetings. In this way, the company was able to enhance the skills of team leaders and examine the process and organization of team meetings to improve effectiveness.

Early in the transition period, meetings were mostly informational, characterized by one-way communication and dense reports of data. There was little discussion and a growing perception among participants that they weren't needed at the meeting. Although these groups were technically productive, they resembled the groups that had met before they were called "teams." They relied heavily upon team leaders for direction and decisions, with reluctance among most members to take risks or offer new ideas. It was also quite costly to involve so many staff members, who were otherwise busy and productive, in meetings in which they had little at stake.

As a result of the facilitation training, a significant shift occurred in the conduct of team meetings. They were now more interactive and participant-centered. The group determined the agenda within a clear sense of team purpose. If staff were needed more in their capacity as expert resources to the group, rather than ongoing members, they were allowed to participate as such. Team participation became viewed less as an obligation and more as an opportunity within the overall workload. In addition, some of the highly technical information items that had dominated agendas were shifted to e-mail reports, accessible at staff members' convenience. The meeting agenda now tended to look more like this:

TEAM AGENDA
April 19th   8:30–10:30 a.m.

1. Check-in/Agenda Review/Q&A about minutes from last meeting (Facilitator, ten minutes)
2. Subcommittee A Report/Discussion/Recommendations for Next Steps (John, twenty minutes)
3. Subcommittee B Report/Discussion/Recommendations for Next Steps (Mindy, thirty minutes)
4. Upcoming Deadlines (Information sharing) (Jose, ten minutes)
   a. What might we need to do to address these deadlines? (Discussion/decision, twenty minutes)
5. Technical Report #80 (Information clarification, Q&A) (Pete, ten minutes)

(Pete sent this to all via e-mail last week)
6. Review assignments, expectations between meetings (Facilitator, five minutes)
7. Next Meeting: Confirm May 17, 8:30–10:30 a.m., Conference Room A
8. Check-out

It is clear that this is a full agenda. However, by clarifying the expectations of each item and identifying all of the items within a full agenda, team members can readily understand what will occur at the meeting. They can also see the importance of advance preparation; Pete's "Technical Report #80" was sent to participants for review prior to the meeting. The team prepares minutes of each meeting, which is an important element of its continuing story. However, a great deal of time isn't spent reviewing the minutes; it is an affirmation of their work and a tool to focus on the issues at hand.

In this specimen agenda, the team facilitator has a certain responsibility for leading discussion on items 1 and 6, as these are procedural issues; other group members take the lead on the substantive topics. Occasionally, the team facilitator may have an important stake in a substantive item. In such circumstances, another team member should take the facilitator role for that phase of the discussion. Finally, note the presence of check-in and check-out within the agenda, as well as confirmation of the group's next meeting time and location. The more the process for identifying meeting times and locations can be simplified, the less likely the group's time will be absorbed with such matters.

This sample agenda meeting form is appended for guidance.

SAMPLE AGENDA MEETING FORM
Name of Group
Date, Location

Responsible Person/Time

1. Check-in
2. Establishing (Reviewing) Ground Rules
3. Minutes Review
4. Agenda Review
5. Item A: Information   Discussion   Decision
6. Item B: Information   Discussion   Decision
> Break (as appropriate)
7. Item C: Information   Discussion   Decision
8. Item D: Information   Discussion   Decision
9. Review assignments, responsibilities between meetings
10. Next meeting date, time, location
    Next meeting facilitator and recorder (as appropriate)
11. Check-out

NOTE

1. An example of this approach in a very different context is offered by Paolo Freire, author of *Pedagogy in Process: The Letters to Guinea Bisseau* (1978). In that situation, educational consultant Freire was engaged by the freshly independent nation of Guinea Bisseau to develop a new educational system. As reflected in his correspondence with the minister of education, Freire resisted the "efficient" pathway of telling them what to do. Instead, he facilitated their own dialogue about the values of their educational program, the barriers to success, and the development of a unique system that would meet their special concerns. He did so in a way that helped foster an internal capacity for the nation to solve its own problems in the future.

Chapter 4

Problem Solving in Facilitated Groups

Predicament, difficulty, quandary, imbroglio . . . no matter how you phrase it, a problem can be reduced to a question in search of a solution. Within groups, problems are typically encountered when strategies used in the past now prove unsuccessful or when unforeseen obstacles disrupt the path to achievement. Problem solving is an *intentional* and *systematic* process by which we seek effective responses and apply them to the situation.

Solving problems is an essential challenge facing any work group. The facilitator's dilemma is to gauge the degree to which the group is ready to address problematic issues: Is it premature, given the group's abilities, to try to solve the problem? Is the problem too complex, given the resources of the group? Do we have sufficient information to identify the problem, and are we confident that solving it is within our mission?

Problem solving helps uncover underlying issues, generates options for responding to these issues, and offers decision-making procedures for ranking choices within clearly understood criteria. The facilitator's challenge is not to be an outstanding problem solver; rather, it is to rally the resources of group members to bring their skills to the process.

PRECONDITIONS FOR EFFECTIVE PROBLEM SOLVING

As groups approach the pursuit of problem solving, they require certain preconditions that enhance their abilities to seek optimal solutions. These preconditions are best conceived as an inventory or checklist to be considered by the facilitator:

An Affirming Environment

An affirming environment is critical to the comfort of group members in the problem-solving process. As identified earlier, participants need to feel safe and respected. They must trust the ground rules in order to share honestly in the raising of potential concerns and in the development and evaluation of possible solutions. An affirming environment is crucial so people can express hesitation, ambiguity, or dissent.

Knowing the Language

Knowing the language (having the tools) is important if people are to participate realistically in each phase of the problem-solving process.   For example, solve this problem:

$$2x + 4 = 8.$$

If you understand algebra, you are capable of solving this problem quite easily. However, if the appropriate mathematical tools (the associative and commutative properties) are foreign to you, it is difficult to understand where to begin. The facilitator must ensure that, as much as possible, all participants know the language of their group and that of the problem to be solved. This approach compares favorably to the typical admonishment to new staff or task force members: "Hang in there. You'll catch on to what we're saying after a few months!" Very competent, experienced people tackle problems despite their uneasiness about terminology and its applications. The facilitator helps group members treat this uncertainty with respect. All members are educated in the vocabulary and customs of the group, in order to participate effectively. They have jargon clarified, so they can follow discussion readily. They are given training in the problem-solving tools of the group, so they can perform meaningful work.

Knowing the Context

Knowing the context or purpose of the problem being posed is also important. Although we may understand the basic technical guidelines for addressing an issue, we may not understand the culture from which the problem has arisen.   In order to identify the right problems and subsequently resolve them, this contextual understanding is critical. For example, the early Peace Corps workers in East Africa witnessed farmers who protected their fields from vandalism with a *kiopo*, a sacred object made from a stick, a coconut, and rooster feathers. In their zeal, these Americans suggested that the *kiopo* was powerless, and that in order to protect their fields, farmers should erect fences. The farmers complied, but found the problem worsened. Because the *kiopo* was perceived as sacred by potential vandals, while the fence was not, it had been a successful deterrent within its cultural context. Solutions that may apply within one milieu may contribute to ineffective problem solving in another.

Often we find that groups have little understanding of the meaning and impact of the work they are asked to perform. Employees see a task force, for example, as management's latest idea to promote change or to protect itself or the shareholders. They fail to recognize the direct link between the opportunity to find solutions and their potential to increase their own power within the workplace. Once function and context are clarified, the group can focus purposefully on its task and assume responsibility for its completion.

Flexibility and Creativity

Flexibility and creativity are key attributes of the successful problem solver. It is important to look at a situation without prejudice and to apply prior experience only as a guide, not as a constraint. As participants become more stressed and uncomfortable with the problems they face, the facilitator becomes central in maintaining flexibility. Helping people engage in a paradigm shift, with totally new ways of thinking, can be among the most challenging and satisfying aspects of facilitation.

For example, people from different departments often engage in conflict over budget allocations. When budget cuts necessitate layoffs, they fight fiercely to protect their respective turf. A powerful transformation occurs when they are willing to set aside historic perceptions of territory, focus creatively on future needs, and uncover solutions that increase collaboration among restructured departments. This flexibility offers the added benefit of helping staff vent frustrations, resolve misunderstandings, and establish new communication mechanisms.

Future-Oriented Thinking

Future-oriented thinking is also critical to effective problem solving. Groups can easily become bogged down, reacting to the problems of the moment. They formulate solutions that address symptoms of problems, rather than underlying concerns. Facilitators should help groups anticipate future problems as a normal component of their work together. Group members must be willing to look ahead one, five, or fifteen years. In this way, they may foresee prospective problems and arrive at present-day solutions that take their probability into account.

In summary, these preconditions form the basis for entering the problem-solving process. (See Figure 4.1.) Within a facilitated group, leadership must help nurture these conditions, so problem solving may occur in a manner that is participatory and effective.

Figure 4.1
Preconditions for Effective Problem Solving

1. An affirming environment
2. Knowing the language
3. Knowing the context
4. Flexibility and creativity
5. Future-oriented thinking

ALTERNATIVE STRATEGIES FOR PROBLEM SOLVING

The focus of this section is to identify some common problem-solving methods to utilize within facilitated groups. Three problem-solving approaches are presented: The first is a classic, linear approach that we call "IDEAL." The second is a less traditional, nonlinear approach known as Mind Mapping. Finally, the Future Problem Solving Model focuses on problems likely to arise in the future and provides tools for addressing such problems. Each approach offers distinct advantages for the problem-solving process. In considering these techniques, facilitators should examine the unique work styles and needs of their groups and how these strategies may apply accordingly.

IDEAL: A Classic Problem-Solving Model

The following model follows the format of most presentations on problem solving (Bransford and Stein 1984, Hayes 1981, Ackoff 1978, Lippitt 1983, Havelock and Huberman 1977). Our "IDEAL" is a synthesis of these classic models, representing our best understanding of the linear, step-by-step approach:

1. *Identify the problem.* The group needs to focus on a specific problem that must be solved. Difficulties in problem solving often arise from misunderstanding the problem being solved. In complex situations, it is especially important to understand which problem is being addressed, as well as whether all parties agree that this issue is worth pursuing. This is the foundation on which the problem-solving process is built and may evoke very different emotional responses within the group.

2. *Develop alternative possible solutions.* It is crucial that evaluation be deferred until several options have been explored. This can be accomplished through brainstorming, where participants together offer as many ideas as possible, piggy-back on each other's ideas, and look at the problem from a variety of perspectives. Options can also be developed independently, through

nominal group technique, where participants privately generate solutions that are later shared "round robin" or together through affinity grouping, where participants write thoughts on small sheets of paper, and pool them for evaluation. Whatever the approach, the likelihood of an optimal solution is greatly increased if several options are generated before evaluation and decision making.

3. *Evaluate alternative solutions according to mutually acceptable criteria.* In some cases, objective criteria may be applied to the evaluation of options. But in most situations, the choices we make about what is "best" are personal and subjective. Good problem-solving teams discuss possible criteria, agree on those to be applied, and use them to make informed decisions. In conflictive situations, taking extra time to clarify criteria can be extremely important in maintaining a willingness to continue the process.

Criteria, such as cost-effectiveness, ease of implementation, durability, and impact on target populations, reflect the values and interests that people bring to the table. The goal of the democratic meeting is to bring forth personal differences and use them constructively in the problem-solving process.

4. *Analyze your preferred solution, using an accepted decision-making process.* There are many systematic approaches to decision making that may be acceptable, depending on the situation. Usually, we seek consensus among all parties, where all group members find the decision to be acceptable. Sometimes, majority rule is utilized where there is a need for efficiency. On other occasions, democratic groups may delegate authority to a subgroup to decide (technocratic decision making), especially if that group is viewed as having a special expertise or stake in the outcome. In effective problem solving, all participants agree on the decision-making process and then use the criteria developed in Step 3 to select the best solution.

In framing a good solution, several benchmarks often prove useful:

1. Fairness, as perceived by all parties
2. Balanced implementation, indicating that all are similarly vested in the solution
3. Realism, given the resources and skills of the parties
4. Interest-based solutions, meeting the true needs and concerns of the parties
5. Sufficient specificity, the understanding of all that is required to implement agreements successfully
6. Consideration of the future, not merely solving the problem for today

5. *Live and learn.* (Implement and evaluate.) This phase of problem solving is characterized by the motto "Life is a pilot project." All too often, people espouse an orderly problem-solving process, then fail to carry out their choices. It is vital that people honor their commitments and apply the results in future efforts. Implementation should include an evaluation component, to determine whether the execution of a solution meets the group's expectations. (See the accompanying chart for a summary of the IDEAL method.) If our assessment merely confirms the brilliance of our efforts, it provides an

opportunity to celebrate. However, evaluation also provides a chance to respond to concerns before they worsen and to create legitimate channels for expressing conflicts before they fester. Evaluation provides the opportunity to uncover developing problems while many viable solutions remain.

IDEAL

IDEAL is a simplified version of the classic problem solving model:

I =Identify the problem. Be as specific as possible. Talk the situation through to clarify why it is problematic.
D=Develop alternative possible solutions. Generate as many possible solutions to the identified problems.
E=Evaluate alternative solutions according to mutually acceptable criteria.
A=Analyze your preferred solution, using an accepted decision-making process.
L=Live and learn. Follow through and implement your strategy as designed. Then evaluate outcomes and try to understand why they occurred.

Mind Mapping

An alternative to the classic approach is a nonlinear strategy, Mind Mapping. This approach begins with a presumed problem, then generates issues and possible solutions, following an associative route through the mind. Rather than locking participants into a linear process, where the intuitive urge to explore tangents is disciplined, Mind Mapping grants participants the creativity of free association and helps diminish feelings of being overwhelmed by complex situations. It helps participants focus realistically on what can be accomplished, while placing related concerns within a broad context.

The concept of Mind Mapping is attributed to Tony Buzan, who has championed the process throughout the world. In his publication *The Mind Map Book* (Buzan 1996) he presents the fundamental philosophy of the approach:

The more you learn/gather new data in an integrated, radiating, organised manner, the easier it is to learn more. From this gigantic information processing ability and learning capacity derives the concept of Radiant Thinking of which the Mind Map is a manifestation. Radiant Thinking (from 'to radiate', meaning 'to spread or move in directions, or from a given centre') refers to associative thought processes that proceed from or connect to a central point. The other meanings of 'radiant' are also relevant: 'shining brightly', 'the look of bright eyes beaming with joy and hope' and 'the focal point of a meteoric shower'—similar to the 'burst of thought'. How do we gain access to this exciting new way of thinking? With the Mind Map, which is the external expression of Radiant Thinking. A Mind Map always radiates from a central image. Every word and image becomes in itself a subcentre of association, the whole proceeding in a potentially infinite chain of branching patterns away from or towards the common centre. Although the Mind Map is drawn on a two-dimensional page it represents a multi-dimensional reality, encompassing space, time and colour.

The brain is capable of making numerous associations and from those, further associations, according to Buzan. (See Figure 4.2.) From such associations potentially optimal solutions arise. Such thinking highly reinforces the process of facilitation. By promoting Radiant Thinking and the use of Mind Maps, we encourage participants to be at their best, both individually and collectively.

A key advocate of the Mind Mapping approach is Future Search, an organization that works with communities to anticipate future needs, identify problems, and clarify barriers that may interfere with responding to those needs. Future Search develops alternative strategies that have acceptance among all community stakeholders, and it ultimately tries to build consensus around solutions that can be implemented through the political process. Future Search has modified Buzan's original process with great success, as presented in their excellent resource manual, *Future Search* (Weisbord and Janoff 1995):

First, we invite everybody to "come on down" to the wall designated for this purpose. We want folks close in. The conference task is written in the center of a sheet of butcher paper 6 feet high by 12 feet wide. We want to map all the external trends that are having an impact on our conference topic now. We mind map as a total group so everybody hears what matters to others. This is an interactive community experience. Ideas and connections trigger other ideas and connections . . . The mind map not only describes your own community, but also you begin to see all the global and national forces that have a bearing on everybody's communities.

The Future Search process has been adapted to a wide range of situations. Recently, a colleague facilitated a future search in order to help his church group make progress with congregational planning. The enthusiasm generated by this approach resulted in renewed energy, rededication of resources, and the reversal of negative momentum that had paralyzed the group.

Mind Mapping is applicable to a wide range of problems. Let's take the question of "Do we need a new computer system?" as an example. In the Mind Map in this chapter, a number of issues have been generated from this initial query. They are not ranked or evaluated, simply connected on the basis of perceived relationships to one another; a map of the problem is thus being constructed. Often, this process helps participants understand their mutual perspectives on an issue. It can transform an overpowering situation into a manageable one and offers feasible starting points for discussion. This generates good will for collecting data (which is often critical) and encourages experimentation along several possible paths in problem solving.

Figure 4.2
Mind Map

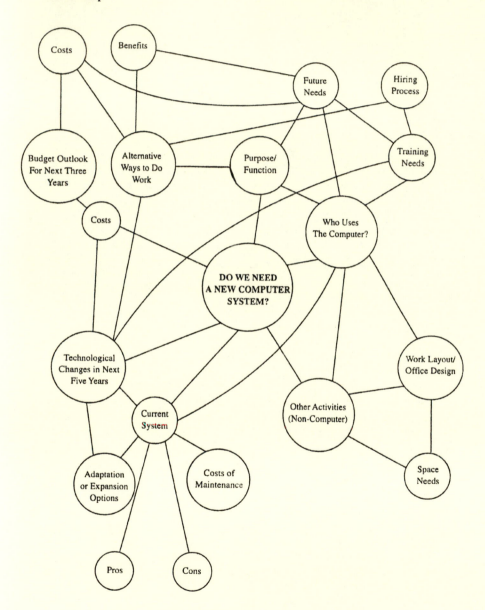

Mind Mapping is especially useful in addressing intractable problems that have reached impasse, a common occurrence in conflict. Disputants often get stuck in destructive, closed patterns of communication, resistant to more formal approaches to problem solving. Mind Mapping can be helpful at breaking such impasse, as it helps participants focus on new possibilities and recognize related issues in a less personalized way. A Mind Map can be a useful homework assignment to give group members during a cooling off period, or between meetings in an ongoing situation, as a tool for refocusing the group.

As with our IDEAL approach, Mind Mapping is an exciting concept. From a training perspective, it is best taught by using a realistic, simple problem, and then practiced with more complicated issues. Problem-solving skills, like many skills, need to be practiced, using an experiential learning approach.

Future Problem Solving Model

The Future Problem Solving Model (FPS) was developed by Alexander Osborne and Sidney Parnes over thirty years ago, and it has been promoted through both Osborne's Creative Education Foundation in Buffalo, New York. FPS is taught by the Future Problem Solvers organization and practiced by teams of school children throughout the world. It is easily adapted to adult instruction in problem solving. By using scenarios, FPS successfully brings attention to issues likely to arise in the future. In combination with other work on strategic planning and conflict resolution, this approach holds promise for democratic groups. The technique has undergone revisions through the years, but its model has maintained several key elements:

1. "Fuzzy situation": The "fuzzy" is a futuristic scenario focusing on a set of situations likely to occur fifteen to thirty-five years from today. Prior to receiving the scenario, problem-solving groups have received materials and background information about key issues.
2. Small group approach: The larger group is divided into teams of four to five participants, in order to maximize participation in the process. This also allows several problems to be addressed, simultaneously, in greater depth.
3. Brainstorming: This approach is key to FPS, both in problem identification and solution seeking. The FPS dedication to brainstorming, a technique taken for granted today, was a generation ahead of its time.
4. Applying criteria to evaluating options: FPS encourages the development and consideration of meaningful, problem-specific criteria. By doing so, the values and beliefs of the problem-solving team are brought to the process in a significant, objective manner. The systematic application of the criteria to decision making allows participants to manage their biases constructively and less emotionally.
5. Synthesis and application: FPS encourages the synthesis of divergent ideas and the opportunity to consider the practical application of strategies. It also promotes flexibility, creativity, and other qualities that enhance the capacity for problem solving.

The FPS Model follows six steps:

1. Read and discuss the fuzzy situation. Brainstorm twenty problems likely to arise in this scenario.
2. Identify an underlying problem presented by the scenario. This is derived from the brainstormed list.
3. Brainstorm solutions to the underlying problem. You are no longer focused on the broad, fuzzy scenario, but on the central issue that your group has identified.
4. Develop five criteria for evaluating possible solutions to your problem. These criteria should be relevant to your issue, forming unambiguous standards by which to separate "good" from "poor" solutions.
5. Rank the solutions from Step 3 according to the criteria developed in Step 4. As a result, the "best" solutions emerge at the top.
6. Describe your responses to the problem, articulating your recommended solution (or solutions, if a few appear to work best together) and any initial thoughts regarding strategies for implementation.

For the facilitator, it is crucial to have a full "tool box" of strategies accessible to support the problem-solving needs of the group. By practicing these alternative approaches, the group is less likely to settle for poor solutions or to perceive a barrier as insurmountable. By modeling adaptability and ingenuity in the face of difficult problems, the facilitator encourages group members to remain engaged in the process and seek satisfying outcomes.

ACTIVITIES IN PROBLEM SOLVING

We often find that groups have had little experience in systematic problem solving. Frequently, they are limited by preoccupation with one or two issues they perceive to be of greatest importance. Although the use of real problems may work well for building confidence, there is great benefit in shifting to hypothetical situations to build skills in problem solving with the big picture in mind. Then the group can apply their insights to real issues. The following activities have all been useful in aspects of our work. Certainly, many other types of activities may be appropriate. Please review the bibliography at the end of this book for additional sources of activities.

One Hundred Carats: A Group Problem Solving Activity

The objective of this exercise (Kreidler 1990) is to create a team name with letters that add up to 100 carats. It builds community and cooperation and promotes effective communication skills. Participants will need paper and writing utensils. The instructions are as follows:

1. Divide participants into groups of four to six. Explain that a carat is a unit of weight used for gems.
2. Ask participants to figure out the following problem: "If the letter A has a weight of 1 carat, B has the weight of 2 carats, C equals 3 carats, etc., what is the weight of your first name?" Provide a key such as the accompanying one to assist participants. When everyone has completed this task, ask them "Who in your group has the heaviest name?" and "Who in your group has the lightest name?" Assign the roles of recorder and spokesperson to the participants with the heaviest and lightest names.

KEY
A=1 B=2 C=3 D=4 E=5 F=6 G=7 H=8 I=9 J=10 K=11
L=12 M=13 N=14 O=15 P=16 Q=17 R=18 S=19 T=20
U=21 V=22 W=23 X=24 Y=25 Z=26

3. Explain the group task: In ten minutes, come up with a team name in which all the letters add up to 100 carats. The name can be one or more words. Nonsense words are acceptable as long as the participants all agree on them.
4. After developing the team name, each group may design a logo that reflects its name to share with the larger group.

The facilitator may use the following questions for discussion:

1. Did everyone in your group have a chance to contribute?
2. What things did you do to encourage everyone to contribute?
3. Did you feel listened to?
4. What did you do as a group member to encourage listening and cooperation?
5. How did your group make sure everyone was satisfied with the team name?
6. If you weren't able to finish in ten minutes, what could you do differently next time?

The World's Fastest Paper Airplane

Ask participants to pull out a piece of scrap paper. Give the group the following instructions: "You have an opportunity to make the world's fastest paper airplane. In the next three minutes, make the fastest paper airplane you can. Test flights are encouraged." After three minutes, ask participants to fly their airplanes across the room. After each attempt, be encouraging and supportive. Then ask the following questions:

1. What assumptions did you follow as you designed your airplane?
2. What were the possibilities and limitations of these assumptions?
3. What possible designs may have emerged with differing assumptions?

Next, take a piece of paper, crumple it, and throw it across the room. "Now, look at the airplane I just made. It went very quickly across the room." Some will dispute the validity of your creation as an airplane. Remind them of assumptions NASA originally made in rocket design, when they thought space capsules would need to have wings. However, for the purpose of fast reentry, capsules didn't need wings. (The space shuttle, created for reuse, required a different design.) Now, reexamine the three processing questions above, in light of this new design.

Goldstein's Delicatessen: A Grocery at the Crossroads

For nearly three generations, Goldstein's Delicatessen has been a neighborhood institution. Located in the heart of an old Jewish neighborhood, the deli has been managed by Alexander and Clara Goldstein and their daughters. They have served a loyal clientele a small but tasty selection of soups, sandwiches, kosher delicacies, and fountain drinks. Clara's Egg Cream Soda was renowned throughout the city, and her recipe was taught to only a few loyal employees over a fifty-year period. Goldstein's has maintained a strong line of Jewish grocery items, a few staples, a kosher meat counter, candies, and magazines. It has become a convenient and friendly place to spend time and catch up on neighborhood news.

Alexander passed away ten years ago, and Clara is nearly seventy. As she looks to retirement, her world has changed. Her daughters have moved away: Sally is a teacher in California, while Susan has moved to the suburbs and owns a restaurant with her husband. Their restaurant is quite successful, especially for people who want to pay a little more for a good meal, and it keeps Susan very busy.

The old neighborhood has disappeared. As young professionals have moved in, new townhouses and apartments have been built through urban renewal. The less wealthy, older clients of the deli have moved away to the suburbs. Bob and Ernie Stein, two brothers who have worked for Goldstein's for over thirty years, are now wondering what Clara will do with the store. Revenues have been gradually declining for several years, and Clara worries about her retirement. She is also concerned that unless something changes soon, there won't be enough money to keep both brothers employed.

The deli still does a brisk lunch business, with less seating than possible customers. However, weekends and evenings are no longer crowded. It is also less safe to work at night, especially with so little business, and Clara feels lucky not to have been robbed. Needleman's Bakery, which had been next store for years, moved to the suburbs three years ago, only to be replaced by a computer store. (Who knows what they do there—what does she know from computers?!) Sally, in California, is urging her to close the deli and move out there. Susan has offered to help out part-time, and her children help on the weekends, but Clara doesn't want to impose on her. She doesn't want to close the store, because there are still many people in the area who rely upon it and don't want to go to the big supermarket. She feels that she will have failed her community if she allows the deli to close.

As Clara sees it, she has two choices: she can close the deli, which she really doesn't want to do, or she can reduce hours and close during off-peak times that are not generating enough money. She has asked your problem-solving team for advice. What should she do? How do you think Goldstein's Delicatessen should move forward from this crossroads?

Once the problem-solving team has developed strategies for Goldstein's Delicatessen, ask them to consider the following questions:

1. In solving this problem, did you consider the range of options available to Clara, or were you constrained by the choices she perceived?
2. Did your problem-solving group proceed systematically, generating options, discussing criteria, and applying them to the problem, or was there a premature rush to judgment? What impact did your approach have on the quality of your eventual recommendations?
3. Did the group recognize new resources (e.g., the computer store next door or the residents of the nearby apartments and townhouses) that could be tapped for developing solutions? Was there recognition that family and business needs in this situation may be quite different?

SCENARIOS FOR FUTURE PROBLEM SOLVING

We have included two scenarios. "Riverside, USA" offers an urban planning problem set over twenty years in the future, while "Campus Scenario: 2010," offers a university planning problem likely to exist in a shorter time frame. In proceeding through each scenario, participants should follow these steps:

1. Divide into small groups, with four or five members per group. Appoint a recorder for the group.
2. Give the scenario to all participants. Provide adequate time (five minutes) to read it, then encourage small groups to discuss their initial understanding of the scenario. (Five to ten minutes.)
3. Ask participants to brainstorm problems likely to arise in the scenario. Have them identify at least ten problems. (Ten minutes.)
4. Then, ask each group to identify a single, underlying problem within the scenario. (Five to ten minutes.) Have them frame the problem statement as an open-ended question in a format such as:

How might we (strong action verb) (object) so that (purpose) (context)?

For example, "How might we create a new university policy so that registration needs can be met over the next decade?"

5. Then, have group members brainstorm possible solutions to the problem identified in the previous step. Each small group will now be focused on a different underlying problem. (Fifteen minutes.)
6. The next step is for each small group to identify four criteria that are appropriate for evaluating possible solutions. This discussion is important and should consider guidelines discussed in this chapter. (Ten minutes.)

7. Finally, they should apply these criteria to the solutions they have generated, resulting in selection of "preferred options" or "best solutions." (Twenty minutes.) As an exercise, it is less important that participants reach an outstanding conclusion; an understanding of the problem-solving process, and strategies that enhance or inhibit its practice, are the goals of a practice problem.

In discussing the exercise, participants may find aspects or adaptations of the FPS model that apply to their work. Participants in an ongoing work group may find insights into their work styles, values, attitudes towards problem solving, or other areas that may prove useful in their future work together.

Riverside, USA

The city of Riverside has experienced dramatic growth over the past thirty years. (See Figures 4.3 and 4.4.) Now, in the year 2020, it is facing a number of problems of which planners in the 1990s forewarned, as well as others that could never have been anticipated—at least that's what the mayor says. She says that more modern, wider roads to accommodate 300,000 people (double the 1990 population) were needed but the state never provided funds. The schools needed renovating and new buildings were required, but it wasn't until 1998 that wary taxpayers approved a local bond referendum. But the 1998 referendum included the stipulation that no new schools could be constructed within the district for twenty-five years. The conservative administration in Washington has systematically dismantled the universal health care system that was instituted in 2007, leaving it to cities like Riverside to provide direct health care services that had been funded by the federal government for over a decade.

Others, however, say that the mayor is wrong to place blame on the state and federal governments, or on taxpayers concerned about runaway government spending. The gentle Dove River running through town was developed in the 1980s to bring jobs and tourists downtown. It worked successfully for several years, but since the 2002 recession, its once flourishing Riverwalk has significantly declined. Downtown is now abandoned to dope peddlers, prostitutes, and gangs. The big indoor River Mall is largely vacant as shoppers use suburban malls, interactive TV networks, and global computer communities to fulfill shopping needs. Downtown Riverside has become a ghost town after dark. Most businesses have relocated to less expensive, more secure locations in neighboring towns.

The mayor, critics say, is responsible. She has failed to provide a pro-business atmosphere, failed to provide leadership and vision to the community, and failed to anticipate the city's economic and social needs during the four years she has been in office. They say a change in political leadership is required.

The mayor recognizes that there are many problems facing Riverside. She has asked you and your problem-solving team to give her your best advice for the 2020s. In that way, perhaps she and the people of Riverside can gain prosperity once again.

Figure 4.3
Age Breakdown of Riverside, USA

	1990	2020
Age 70 and older	2%	12%
60–69 years	12%	18%
40–59	30%	30%
20–39	30%	20%
5–19	15%	12%
Under 5 years	11%	8%

Figure 4.4
Racial/Ethnic Diversity of Riverside, USA

	1990 Total	Percent	2020 Total	Percent
African American	28,080	18.0	48,640	16.0
Hispanic American	4,680	3.0	24,320	8.0
Asian/Pacific American	780	0.5	12,160	4.0
Native American	780	0.5	3,040	1.0
Foreign Born*	1,560	1.0	18,240	6.0
Caucasian American	120,120	77.0	197,600	65.0
Total	156,000		304,000	

* Foreign born have been primarily immigrants from Eastern Europe, after the fall of communism in the 1990's led to instability, civil wars, and the famine/depression of 2003–2005.

Campus Scenario: 2010

It is the year 2010 at the University of the Heartland. As the winter thaws and spring emerges this new year, there is an air of apprehension and concern mixed with excitement, for many changes are coming about: The new chancellor has announced a bold initiative, the Campus Creative Conquest Consortium, to bring together the diverse and disparate campus departments and factions into one collaborative effort. She has asked your Future Problem Solvers team to make recommendations regarding the best ways to achieve this goal.

The campus has grown over the past decade. A new sports center has opened, near the High Rise Residence Halls, bringing many new events to campus. Enrollment has grown 20% to 50,000 students, despite efforts to control it. Growth is due to the new training programs for displaced workers, nontraditional students, and immigrants from the former Soviet Union who came to Heartland in the late 1990s during their civil war. But staffing is at 1996 levels, so stress increases each year, as university staff manages an increased workload with no corresponding increase in staff. Increasingly, they rely on student help and temporary workers who lack experience and commitment.

President Gore expanded Clinton's community programs, but the Republican Congress reduced funding for education. Students are increasingly taking service time and five-and-a-half-year degree programs. Universal health care, in place since 1998, is a bureaucratic nightmare for the campus. The university interacts with a maze of managed-care providers and regional insurance brokers throughout the United States. University Hospital has more patients than ever before, due to independent marketing and research grants it obtained under the new health system, but its 1970s facility is showing signs of wear. The inflation of the past five years has reduced purchasing power, and state revenues are flat. Finally, the federal deficit is now over $1 trillion annually, despite balanced-budget goals of the late 1990s. With Social Security about to come of age as a significant drain on resources for an aging population, the national economic outlook is bleak.

Technology has dramatically changed the student experience. All residence halls are hardwired and networked to instructors, some of whom teach from elsewhere in the world. Grades and lessons are communicated through electronic mail and the Internet. All lectures are available on interactive video, which students choose over going to class. But students with fewer skills need more student services than ever before, and counseling and tutorial assistance are high priorities for students entering a depressed work force. Finally, as the Asian Continental Conflict threatens to become a world war, the United States has reinstated the draft this past summer.

What key issues do your problem solvers see in this scenario? What advice would you offer the chancellor ?

CASE STUDIES IN PROBLEM SOLVING

Using the Future Problem Solving Model with a City Government

A facilitator was contacted by officials of a small, growing city—we'll call it Middletown—regarding difficulties they were experiencing at the time. Middletown had grown dramatically in the past decade, as the surrounding region had grown more urbanized. With the growth came new problems: sprawling development; new transportation needs; increased demand for basic services; and elevated crime rates. Although financial resources were greater than before, they were not keeping pace with the demand for services. The mayor explained that department heads had little experience working cooperatively, that the city council undermined any efforts at planning through polarized political partisanship, and that short-term problem solving was the only mode known to their community. Citizens seemed happy when garbage was picked up on time and unhappy when it piled up. Beyond immediate concerns, the city was characterized by single-issue politics that made it difficult to take a large, long-term view of issues.

After a preliminary needs assessment with all department heads, the facilitator brought the group together for a training in problem solving. The first session focused on expectations of the group as a management team, a concept that was initially a major jolt to the group. They had never thought of themselves as a management team, unified by a common purpose or commitment. Through the "Outcomes Identification Exercise" (see Chapter Seven on team development for this activity) a new sense of dedication and clarified goals emerged. They also had an opportunity to discuss and resolve conflicts that had accumulated over the years. From this point, the group was able to return to its previous agenda and develop problem-solving skills.

The Future Problem Solving (FPS) model was utilized as a tool for this group. FPS was selected by the facilitator because it is dynamic in sparking visionary strategies. FPS generates creative approaches to problems without being either a visioning exercise or a strategic planning exercise. These would have been too directive and vested too much power in the mayor. By utilizing the creative, future-oriented process of FPS in a hypothetical situation (they used the "Riverside, USA" scenario), the group was able to learn and practice problem-solving skills in a safe environment.

As a result of this exercise, the group critiqued their own situation. They realized that Riverside was very much like Middletown. They related the problems likely to arise in Riverside to their own issues of urban sprawl, increased crime, declining infrastructure, and uncontrolled land use. They also discussed relationships with nearby towns and cities and the potential value of cooperative forums for addressing common concerns. Finally, they also recognized the power of developing a joint vision for the city that could guide their work together. If Middletown were to prosper in the future, it was important that they view themselves as a future problem-solving team.

The Middletown management team used the FPS exercise as a springboard to two crucial activities. First, they developed a vision statement together, building it from ideas developed in three small groups and merging these ideas into a consensus statement of the larger fifteen-member team. They identified strategies for achieving this vision, using desired outcomes and expectations from the previous "Outcomes Identification Exercise" to focus their efforts. Second, they utilized their internal expertise to construct a "Middletown, USA" scenario approximately fifteen years into their city's future. Using the FPS model to guide their work, they devised a process that allowed them to develop a preferred future for Middletown. They generated a mechanism for working with the city council that was independent of political dictates.

Although Middletown did not fully resolve the structural issues that had historically hindered its progress, the department heads and mayor made a significant transition in their relationships together. They utilized a facilitator as training resource and consultant but developed an internal capacity to carry their work forward. By reframing their association as a management team, the facilitator helped them recognize common concerns and goals that allowed a face-saving way to move beyond historic divisions. By mediating specific conflicts within the group, the facilitator eliminated past issues that prevented substantive progress. He modeled a stance that could be adopted by group members in subsequent work together and with their staffs. By offering the Future Problem Solving model as a procedure that could easily be adapted to meet the needs of their situation, the facilitator gave the group a tool that was easily learned and relevant to their needs. This is an excellent example of how a facilitator can assert for process while allowing a group to retain important power to address substantive concerns.

Mind Mapping Out of a Stalemate: A Supervisor's Tool

One the greatest difficulties facing supervisors is the task of improving morale and motivation when they lack effective power. Middle managers frequently bemoan situations where staff gossip and complain, try to do as little as possible, and apparently resent direct efforts to improve behavior. They seem to have behaved this way for many years and are stuck in a relentless pattern of self-pity and derision of the system. Supervisors in such situations are desperately seeking help. They form a challenging group for using problem-solving tools and strategies to improve their circumstances.

A facilitator found herself working with such a group of supervisors at a medium-sized college food service unit. The supervisors complained that there were two types of employees who were impossible to motivate. The first was long-term, older employees who were in a rut, not interested in learning new skills and resistant to changes in technology and procedure. The other type, students, were fast learners but preoccupied with their studies and their social lives; work at food service was just a job for them. They often skipped shifts or were otherwise unreliable. In addition, students often left after only a few months, leading to further resentment among older employees. Overall, there was a labor shortage on campus that further complicated efforts to improve the quality of work.

The facilitator utilized a Mind Map as a tool for helping this depressed group break their impasse. After creating a list of typical problems, she asked the group to identify effective strategies they had used in addressing them. She discovered that the group perceived no effective strategies. In short, they were overwhelmed. That's when the facilitator suggested a mind map: "Earlier, you identified the challenge of low morale as an important issue needing attention. Could one of you frame this issue more specifically for us?" A volunteer then outlined the situation. After he did so, the facilitator asked the group, "Now that you've heard Joe's presentation of the problem, do any of you see issues that would need to be considered in solving it? Just brainstorm or throw out any ideas that occur to you. Also, feel free to ask Joe questions to try to further clarify his view of the problem." From the ideas offered by the group, the accompanying Mind Map emerged.

At this point, the facilitator asked Joe if he saw any issues that now appeared to be important aspects of a possible solution. He reported several, including the need to clarify expectations of staff and management and to estimate the true costs of lost labor through attrition and low productivity. Joe went on to critique the training program now in place. He felt that it would be helpful if a new program, individually tailored by supervisors and employees to meet the needs of the unit and shift, were developed. A supervisor/subordinate contract could follow, within the framework of an overall commitment by food service employees to quality work. Ongoing training would be provided that supported a new, specific definition of work competencies. Experienced staff would be employed as mentors to new staff, providing a new role that could creatively engage them. Joe (and the others in the group) now felt less stuck and had several ideas worth exploring further.

This experience underscores the value of Mind Mapping as a problem-solving process. Although the Mind Map didn't suggest the actual solution to the problem, it helped visually organize the concerns in such a way as to make them less overwhelming. By providing such a picture, the Mind Map freed the group to examine the problem systematically, as any other issue, rather than feel powerless to address it. Furthermore, by drawing associative connections among ideas, it provided a visual map that gave participants a specific pathway to seeking solutions.

Figure 4.5
Food Service Unit Mind Map

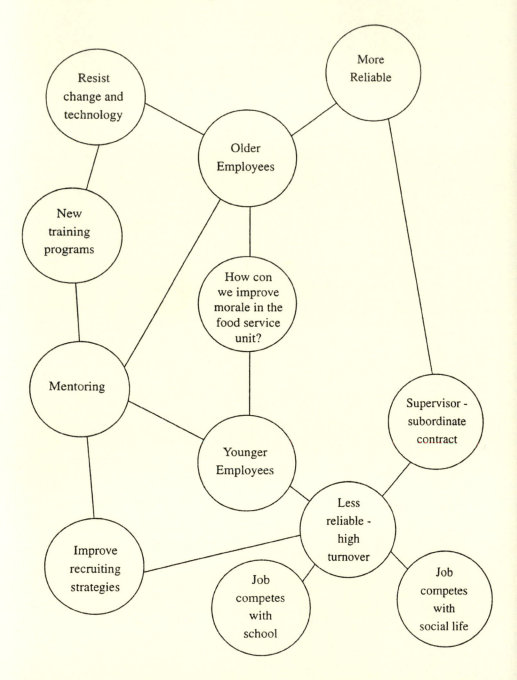

Helping a Community Group Get Beyond Personal Issues and Set a Plan of Action

A community organization, New Horizons, was dedicated to providing quality educational, counseling, and other support services to low-income families. Through largely volunteer efforts, they had been quite successful over the years. However, for the past five years they had witnessed a decline in volunteer involvement, a rise in bickering between staff and volunteers, and a drop in the number of clients served. In addition, significant cuts in federal and state funding had reduced their capacity to respond to non-routine community crises. Key staff members had left the agency for more stable positions elsewhere. Leadership from the board of directors initiated work with a consulting facilitator to help them determine a renewed plan of action for the future.

Through an initial needs assessment, which included some discussions and many pen and paper surveys (the group numbered nearly forty members), the facilitator discovered that there were longstanding fears and difficulties that existed within the group. These included staff/board conflicts, differing philosophies of the purpose of the organization (e.g., *Do we try to serve as many as possible, or do we focus on a few services and do them well?*), and historic animosities that related to roles formerly independent groups had played prior to merging as New Horizons twenty years ago. These unresolved issues led to alliances within the group, preventing collaborative responses to common problems.

The facilitator sorted the forty participants into five groups of eight members. Within each group, various factions and stakeholders within New Horizons were represented. In addition, each group was asked to appoint an internal facilitator and recorder. Finally, ground rules were established to encourage positive discussion within a safe environment. The following questions were posed to the small groups:

1. What are our expectations of one another in our work together?
2. What are some key issues that need to be addressed by New Horizons in the next two years?
3. What are some possible strategies we might use to address these issues?
4. What barriers, if any, prevent us from meeting these expectations or addressing these issues?
5. Given this discussion, what next steps would be useful to the group? Can you recommend a "plan of action" to the larger group?

Each group was given twenty minutes to address each question. Rather than considering these questions as discrete entities, the groups examined them as interconnected pieces in a bigger puzzle, and soon interactive dialogue was flowing between previously disputing factions. After discussing each question for twenty minutes, the facilitator had the groups provide brief reports to the large assembly, so all were able to appreciate the tenor of the debate. By the time they addressed the "next steps" issue, all groups were in agreement about issues they felt were important for the larger group to address. The facilitator helped frame the problems being identified, supported the challenges faced in stating some longstanding issues that were often taboo to discuss so explicitly, and clarified preferred subsequent actions. Everyone then left the session to share in a potluck lunch together.

There was significant overlap among groups, both in problems identified and barriers perceived. There were also great commonalities in expectations that were easily synthesized into a broader set of ground rules for the agency. While the next steps that came from the groups were somewhat different, they easily came together as a plan of action for the year.

The IDEAL problem-solving model was utilized by the facilitator in this situation. He helped the group identify a large number of possible problems, then focus on key issues in small groups. They listed potential solutions, then evaluated these solutions through the discussion of barriers. The small groups developed criteria for evaluating options through fluid conversation, rather than rigid procedural steps. Finally, the group agreed on next steps, first in smaller groups, then by agreement of all forty members. They adopted a plan of action for the year, recognizing the value of implementation and evaluation in the process.

It was obvious that the plan of action required ongoing efforts in implementation. Through representative ambassadors from each of the small groups, New Horizons established an ad hoc Problem-Solving Task Force. The task force assumed responsibility to monitor implementation of the plan of action and report to the board on a quarterly basis during the coming year. The task force also agreed to meet with the facilitator six weeks after the session.

The next meeting with the facilitator helped the representatives evaluate what had occurred thus far. They learned to appreciate their progress and identify possible stumbling blocks that could need attention in the future. Since they now had the previous experience with the IDEAL model, the facilitator supported them in trying it on their own at subsequent meetings. Over the course of the next year, many of the ideas developed in that initial meeting were implemented, while a few failed. More importantly, the goodwill that had developed energized New Horizons and reinvigorated the staff and volunteers to persevere. By shifting many of their interpersonal and political concerns into shared problems, the group was able to transform its manner of working significantly.

Chapter 5

Facilitation and Conflict Resolution

A conflict is a situation characterized by disagreement between two or more parties, in which the parties perceive a threat to their needs, interests, or concerns. Parties in conflict tend to perceive limited options for solutions and finite resources available to manage their differences, often resulting in the adoption of positions that protect their interests (Thomas and Killman 1977, Auvine et al. 1977).

Key elements of this definition must be understood by facilitators. First, conflicts are more than mere disagreements; they are situations in which parties perceive threats to their needs. As the perception of threat increases, the tendency to protect interests is heightened. Therefore, if facilitators can help manage the intensity of that threat, less rigidity may be required of the parties to protect their interests.[1]

Second, people's responses to conflictive situations are governed by their *perceptions* of those situations, rather than by objective reality. Efforts should then be made to facilitate understanding of the disputants' perceptions. Such efforts can differentiate legitimate areas of difference from issues that simply result from misunderstanding.

Third, there is a tendency to recognize the *limitations* of conflictive situations, rather than *opportunities* for collaborative solutions. If facilitators can model and encourage flexibility, creativity, and openness in the negotiation process, the likelihood of optimal, interest-based solutions is greatly enhanced. By focusing on opportunities, disputants can gain confidence that can be applied to the greatest challenges of the conflict.

There is a final element to be considered that poses a paradox for the facilitator. The intractability of conflicting parties in protecting their interests is counterproductive, as it undermines their efforts to meet their needs. The best interests of the parties will often be served most successfully by setting aside substantive positions and focusing on the procedural and psychological aspects of the conflict. In order to do so, however, fears of loss (of power, leverage, control, dignity, etc.) may initially increase, putting further stress on the dialogue. Helping parties navigate the *process* of conflict resolution is, therefore, among the most significant challenges for a facilitator.

THE CONFLICT CYCLE: ATTITUDES AND BELIEFS ABOUT CONFLICT

Beliefs

As we approach a specific conflict, we bring with us our beliefs about conflict—experiences, values, skills, and knowledge that we have accumulated throughout our lives. It is through such beliefs that we filter our initial responses to a situation. Therefore, it is helpful to facilitate self-awareness among group participants about these beliefs and for members to share these insights together, as appropriate. For example, in a staff group we might find that there are several members who believe that conflict is bad, should be avoided, and that the expression of anger should be minimized. Others may believe that "mixing it up" is healthy and appropriate, that if people want to deal with real issues, a little argument can be worthwhile.

It is the facilitator's role to help participants understand these beliefs and recognize how they contribute to responses to conflict. Then he or she can problem-solve regarding the management of such differing beliefs within the group. It may be appropriate, for example, for the group to revise its ground rules, to check whether people feel it is safe to participate, or to clarify who has a vested interest in addressing certain issues. Although the underlying beliefs about conflict cannot be readily changed, specific attitudes and behaviors in key situations can be managed more effectively.

Responses

There are four general categories of responses to conflictive situations:

Behavioral responses. Behavioral responses, illustrated by the conflict styles that we will discuss shortly, are actions in response to conflict. They include screaming, stomping, walking out, getting quiet, negotiating, listening, pacing, and the like. They often occur as a first reaction to a dispute.

Emotional responses. Emotional responses relate to our feelings in a conflict, and they may range from anger and fear to despair and confusion. Emotional responses are often misunderstood, as people tend to believe that others feel the same as they do. Thus, differing emotional responses are confusing and at times, threatening.

Cognitive responses. Cognitive responses are our ideas and thoughts about a conflict, often present as inner voices or internal observers in the midst of a situation. Through sub-vocalization, we come to understand these cognitive responses. For example, we might think any of the following things in response to another person cutting in line at the bank:

"That jerk! Who does he think he is?! What audacity and sense of entitlement!"

or:

"I wonder if he realizes what he has done. He seems lost in his own thoughts. I hope he is okay."

or:

"What am I supposed to do? If I let him cut in front, others are going to think I let him. That's embarrassing! Maybe I should say something to him, but what if he gets mad at me? Just let it go . . ."

Such differing cognitive responses contribute to emotional and behavioral responses, where self-talk can either promote a positive or negative feedback loop in the situation.

Physical responses. Finally, there are also physical responses to conflict that play an important role in our ability to meet our needs. Physical responses include heightened stress, bodily tension, increased perspiration, tunnel vision, shallow or accelerated breathing, nausea, and rapid heartbeat. These responses are similar to those we exhibit in other high-anxiety situations, and they may be managed through similar techniques (McKay et al. 1981; Heitler 1990). Helping people in the group become aware of their physical responses and being observant of this element of the reaction is important for the facilitator. Establishing a calmer environment in which emotions can be managed is more likely if the physical response is addressed effectively. Participants may practice diaphragmatic breathing, progressive muscle relaxation, or positive imagery, for example, which may prove valuable in highly stressful situations. These four elements of the personal response to conflict (behavioral, emotional, cognitive, and physical) conspire to form our collective response to a situation. They may be conceptualized and managed independently, but there is also value in understanding how they interact and participate in the conflict cycle.

The Conflict Cycle

Phase One: Attitudes and Beliefs. The cycle begins for all of us with our beliefs and attitudes about conflict, which stem from many sources and affect how we will respond when conflicts occur. In a hypothetical situation, Bill is Roberta's supervisor at XYZ Corporation. During a meeting they voice their disagreement over planned company growth: Bill advocates steady growth in established areas, while Roberta believes this is a time for XYZ to take risks and put resources into new ventures.

This is an understandable philosophical disagreement that could, at first, be addressed as a problem to be solved. However, it is filtered through Bill's belief that subordinate staff should never openly express disagreement, especially in front of others from different departments within the company. Roberta fears that, unless the company take risks, she will lose her job. She also believes that only through healthy dialogue and advocacy, both inside the meeting and outside of it, will the best ideas win the debate.

Phase Two: The Conflict. In the next phase of the cycle, the conflict occurs. In this scenario, Bill gets very quiet and noticeably flushed when Roberta expresses her ideas at the meeting. He becomes visibly upset when others assert that they share Roberta's position and that they have discussed their ideas prior to the meeting. Bill says nothing, except that he feels it is premature for the group to reach any decisions. Suddenly, he indicates that he is late for another meeting and leaves hastily.

Although Roberta and Bill haven't had an argument at the meeting, a conflict has occurred. Both perceive threats to their needs. Roberta's response is to raise issues and encourage discussion and debate. Bill's response is to avoid the conflict and withdraw from the meeting.

Phase Three: The Response. The response is the point where we take action. We might begin to shout, to attempt to talk about the situation, or simply to leave. Given our personal beliefs, we will often react in the same general way, no matter what the particular conflict. Thus, these reactions can tell us much about ourselves and our patterns in conflict situations.

In our case at XYZ Corporation, Bill's initial responses have now occurred: anger, embarrassment, quiet, and walking out of the meeting. Roberta's responses are surprise, anger, frustration with him for leaving the meeting, fear of consequences, and a heightened sense of insecurity. She retreats from her advocacy for the risk-taking strategy and allows others to participate more actively in determining the solution to the problem. She goes to the bathroom, and when she returns to the meeting appears distracted and unfocused.

Phase Four: Integrating Experiences into Belief Systems. Responses, in turn, lead to consequences. The apparent consequences of Bill not dealing directly with Roberta are failure to find resolution and lack of honesty between the two colleagues. The group is unable to provide input or participate in an important discussion. There is confusion about what is happening, anxiety about Bill's future participation, and a general malaise among the group members. For Bill and Roberta, there are cognitive, emotional, and physical consequences. These consequences serve to reinforce Bill's belief that conflict is negative and that it causes psychic pain. This, in turn, brings him back to the beginning of the cycle. For Roberta, the experience heightens fears about her work situation. Given her attitude that conflict should be openly and directly addressed, she focuses frustration and anger on Bill. She comes to believe the conflict is his fault. She becomes reluctant to initiate a resolution, despite her belief that it would be healthy to do so. If Bill and Roberta have historically managed conflicts in this manner, it is likely to continue. For most of us, the results of the cycle reinforce our belief system and lead to the perpetuation of the pattern.

These four phases of the conflict cycle are diagramed in Figure 5.1.

Figure 5.1
The Conflict Cycle

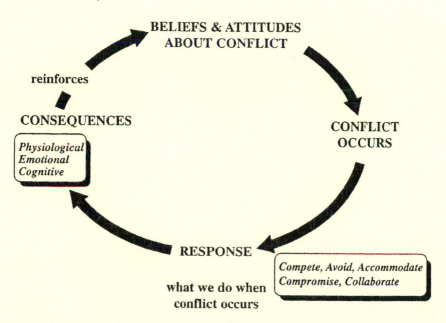

A way to break the conflict cycle is to gain greater awareness of our personal responses and consciously choose to change them. A good place to start is to *change the behavioral response* to conflict (i.e., conflict style, see following section). Such changes are generally more within our control and lead to modified actions by others. We may continue to feel angry. However, if we stop shouting and try to listen, others are more likely to understand us. From here, we can begin to change our physical, cognitive, and emotional responses to conflict.

The group facilitator's role is to help participants to fully understand the experience of conflict, so they may proceed to resolve their issues in a collaborative manner. By helping participants understand conflict as a normal part of life, the facilitator helps manage the transitions of discarding old beliefs (and their consequent behaviors) and replacing them with new understandings and agreements.

OVERVIEW OF CONFLICT RESOLUTION STYLES AND THEIR CONSEQUENCES

Conflict is often best understood by examining the consequences of various interpersonal behaviors at moments in time. These behaviors are usefully categorized according to conflict styles. Each style is a way to meet one's needs in a dispute but may impact on other people in different ways.

Competing is a style in which one's own needs are advocated over the needs of others. It relies on an aggressive style of communication, low regard for future relationships, and the exercise of coercive power. Those using a competitive style tend to seek control over a discussion, in both substance and ground rules. They fear that loss of such control will result in solutions that fail to meet their needs. Competing is known as a conflict escalator (Kreidler 1990), for it tends to result in responses that increase the level of threat.

Accommodating, also known as smoothing, is the opposite of competing. Persons using this style yield their needs to those of others, trying to be diplomatic. They tend to allow the needs of the group to overwhelm their own, which may not ever be stated. Accommodating is thus characterized by submissive communication. For those who accommodate, preserving the relationship is seen as most important.

Avoiding is a common response to the negative perception of conflict. "Perhaps if we don't bring it up, it'll blow over," we say to ourselves. Perhaps so. But generally all that happens is that feelings get pent up, views go unexpressed, and the conflict festers until it becomes too big to ignore. Like a cancer that may well have been cured if treated early, the conflict grows and spreads until it kills the relationship. Because needs and concerns go unexpressed, people are often confused, wondering what went wrong in a relationship.

Compromising is an approach to conflict in which people gain and give in a series of tradeoffs. While satisfactory, compromise is generally not satisfying. We each remain shaped by our individual perceptions of our needs and don't necessarily understand the other side very well. There is a tendency to remain focused on initial positions rather than to truly understand the range of potential solutions and resources available. Compromising is often premised on a lack of trust and an aversion to risk taking.

Collaborating is the pooling of individual needs and goals toward a common goal. Often called win-win problem solving, collaboration requires assertive communication (see Chapter Two) and cooperation in order to achieve a better solution than either individual could have achieved alone. It offers the chance for consensus, the integration of the needs of the parties, and the utilization of resources previously unknown to the participants. Collaboration offers the potential to exceed the "budget" of possibilities that previously limited our view of the conflict. (See Figure 5.2.) It brings in new time, energy, and ideas to resolve the dispute meaningfully.

Figure 5.2
The Conflict Budget

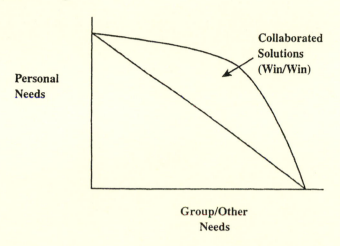

In Figure 5.3, the needs of two parties are represented in a given situation, with my needs along the y-axis and another's, perhaps yours, along the x-axis. As we move out from the graph's origin, we encounter the spectrum of conflict management styles. For example, if my needs are met completely, at the expense of yours, that would indicate a competing style of conflict management on my part. When both sets of needs are somewhat satisfied, but not completely, a compromising style is most likely being used by both of us. When my needs and your needs are both taken fully into consideration, collaboration is possible.

Figure 5.3
Conflict Management Styles

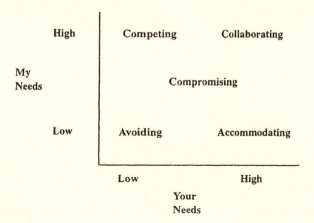

We should not focus on outcomes to distinguish between compromising and collaborating styles. The outcomes of collaboration may not always appear to be win-win, but the process encourages people to broaden their discussion and strengthen their relationship. Collaboration allows us to consider the underlying needs of the parties in a manner that is often precluded by the quick, positional, compromising approach.

Although we do promote a collaborative ethic in our teaching about conflict resolution, we do not wish to leave the impression that collaboration is always the best style. In an emergency, it may be crucial for an individual with critical skills and information to take charge and force the group to adopt a particular course of action (competing). Or there may be times when it's appropriate to smooth things over in a relationship while feelings run high (accommodating), or to ignore certain conflicts that don't matter that much in the big picture of a relationship (avoiding). However, when the resources are there and the willingness to work is present, we try to collaborate with others and seek a solution that is best for all.

The facilitator plays numerous roles with respect to conflict management styles:

1. To assist the group in understanding the normal role of conflict without assigning blame;
2. To help individual group members understand their own personal responses to conflict and conflict styles;
3. To create an affirming environment with clear ground rules for resolving disputes, which enhances the group members' abilities to deal constructively with conflicts; and
4. To promote the use of collaborative, interest-based negotiation for managing differences, whenever possible.

Group members frequently experience a natural tension between the satisfaction of personal needs and those of the group. There are those who believe that conflict resolution only works when there is an altruistic, caring relationship and shared vision. Although this is occasionally true, it is not usually the path through which collaboration occurs. Collaboration is generally pursued out of *self-interest*; in other words, "I recognize that the best way to achieve my needs is to work with you" (Fisher and Ury 1981; Fisher and Brown 1981).

The "Prisoner's Dilemma" and Its Practical Applications

The "Prisoner's Dilemma" refers to a game that is useful in understanding cooperation and competition, as well as aspects of interpersonal conflict resolution. The game gets its name from a hypothetical problem: Two prisoners have been arrested for a crime, and both face potentially long jail terms. Either alone can confess against the other, resulting in defection (abandonment of concern for the other in favor of his own self-interest). If defection is chosen by one of the prisoners, it will result in a full jail term for the other prisoner and an immediate release for the confessor. If both prisoners defect by confessing against each other, both will serve full sentences. On the other hand, if both prisoners cooperate by refusing to confess, both will be convicted on minor charges, and both will serve short jail terms. (See Figure 5.4.)

Figure 5.4
Payoffs for the Prisoner's Dilemma

	Player B Cooperates	Player B Defects
Player A Cooperates	A gets 3 B gets 3	A gets 0 B gets 5
Player A Defects	A gets 5 B gets 0	A gets 0 B gets 0

Axelrod (1984) explored when it is most advantageous for a person to cooperate and when to act solely out of self-interest. He invited game theorists from diverse backgrounds (economics, psychology, sociology, political science, and physics) to submit computer programs for playing "Prisoner's Dilemma." The winning program, "Tit for Tat," developed by Professor Anatol Rapoport of the University of Toronto, was the one that allowed players to earn the highest number of total points over multiple rounds of play. "Tit for Tat" begins with a cooperative move and then proceeds by returning cooperation for cooperation and selfishness for selfishness.

Axelrod discovered several principles that are quite practical for dealing with everyday conflicts:

1. Starting nice and then returning kindness for kindness and competition for competition proves to be the most successful long-term strategy. By making a personal decision to extend an olive branch, participants increase the likelihood of a similar response to get negotiations moving along.
2. Acting on pure self-interest may maximize gains in brief encounters. However, over the long term, solutions that optimize what both players receive yield the higher gains, rather than those that attempt to maximize one player's gains at the other's expense. Consequently, in ongoing relationships, such as those between family members or co-workers, cooperative, rather than antagonistic, attitudes should have the best payoffs.
3. Niceness pays. Niceness refers to initiating the relationship in a cooperative fashion. This can be especially difficult to implement in the face of conflict. For example, if two co-workers have had a long period of hostile interactions, it may take some encouragement before they are convinced that niceness does have potential for better payoffs than continued hostile encounters.

4. Selfishness costs. In "Tit for Tat," frequent, unprovoked selfish moves typically result in overall low scores. Likewise, in relationships, selfishness breeds resentment and lack of trust.
5. Excessive pessimism can be similarly expensive. Pessimism is defined as the expectation that the other will make selfish moves. This can cause needless losses, as operating under pessimistic expectations promotes overall negative behaviors. By contrast, optimism, the expectation that others will cooperate, enhances the effectiveness of "Tit for Tat."
6. "Tit for Tat" is highly responsive. Only one defection is necessary to reverse the pattern of cooperation, and only one cooperative move can, in turn, reverse the pessimism.
7. Forgiveness, defined as the propensity to cooperate at least once more even after the other player has defected, heightens the effectiveness of "Tit for Tat." Couples, co-workers, teammates, and others who work and/or play together need to accept their own and their partners' occasional mistakes.
8. Increasing the degree of retaliation seems to decrease the game's effectiveness. In general, slightly overdoing the forgiveness seems to enhance effectiveness, while overdoing retaliation seems counterproductive.
9. Clarity is a major benefit. Clarity of response elicits trust and long-term cooperation. In continuing relationships, it is important to explicitly state agreements and expectations. In this way, implementation and evaluation opportunities are enhanced.

In conclusion, these insights offer the facilitator additional reference points for encouraging collaboration within the group. As noted earlier, the argument is often made that collaborative approaches to conflict management only work when both parties are caring, empathic, and committed to the larger goal. However, there is also validity to the view that collaboration is possible in the face of resistance and skepticism. Since collaboration flows from self-interest rather than from altruism, the strategy has utility in a broad spectrum of conflicts.[2]

MANAGING DIVERSE NEEDS IN NEGOTIATION: SUBSTANTIVE, PSYCHOLOGICAL, AND PROCEDURAL CONCERNS

As noted earlier, conflicts occur because people perceive a threat to their needs, interests, or concerns. In efforts to manage conflict, it is therefore critical that facilitators understand these interests and facilitate their expression within the negotiation process.

In any dispute, parties have substantive, psychological, and procedural concerns. Substantive concerns are those issues that most of us view as the basis of the problem to be solved, such as resolving policy dilemmas, finding equitable solutions, or determining how to proceed on a project. But when we examine these issues, we find there are aspects of the conflict that have little to do with substance.

Psychological concerns are those related to the well-being of the disputants. As we adopt a new office policy, for example, do all parties feel comfortable with it? Do they feel their input is heard and understood? These emotional components of the problem can be, for many, the key to addressing substantive concerns.

Finally, there are procedural concerns, those issues that relate to process in problem solving. Do all parties feel the process was fair? Are procedures in place to manage future disagreements? Were any key issues excluded from discussion that may undermine the effectiveness of our solution? These types of procedural questions are often linked in subtle ways to psychological issues, and they make significant impacts on substance. For example, in the famous Paris peace talks to negotiate the end of American involvement in Vietnam, the shape of the table was a key hurdle to overcome before substantive negotiations could be held. In the more recent Middle East peace talks, the issue of flags on the table was directly related to who had standing to negotiate and, ultimately, whether discussions could occur at all.

In multi-party disputes, these concerns may vary in priority from person to person. Among the tasks of the facilitator in conflictive situations is identifying these concerns and ensuring that they are given a voice at the table. Participants must then remain flexible regarding the agenda of issues to be addressed.

As illustrated in Figure 5.5, the diverse needs of participants exist side-by-side in all negotiations. They frequently overlap as well, forming hybrid concerns. For example, when discussing ground rules for the meeting, we are solving a procedural problem. However, by establishing such procedures, we are creating a more affirming environment, meeting an important psychological concern. Similarly, by clarifying specific protocols for communicating future problems (a procedural concern), we are addressing a substantive need that helps the parties work out problems in the future.

Figure 5.5
Triangle of Needs in Negotiation

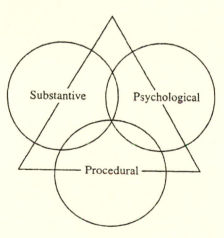

THE IMPORTANCE OF TAKING A "LISTENING STANCE" INTO CONFLICT

Throughout this book, the importance of listening within the facilitated meeting has been emphasized. Listening enhances communication about the various issues addressed within the meeting. The modeling of effective listening skills by the facilitator is especially important. There is no place where listening is more central than in efforts to manage and resolve conflicts within the group. However, when we examine people's tendencies within conflict, the ability to listen is tested, strained, and often abandoned.

Taking what we call a "listening stance" is the most powerful tool of conflict resolution. It reflects the paradox of communication identified earlier: by making a commitment to listen to your point of view, I greatly improve the likelihood that you, in turn, will understand my concerns. This commitment to active listening (see Chapter Two) is crucial if people are to problem-solve together. Otherwise, emotional resistance will remain, based on perceived differences that are far greater than actual differences.

Implicit in this discussion is the importance of genuine empathy as a characteristic of participants in this process. The ability to understand not only what a person says, but how that person has come to hold that belief, is a significant struggle for any listener, but an especially important task for a person in conflict. The facilitator, as mediator, is personally challenged in this process to set aside biases. One must tolerate and respect the beliefs of disputing parties and use this opportunity as the basis for transforming their behaviors. As difficult as the problem-solving phase of negotiation may be, we can think of no greater challenge to the facilitator than to be an empathic listener.

PEACE/6: A SIX-PART MODEL FOR CONFLICT RESOLUTION

Many of the tools and strategies emphasized earlier remain appropriate to the mediation of conflicts. Setting the tone, establishing ground rules, and promoting a clear agenda for action remain important guidelines for this process. However, the structured process of conflict resolution benefits from the model outlined below. This model, which we call "PEACE/6," synthesizes our experiences in dispute resolution with the ideas of Heitler, Fisher, Ury, and others, in a dynamic approach to the collaborative management of disputes. We have found it does an excellent job of assimilating key concerns in conflictive situations. It offers facilitators a guide to the mediating role they must now play within the group.

Step I: Personal Needs Assessment (P)

Prior to bringing parties together to discuss a conflict, it is valuable to create an opportunity to understand their independent perspectives, including their attitudes regarding the upcoming negotiation. This phase within the facilitated meeting is analogous to the pre-negotiation phase discussed in Chapter Three. It provides parties with the chance to clarify issues while building rapport with the facilitator for the conflict resolution process.

A critical element of personal assessment is the exploration of each participant's BATNA, or Best Alternative To a Negotiated Agreement.[3] In other words, if this dispute isn't settled, what is the best result that can be expected? It is also vital to examine each party's WATNA (Worst Alternative To a Negotiated Agreement) and MLATNA (Most Likely Alternative To a Negotiated Agreement). Helping disputants understand their own options puts a realistic presence into the negotiation and may clarify areas of common ground and areas of disagreement.

Step II: Establish Ground Rules (E)

The commitment to ground rules is the foundation from which the rest of the process builds. As noted earlier, the ritual of establishing ground rules together can be an important group experience. In the latter stages of the process, this ritual can be a source of energy and support.

Step III: Address Initial Positions (A)

The expression of the conflict, as perceived by all parties, fulfills important needs. If combined with a commitment to active listening, this phase clarifies the disparity between perceived differences and actual differences. Moreover, since all parties have a fair opportunity to be heard, the desire to violate the ground rules is reduced. Any conflict resolution process that hurries through Step III is significantly impeded; such efforts at efficiency tend to ignore emotional and procedural needs. By focusing prematurely on substantive differences, parties remain positional and tend to become inflexible. If there is to be a genuine transition to Step IV, in which underlying concerns are addressed, facilitators (and participants) must summon the patience to hear all points of view and to listen with respect.

Step IV: Clarify Underlying Concerns and Needs (C)

The heart of this stage is the ability of the facilitator to hear, understand, and frame initial statements as expressions of needs rather than wants. Participants may do well to hear others' positions, but it is unrealistic to expect them to both understand and verbalize the underlying needs of the conflict. Frequently, participants will emerge from Step III in impasse. In terms of initial positions, they may be diametrically opposed. However, by taking pains to reframe these positions in terms of needs, some of which may dovetail, the facilitator helps the group move to problem solving.

For example, imagine staff members discussing the relocation of a busy fax machine in a shared office. Kim wants to move the fax away from her desk, closer to the door. Sergio, who sits nearest the door, wants the fax to remain next to Kim's desk. While Kim and Sergio have opposing positions, facilitated discussion reveals that they actually share an underlying concern: both want to reduce the noise and activity levels by their work areas in order to remain productive. Once they discover a shared fundamental need, Kim and Sergio can move from positional arguments to a fruitful discussion of arranging efficient and quiet work stations.

Vital to this transition is a thorough discussion of the disputants' criteria for choosing solutions. By developing objective and mutually acceptable guidelines, participants are able to make choices that meet their underlying concerns. The facilitator helps participants dwell less on impasse and more on opportunities by recognizing that many different criteria may be applied to a situation.

Step V: Evaluate Options to Build an Agreement (E)

The facilitator's role in this stage is to help the group work thoroughly. As they proceed through various issues, some may be discarded or forgotten. The facilitator should attempt to track the discussion, bring up unresolved issues, identify any possible items for future debate, and support participants in reaching closure. In building an agreement, the facilitator looks for hallmarks of a good solution, as discussed in Chapter Four on problem solving: fairness; balance; realism; response to underlying needs; sufficient specificity and clarity; and consideration of the future.

Step VI: Live and Learn (/6)

Finally, participants should evaluate the process before they leave. This provides a chance for positive reflection on having navigated a difficult time together. It is also an opportunity for the facilitator to validate their work and congratulate them on their progress. At this point, it is important to implement the ideas that have been developed and clarify mechanisms for evaluating their success. Addressing conflict is a predictable aspect of working together. It can be illuminating for facilitators to appreciate the place of such disputes within their evolving mission.

As we examine this model, we find reaffirmation of key components of the facilitation process. (See Figure 5.6.) First, before proceeding to problem solving, it is crucial that we establish ground rules that are accepted by all participants. Second, an environment that promotes honest communication of concerns, even if that means the expression of harshly opposing viewpoints, is to be encouraged. The heat of battle and its associated energy may only be used constructively if it is allowed to be expressed. Third, the initial expression of positions must be patiently transformed into an understanding of underlying

Figure 5.6
PEACE/6: A Six-Part Model for Conflict Resolution

I. **PERSONAL NEEDS ASSESSMENT**
    Understand personal needs including: substantive, procedural,
      and psychological needs
    Determine desired outcomes
    Explore BATNA

II. **ESTABLISH GROUND RULES**
    Create ground rules that reinforce a respectful environment
    Facilitate enforcement of the ground rules
    Gain commitment from all involved

III. **ADDRESS INITIAL POSITIONS**
    Express the conflict
    Use effective and empathic listening skills
    Attempt to express concerns assertively
    Provide equal "air time" for all participants
    This is a start, not a settlement—don't rush the process

IV. **CLARIFY UNDERLYING CONCERNS AND NEEDS**
    Explore underlying concerns free of attack, debate, or judgment
    Cooperate; try to remain flexible
    Focus on interests, not positions
    Identify mutually acceptable criteria to apply to problem solving
    Talk it through in depth and detail

V. **EVALUATE OPTIONS TO BUILD AN AGREEMENT**
    Actively participate
    Genuinely ask, "So, what shall we do to solve this?"
    If impasse is reached, refocus on an earlier stage of the process
    Select a solution

VI. **LIVE AND LEARN**
    Regularly assess what went well and what didn't
    Develop new strategies and/or solutions as needed

                    A GOOD SOLUTION:
                      * Is perceived to be fair
                      * Is balanced in implementation
                      * Is specific and clear enough to be implemented
                      * Is realistic given the parties' resources
                      * Meets underlying concerns
                      * Considers future needs

needs, interests, and concerns. The seeds of collaborative solutions lie within this crucial phase of the process. Finally, effective problem solving is characterized by a willingness to be flexible in understanding differing criteria for solutions, including durability. If facilitators are able to guide their groups through this process, there is great opportunity for members to gain insights that will transfer to other nonconflictive situations.

STRATEGIES FOR MANAGING IMPASSE WITHIN FACILITATED GROUPS

As participants proceed through the conflict resolution process, they are likely to experience impasse, a period of protracted inability to find acceptable solutions. Such periods are characterized by many attributes of "stuckness": frustration, powerlessness, anger, anxiety, rigidity, and blaming are common. Impasse is often viewed, by participants and facilitators alike, as something to be avoided or, at best, efficiently managed. However, we have come to view it as an important, natural time in the evolution of conflict that should be embraced as an opportunity for transformation. Paradoxically, we welcome impasse as an opportunity to confront the most significant underlying concerns of the conflict. Perhaps we may move beyond initial issues into more meaningful ones. It is in this light that we offer the specific strategies for managing impasse which follow.

Discuss Feelings About Impasse

Ask participants to discuss their feelings about impasse. Often, we assume certain emotional responses to impasse that are inaccurate. Also, by focusing only on the issues of the conflict, we lose sight of the emotions experienced by the parties. Having people discuss their feelings about being stuck brings a renewed sense of understanding and empathy to the issues at hand.

Shift from Substantive to Procedural or Psychological Issues

Usually, groups are at impasse over substantive issues. By setting such issues aside for a while, and shifting to a procedural concern, they can regain confidence in themselves as problem solvers. Next, take a psychological concern to further build trust. After such a shift, there may be more success with substantive issues.

Reframe the Problem

Often, we get stranded with initial, inadequate definitions of a problem at hand. We may find that new ways of describing the situation help us appreciate other elusive dimensions of the dilemma. We also like to reframe our style of approaching the issue, not just its definition. For example, an office staff was frustrated over how to solve a problem where people lacked appropriate access to a copier and fax machine. As facilitators, we took common desk items and physically moved them around the table to test alternative arrangements that represented the office. On other occasions, we have had participants draw pictures to redefine their situations. By taking the problem out of an abstract, verbal mode and putting it in a concrete, visual mode, we can create new ways of viewing the situation that promote flexibility.

Consider a Structured Break

A break is a relatively easy way to change the energy of the room. In impasse, people often come to feel personally attacked and emotionally drained. They tend to benefit from relaxing for a few minutes, going to the bathroom, or having a beverage. Rather than just having people adjourn for ten minutes, however, we suggest that they consider a response to a focus question during that time. For example, we might say:

We'd like to suggest a ten-minute break at this point, just to give people a rest from their hard work. We really appreciate how challenging it is to work on these issues, as you have, and we are confident that good solutions remain for you. During this break, we'd like you to consider two things. First, reflect on how you feel right now about being stuck, and, if you need anything from the group before proceeding, what that might be. Second, we'd like you to consider alternatives, should we fail to reach an agreement this afternoon. In other words, what will happen for you if we don't successfully work things out today? When we return from break, we'll check in with each of you to understand what you have discovered about these questions.

We find that such a structured break often leads to robust, meaningful discussion when people return, including the proffering of olive branches that were previously not forthcoming.

An Olive Branch Can Be the First Step Toward Peace

Much as we would prefer that another person be the first to demonstrate flexibility, we are often confronted by the harsh reality that our own needs may only be met by making the first offer. As discussed earlier in the "Prisoner's Dilemma," it is self-interest that motivates the extension of the olive branch. However, one caveat should always be kept in mind: One should not extend a hand that one cannot afford to have refused. The other party may refuse the initial gesture of peace for important reasons, and this could further erode confidence in the negotiations. The facilitator should remain calm and patient about such situations, recognizing the continued legitimacy of the refusing party's position. We must also help the initiating party understand the consequences of this refusal.

When in Doubt, Restate

Active listening remains central to the management of impasse, for several reasons. First, restating clarifies your understanding of the parties' positions and offers a face-saving way for them to modify their positions based on your restatement. Second, it provides you with a chance to consider other strategies; by restating, you keep your focus and buy time for problem solving. Finally, restating can be a useful way to embrace areas of agreement and validate them again for the group. Often, these agreements have been lost in the focus on disagreement, and the summarizing process brings the conflict back into perspective.

Consider the Use of Caucus

Caucus, or meeting separately with each party, allows people to terminate dysfunctional communication. It also reestablishes elements of safety within a situation that may have become dangerous. Caucus allows flexibility and the consideration of creative options in a more relaxed, less pressured manner. The facilitator can be an agent of reality here, helping participants accurately evaluate the situation. Caucus risks the neutrality of the facilitator if improperly handled, and it also has the participants speaking with the facilitator, rather than one another. However, it can be a useful strategy when direct communication has broken down.

Consider BATNA, WATNA, and MLATNA Before Negotiations Are Terminated

We have previously described considering best, worst, and most likely alternatives to a negotiated agreement as important motivators. In times of impasse, it can be tempting to settle for an alternative to collaboration. The facilitator can help by reminding the participants of the consequences of such options. It is imperative that people calm down sufficiently to see their alternatives clearly. Whether such consideration occurs in open session, during caucus, or through a break, weighing alternatives is an effective strategy in impasse.

Reaffirm the Ground Rules

As stated previously, ground rules serve as the foundation for risking functional, honest communication. As such, they are often endangered during impasse. By reaffirming the group's commitment to these rules at this time, participants are reminded of their common commitment to a respectful process. They may find that the ground rules need to be revised in light of new insights. Thus, a new set of procedural issues has been formed, which can positively impact the meeting environment.

Engage the Wall: The Force Is With You

As we noted in the introduction to this section, we view impasse as an important opportunity for achieving meaningful dialogue and significant solutions. A fitting metaphor for impasse as opportunity is a wall. Envision impasse as a time in which the disputants have constructed a wall between them across the center of the table. The deeper the impasse, the higher and stronger is the construction of this wall. Our initial feeling about the wall is that it is bad and should be eliminated. We are, therefore, encouraged to consider destroying, circumventing, or rebuilding the wall to protect ourselves or, perhaps, giving up and withdrawing altogether. Rarely do we recognize that the wall contains within it the answers to our questions and the solutions to our problems. By calmly engaging the wall and seeking to understand it, we often find that its power is transformed to one of insight.

A more concrete analogy is a wooden stockade wall, such as the kind found in outdoor obstacle courses or military training camps. It is difficult, if not impossible, to scale the wall without ever touching it, solely by shimmying up one of the ropes dangling from the top. It is much easier to grasp a rope and walk up the wall, using the force of the wall against one's feet to assist with the ascent.

Those who prefer a more metaphysical metaphor can appreciate the *Star Wars* movie trilogy (Lucasfilms: 1977, 1980, 1983), in which the hero, Luke Skywalker, attempts to become a Jedi knight to overcome the evil dark side of a mysterious force. Luke's early efforts, spent combating the force, are a failure. But when Luke is able to calm himself, find patience with the process, confront his deepest fears, and seek good within his adversary, Darth Vader, he gains understanding of the Force. Thus, he is able summon his own courage and energy to trust the Force to be with him. Similarly, the group facilitator must trust the energy of the group at times of impasse. If we can remain poised and considerate at such times, we encourage conflictive parties to do the same. If we trust their capacity to find solutions, such solutions may be found. However, if we abandon such faith through our own impatience, ego, fear, or arrogance, we undermine the process we are seeking to protect.[4]

In conclusion, numerous strategies exist that may prove useful during impasse. (See Figure 5.7.) It is important to understand the experience confronting the group and help them proceed by using tools that are situationally appropriate. If the impasse is characterized by high energy and continued commitment to ultimate solutions, there remains a very real opportunity for success. If, however, the meeting is now characterized by little energy and a sense of resignation, the facilitator must help participants understand the true consequences of no agreement and assess the options before them. Just as groups pass through distinct phases of development, each requiring unique forms of facilitated leadership, so may specific meetings evolve. By understanding this, facilitators can provide useful leadership to successfully navigate the perils of impasse.

Figure 5.7
Strategies for Managing Impasse

1. Ask participants to discuss their feelings regarding being at impasse.
2. Shift from substantive to procedural or psychological issues.
3. Reframe the problem.
4. Consider a structured break.
5. An olive branch can be the first step towards peace.
6. When in doubt: restate.
7. Consider the use of caucus at this time.
8. Consider BATNA, WATNA, and MLATNA before negotiations are terminated.
9. Reaffirm the ground rules.
10. Engage the wall: The Force is with you.

SPECIAL CONCERNS WHEN FACILITATING MULTI-PARTY DISPUTES

Facilitators often encounter multi-party disputes, or conflicts in which there are more than two opposing parties. Although the strategies previously developed are helpful in these cases, several special tactics should be considered, as follows.

Extra time spent in pre-negotiation and personal needs assessment, either directly or indirectly, helps gain a sincere commitment to the process from all participants. Pre-negotiation can be used as an opportunity to learn participants' perceived needs, expectations, and hesitations, as well as to build rapport. The facilitator should attempt to negotiate actively for the establishment of clear ground rules, the identification of appropriate participants, and the definition of space needs.

Opening statements are an opportunity for each person to share initial positions and to be understood. As important as this is in two-party mediation, it becomes even more complex in multi-party negotiations. An extra restating ground rule may be appropriate, where participants are asked to restate the previous person's viewpoint before presenting their own. Don't rush past initial statements, despite pressure to get on with business.

It may be helpful to seek common ground early on. This is not to minimize areas of difference, but to clarify them. By identifying issues that can be resolved in light of these areas of agreement, support can be built for continued dialogue. The more parties are able to accept mutual territory, the more goodwill is cultivated that will be valuable in resolving true differences.

Often, several levels of negotiation need to occur. Cross-group discussion is the primary focus of substantive negotiation, but within-group communication is important to psychological needs in the conflict. Try to allow time for dialogue within smaller groups, increased use of caucus, and periodic breaks, while keeping large group discussions on the explicit tasks of the group.

The formation of subgroups that break down old coalitions may offer participants the chance to shift from adversarial to solution-oriented relationships. If the group has multiple meetings, they provide excellent opportunities to establish task forces, project teams, and information gathering groups, which rearrange traditional alliances.

There is an inevitable tension between *being (social cohesiveness)* and *doing (task effectiveness)*, which requires sensitivity on the part of the facilitator. Disputants often find it a profound experience to "know the enemy." This is valuable for its own sake, aside from aiding substantive progress, and could translate into goodwill that representatives take to other settings. It is important that the facilitator not become preoccupied with solutions if group members are not so inclined. However, it is critical to check with members regularly, support what may be changing perspectives on progress, and help the members realistically comprehend consequences of their decisions.

Moderates and extremists may play an important function within the meeting. Moderates are defined here as members who demonstrate flexibility in negotiation. This includes a willingness to consider a variety of options and a desire to attend to others' needs in negotiation. Unfortunately, moderates tend to be reluctant to speak, as they may see themselves as less passionately committed to a position. Extremists in this context are members who rigidly hold on to a minority position. They narrowly define the agenda and often sabotage efforts by others (even in their own camp) to negotiate. Extremists tend to dominate discussions, fearing that their concerns will lose out if they don't argue forcefully. The challenge for facilitators in such situations is to empower the moderates, encouraging them to participate and model flexibility. The result is that the overall sentiments of the group are more accurately represented and a mainstream set of positions emerges. Facilitation is premised on a willingness to participate, which some influential parties may be reluctant to demonstrate. While this should be addressed in pre-negotiation, it may need to be revisited in determining who should join an ongoing group and how people are invited or uninvited.

The facilitator should take care to continue as a neutral party during any further discussion between meetings. Major issues raised by interim subgroups should be brought back to the larger group for resolution. The facilitator should also recognize potentially biased responses that he or she may have to certain extremists within the group. Since they are exhibiting attitudes that may differ from those of the facilitator, biases may lurk just beneath the surface of the meeting. Having opportunities to discuss one's own personal responses with a colleague can be quite valuable in such circumstances.

Figure 5.8 sets out these special concerns when dealing with conflicts in which there are more than two opposing parties.

Figure 5.8
Special Concerns When Facilitating Multi-Party Disputes

1. Spend extra time in pre-negotiation and needs assessment.
2. Use opening statements by participants as an opportunity for each person to share initial positions and be understood.
3. Actively seek common ground early on, not to minimize areas of difference, but to clarify them.
4. Recognize that several levels of negotiation need to occur.
5. Whenever possible, have subgroups form that break down old coalitions.
6. Be sensitive to the inevitable tension between being (social cohesiveness) and doing (task effectiveness).
7. Be especially sensitive to the roles of moderates and extremists within the meeting.
8. Continue to be vigilant regarding your neutrality throughout the process.

ACTIVITIES FOR TEACHING CONFLICT RESOLUTION SKILLS

My Conflict

"My Conflict" is an activity designed to increase personal awareness of one's role in conflict. The primary purpose of this activity is to explore what works well in conflict and what needs to be changed. Participants probe underlying assumptions, attitudes, and beliefs about conflict, as well.

First, participants are encouraged to relax and clear their minds of extraneous thoughts. Taking a couple of deep breaths, stretching, or shaking out one's hands and feet can encourage relaxation. Then, have participants focus on your voice as you encourage them to recreate in their mind's eye a recent conflict. (Note: They should be informed that the conflict chosen should be one they feel comfortable sharing with a partner or others in a group discussion.) Participants are guided through remembering the conflict and encouraged to create a vivid visual recollection of the conflict. They are given the following verbal cues from the facilitator:

1. What did you see in the environment?
2. What did the other person look like (e.g., clothing, body posture, facial expression)?
3. What did you hear (e.g., what the other person was saying, what you were saying, tone of voice, peripheral noise)?
4. What were you feeling (e.g., excited, scared)?
5. What were you thinking (e.g., "This is a great opportunity," or "I hate this.")?
6. How was your body feeling (e.g., relaxed, muscles tense, butterflies in stomach)?

MY CONFLICT

Think about an interpersonal conflict you recently experienced. Try to recreate, in your mind's eye, where the conflict occurred, who was present, and how you were feeling (both physically and emotionally). Consider what you were thinking just before, during, and after the conflict. Take your time to create a complete mental image, and then answer the following questions:

How did the conflict start? _____

_____

_____

_____

How did I contribute to it? _____

_____

_____

_____

What did I do during the conflict? _____

_____

_____

_____

What consequences did I experience as a result of this conflict? _____

_____

_____

_____

Is this a common pattern for me in conflict? _____

_____

_____

_____

What attitudes or beliefs do I hold about conflict? What parts of my belief systems contributed to this conflict unfolding as it did? _____

_____

_____

_____

Allow participants about five minutes to reflect. Encourage them to record their responses on the accompanying "My Conflict" sheet.

After completing the "My Conflict" sheet, ask participants to discuss their conflicts with a partner (ten minutes). Then seek insights from the larger group, reviewing the basics of the conflict cycle and analyzing individual scenarios using the following questions:

1. Identify or describe the problem.
2. What conflict style was used?
3. What were the external consequences?
4. What were the internal consequences?

5. What would I do differently?
6. Is this how I usually behave when in conflict?
7. What are some of my personal attitudes and beliefs about conflict?

Global Deadlines

"Global Deadlines" is a powerful tool for teaching conflict resolution skills. We have adapted it from another exercise developed by the Stanley Foundation (*Teachable Moments* 1989), using it as an activity in dialogue and negotiation. It is best employed when all participants have had an opportunity to get to know one another and have previously worked together on listening skills. It is important to allow time for participants to evaluate the effects of this activity on them. It is recommended for groups or subgroups of six to nine members. The instructions are as follows:

1. List all of the "global deadlines" on the board so they are easily read (some suggested deadlines are listed at the end of this exercise). Ask participants to look over the list and silently choose one global deadline that they feel is the most important and deserves immediate attention. In reviewing this list initially, be sure to point out that each issue has merit. (1–2 minutes)

2. Ask participants to mill around, looking for people with similar viewpoints. In other words, they should form clusters of people who are in agreement about which deadline should receive first priority. You may offer the option to any who find themselves alone at this point to either go solo or join a group with a second-best alternative. At this point, people are already beginning to view this as a competitive exercise. (2 minutes)

3. Have participants identify up to three compelling reasons why their deadline is the most important and most deserving of immediate attention. Be sure to emphasize that all group members should be prepared to defend their choice. (5 minutes)

4. Form a circle of chairs for the next phase of the exercise. If the numbers justify, have the group break into subgroups. Try to have as many different positions represented in each subgroup as possible, with proportional representation of each cluster. Give the instructions that:

A. Each position is to be presented in an order determined by the group. One person per position should present the three compelling reasons as concisely as possible. Continue around the circle until all positions have been presented.

B. In proceeding from one person to the next, it is each presenter's responsibility to restate the previously presented position to that person's satisfaction. This ground rule should be honored until all positions have been presented (the first presenter restates the last).

C. After all positions have been laid out, it is the task of the group to reach consensus regarding the one global deadline that is the most important, deserving immediate attention. Consensus is interpreted here to mean that all group members find the decision acceptable; if one blocks agreement, this must be honored and respected. In conducting this phase of the discussion, all members are free to speak in any order. They are encouraged to retain the restating rule, making certain that people feel understood.

D. Discussion continues either until consensus is reached or time expires. We recommend 40–60 minutes for this effort to reach consensus, including time for initial presentations of positions. Additional time could be allocated, if group size warrants it.

E. After the discussion ends, ask each group member to spend a few minutes evaluating the process: *Did I feel I was heard and understood? Were my ideas respected? How did the restating affect the process? What do I mean by consensus?*

Evaluation and Synthesis

Global Deadlines is a highly conflictive exercise that reflects the personal values and experiences of the participants. It is important that it be debriefed with sensitivity and respect. Typically, a few participants will become oppositional and dominate the discussion for a time. Often, some will fall silent, uncomfortable with the conflict. It is also common for certain members to play a facilitative role, assisting the group in its search for underlying interests that exist in common. This results in a redefinition of the problem and often results in consensus.

We emphasize that consensus is not merely an outcome, it is a *way of being*. How people behave with one another, that is, the *process* of their decision making, is far more important in the long run than any short-term conclusions. "Global Deadlines" assimilates collaborative problem solving, integrative negotiation, mediation, and communication skills in one exercise.

Global Deadlines

The global deadlines may change over time. This list is merely a starting point for generating your own list of global deadlines:

1. The deterioration of the environment: air, land, and water.
2. The spread of HIV and increasing mortality due to AIDS.
3. The persistence of racism, prejudice, and intolerance.
4. The proliferation of violence and weapons of mass destruction.
5. The decline of morals, values, and the institutions that support them.
6. Overpopulation, and the persistence of high human reproduction.
7. Denial of basic human rights: freedom of expression, religion, and political beliefs.
8. The lack of basic human needs: food, water, shelter, sanitation, and health.

CASE STUDIES IN CONFLICT RESOLUTION

A Staff Team Stuck in the "Gunk"

A facilitator was hired to address a conflict within a city parks department. The director, Frank, had been with the department for fifteen years, ten as the director. The staff of eight men included a few more recent arrivals, but most had been there for over twenty years. The staff included Jim, nearing retirement after spending his whole career in parks. At one time he had been in charge, too, until he had been demoted for poor work performance. There was also Bob, the person who had called attention to flaws in Jim's work nearly twenty years ago. Bob believed Jim had held this against him ever since that time. The six other men in the department felt that they had to take sides with either Jim or Bob as a condition of work. The parks department staff had been divided for a long time, and the director had been told by the city manager to fix the problem.

The facilitator worked to engage all eight men in the process (*pre-negotiation*). These men were not inclined to speak much, and they preferred to avoid the whole matter. The exception was Bob, a loud and angry individual who felt he had been held back by the system because he had used it to blow the whistle on Jim years ago. He and Jim never talked, he said, but he got along with almost everyone else. Jim was quiet: "I don't want to cause any trouble. Bob has always had it in for me, and he always will. I'll be ready to retire in a few years and don't want any trouble." The director felt powerless, valuing Jim's experience and Bob's energy (when properly channeled). Others just tried to stay out of the way, but they raised concerns about the quality of leadership from Frank. They didn't feel he had handled Bob properly, and they wondered whether he appreciated all they were doing.

The initial meeting of the group began in this context. The facilitator tried to set a tone of openness and respectful discussion (*opening statement*), but most said little. Frank tried to encourage his staff to open up, but they were silent. The only exception was Richard, a young man who considered himself outside the group. He said, in a somewhat self-righteous manner: "Come on, guys. Let's not waste time here. We all know what the problem is. Jim has hated Bob since he got him demoted in '75. Bob is lazy, drinks too much, hates everybody, and is always looking over his shoulder. Frank hates conflict and just wants us to get along. And most of us are upset because we're stuck doing this lousy job with no recognition from anybody!"

The facilitator summarized Richard's remarks, while others uneasily moved back from the table. He identified longstanding, unresolved feelings between Bob and Jim as key, lack of recognition for the entire group as a concern, and an avoidance of conflict by the director as a contributing factor (*active listening*). The facilitator sought further participation from the group. At this point, Jim offered that he didn't hate Bob. He resented Bob for what he had done twenty years ago, but he had long ago come to terms with his own responsibility for the flaws in his work and had moved on. He didn't like Bob's attitude at work, but it wasn't his job to discuss such concerns. Others in the group expressed appreciation for Jim, and respect for his experience. They also raised concerns about Bob's attitude. Bob felt ganged up on, but the facilitator helped him discuss his feelings about the workplace and not leave the meeting. After an intense ninety minutes, the group took a break (*managing impasse*).

Upon returning, the facilitator separated the issues and offered an agenda for problem solving. They began with the issue of recognition (*psychological need*), and successfully identified several ways they could both give one another positive support and seek it from the city. From there, the group easily focused on ground rules to guide their communication, both in staff meetings and informal workday interactions (*procedural need*). They agreed to try these ideas for one month and reconvene to continue their work (*evaluation/tasks between meetings*).

The facilitator returned a month later and found most people felt there were improvements. At check-in, Richard was particularly philosophical. "There is a special challenge, when changing long-held patterns," he said, "but there has been progress." The exception was Bob, who initially offered the observation, "I'm here to do my job, punch the clock, and pick up my paycheck." Other didn't say much, only that things were somewhat better than before.

The facilitator took each element of the initial agreement and reviewed it with the group, point by point. This led to little initial discussion. Finally, another staff member, Pete, who had said very little in the previous meeting suddenly blurted out, "Look. There's no reason for us to talk. The director is sitting over there keeping track of everything. It's not safe here!" Of the facilitator, he asked, "What do you want? We came, we talked, we made some progress. Let's put this stuff away!" A few others nodded in agreement. At this point, Frank responded directly to Pete, "Hey, Pete, I hate this stuff. But we've got to trust one another enough to get to the bottom of this crap. If I'm not doing something you need, or if I am doing something that rubs you the wrong way, I have to know!" It was easily the most honest emotion that had been seen in the two meetings (*problem identification*).

Pete and Frank then engaged in a ten-minute discussion that others witnessed, in which Pete outlined various ways he had felt disrespected through the years and how he wanted Frank to behave instead. Frank listened well and promised to make improvements in the areas Pete had identified. Pete listened well, and offered positive support for certain changes Frank had already made to improve things. The facilitator summarized the discussion, then asked the group for observations and comments, going "round robin" to ensure that all had a chance to participate. Several of the more reticent members offered support to Pete and the director for their courage, and added more insights to the discussion. Jim supported them as well, saying it was the kind of honesty that was needed (*validation*).

Finally, Bob turned to Jim: "Are you ever going to forgive me, old man? Enough, already." Jim then looked Bob in the eye: "I let go of it a long time ago, Bob. I forgive you for what you did. It was your job and I was wrong. I just don't need to be reminded of it every day. Let's move on." Bob agreed, and the two men shook hands. Nothing more needed to be said (*agreement*).

Facilitating resolution of long-term workplace conflict is highly energized and emotional. This case involved a group of work hardened men who would never willingly submit to a discussion of emotional needs, yet they required understanding of their feelings in order to solve their substantive concerns. They needed a safe, affirming environment to articulate their needs and courage to honestly express themselves. Their courage to speak openly was fostered by the ground rules and order of the facilitated meeting process. By removing the "gunk" that had accumulated over twenty years, the group was able to focus on substantive problems facing the parks department that required their full attention.

We commonly encounter long-held conflicts in our work. Sometimes frankly, we are amazed at how long people have maintained such disputes. We are also surprised at how people are often able to accomplish many of their work tasks in spite of such differences, masking their true cost to the business or organization. However, when these disputes are properly facilitated, it can free resources and energy that have been trapped by conflict for years. All too often, people report at the start of the process that they dread coming to work and see no prospects for improvement. Trust is a scarce commodity in such situations. However, if disputants are able to extend professional respect to a degree that creative channels can be opened, a renewed desire to come to work can be encouraged. Our professional satisfaction frequently derives from witnessing changes in such attitudes and the outstanding work that results.

"He's the Person to Blame": Reframing the Issue

Among the great hurdles to clear in facilitation is a client's belief that an individual or small group should be blamed for the ills facing an organization. The facilitator must approach each situation with neutrality and support for equal, responsible participation—a challenge with groups in which a person, especially in a position of leadership, is commonly perceived to be "the problem." In approaching such conflicts, the facilitator must constantly check his or her own biases as they encroach upon the situation.

A facilitator was retained by an auto dealership, Main Street Motors, to resolve an internal staff dispute. She was contacted initially by Doug Smith, president and CEO of the company, who sat down with her to outline the situation: It seemed that Smith's sales manager, Ron, had so alienated his sales staff that three had left and others were threatening to quit. Ron had been with Doug and Main Street Motors for over twenty years, and they were like family together. Doug didn't want to fire Ron, or lose him, but he wanted Ron to understand how he contributed to the problem and to change his behaviors. It seemed that Ron was moody, unapproachable (especially at times of stress), and autocratic. He was a tireless worker, putting in one hundred hours a week, so his staff often felt they had to work that hard to stay in his good graces. Doug was clear: "Ron is the problem. He's the reason people are leaving, and we can't afford to lose good people. But he's family, so I have no desire to let him go. Besides, I'm afraid he might 'lose it' if he couldn't work here." This last comment indicated to the facilitator that mental health concerns were present, and Doug confirmed her suspicions that Ron suffered from depression.

In approaching this dispute, pre-negotiation was especially important. Was Ron really the core of the problem? What were Doug's options? How might Ron respond to a facilitated meeting? How might others treat him, especially if they were concerned about him? Were other resources required in order to assure safety in this situation?

From the pre-negotiation, the facilitator gained answers to these question. First, she discovered that there was more to this conflict than had been understood by Doug. There were other department heads who had found Ron difficult to work with, leading to a much deeper breakdown in the company. There were some who now doubted Doug's resolve to deal effectively with Ron. These perceptions confirmed the consensus that Ron was "the problem," but led the facilitator to consider other contributing factors. She learned that staff meetings were closed and dysfunctional, with little willingness among the managers to openly criticize Doug. They feared that, since he's the president and primary owner of Main Street Motors, he could not be criticized. For his part, Doug apparently sought honesty, but admitted that he could be closed to criticism and had called people on the carpet in years past.

Rather than solely bringing the sales staff together, the facilitator brought a larger group together in the guise of a conflict management skills workshop. This approach, rather than the formal approach of a facilitated or mediated meeting, was a way to get people discussing their issues and learning together. The approach worked. In initial activities, small groups were encouraged to identify conflicts at work, factors that interfered with successful responses, and other concerns. As the small groups reported back to the larger staff of twenty, a pattern emerged: "We at Main Street Motors don't deal with conflict very effectively and, due to job stress, don't feel we have the time to do so."

The group went on to acknowledge a few key issues and developed strategies for addressing them. They were a very capable group, with strong problem-solving and communication skills that had previously been applied only to clients. Therefore, the facilitator needed to create opportunities for them to apply these talents to their own conflicts. Quite efficiently, they developed a set of ground rules for dealing with concerns, as well as mechanisms for contending with those that were not satisfactorily resolved. The group adjourned from its first session feeling quite invigorated.

Nevertheless the facilitator remained concerned. If Ron was the problem, she thought, why were they now so willing to move on without confronting him? And what of the sales staff that now seemed so cosy together? She expected a problem to arise, and within two weeks it did.

One Friday, Ron blew up at Maria, one of the sales associates, in front of customers on the showroom floor. Apparently, Maria had failed to properly complete some paperwork from a sale earlier in the day, and Ron had to fix it. As Doug described it, Ron had thrown a tantrum and stormed away. Maria, being a professional, minimized the situation to the customer and found another sales associate to help them. However, she then was so upset that she had gone to Doug's office, demanding either that Ron goes or she'd go. Doug had no idea how to proceed.

The facilitator listened to Doug's concerns, then reminded him of the agreements reached in the previous session. Either Doug could try to help Maria and Ron resolve these issues, or the facilitator could return, holding a session with all three of them. Doug didn't want to mediate—he wanted to fire Ron and get the problem to go away—but he remained open to the facilitator's suggestion that she speak individually with Maria and Ron before determining a next course of action.

The facilitator then contacted Ron, who was most upset with himself for blowing up at Maria. He went on to explain that personal issues had made him distraught lately. He felt he was moody, and he was seeking professional assistance to help. He was afraid to let Doug know this, fearing that Doug would lose respect for him. He wanted to talk with Maria and apologize. Maria, when contacted, was still quite upset, as well. She was also concerned that she had put Doug in an unfair position with her ultimatum. She had no desire to leave the dealership, but she hated it when Ron embarrassed her. She had screwed up with the paperwork, she admitted, but that didn't entitle him to harass her in front of others.

The facilitator then lobbied Doug for a group session. He agreed, but he was skeptical of success. In addition, now that he had finally decided to fire Ron, he wanted to implement his decision. She reminded him that, as facilitator, she had no position regarding whether or not he would retain Ron. However, one of the terms of the staff agreement had been to sit down together in the time of conflict, and this had not yet occurred.

The meeting was actually fairly brief. Ron began with his apologies and insights, as well as an honest statement regarding his personal issues. Maria accepted his apologies and clearly stated her needs regarding future behavior on his part. Doug, while being supportive of them both, clarified that such outbursts would not be tolerated in the future. As valued employees, he said, it was in his interest for both to stay and do their jobs well. He never told Ron of his earlier decision to fire him.

When the larger group met for its second conflict resolution skills workshop later that month, Doug, Ron and Maria shared how they had resolved an issue together. They supported the agreement reached by the group and the facilitated meeting process as key to their progress. While they were not yet confident of success, they knew they had a framework that could help them achieve their goals. With this crisis behind the group as a test of its mettle, they were able to make significant improvements in the future.

In this case study, the facilitator actively negotiated for the process at critical junctures. Initially, she was told that Ron was the problem. By resisting such portraits of the scenario, she remained flexible to find other concerns within the situation. Later, Ron's tantrum could have easily led to the judgment that he was incorrigible and that the process had failed. Again, the facilitator asserted the value of the process within the ground rules adopted by the group. Through separate negotiations, she was able to gain a willingness to return to the table. Once there, the participants were able to understand one another and resolve their issues.

Frequently groups view an explosion as the end of a conflict, but it is merely one phase, often a necessary one, for the expression of the issues fulminating beneath a deceptively peaceful surface. The initial training session, while helpful, had not uncovered some of the incendiary concerns within the sales staff. Only through Ron and Maria's conflict could the larger group gain insights they all needed. By staying true to her responsibilities, the facilitator was able to help empower the group to develop its best long-term solutions.

Facilitating a Conference Around a Highly Contentious Issue: The Common Ground Network for Life and Choice

In May 1996 an unusual group of people came together in Madison, Wisconsin. They arrived from about forty states and Canada, prepared to discuss an issue most were reluctant to face together. The issue was abortion, and the conference was called "Reaching for Common Ground on Abortion." Sponsored by the Common Ground Network for Life and Choice, a project of Search for Common Ground in Washington, D.C., the conference was the first effort to bring together leaders of pro-choice and pro-life organizations, as well as others who feel strongly about the abortion issue and operate as grass-roots activists. They came to discuss their feelings within the structure of facilitated dialogue.

Some had been involved in such dialogues in their communities before, while others were experiencing the opportunity to sit with their adversaries for the first time. The conference attracted over two hundred participants, and its size was intentionally kept small by the organizers. In order to attend, potential participants were asked to agree to a set of conference ground rules, including the willingness to treat one another with respect and maintain confidentiality within the sessions. Members of the press who had covered abortion and previous common ground efforts were invited to attend the conference. Specific opportunities were arranged for confidential observation of sessions, open plenaries, and press conferences. A group of pro-life demonstrators outside the conference, who raised concerns regarding one of the funding sources of the event, were engaged in discussion by organizers and invited to participate. An open, nondenominational prayer service for peace helped bring closure to the four-day event. Overall, it was a time of great discussion, powerful learning about how to change the tenor of the abortion debate within our communities, and insight regarding the relationships of activists to society's polarizing institutions.

The conference offers a useful case study in facilitation on a large scale, involving a value-based dispute. This presentation differs from others we have covered in this book in several respects. First, we are sharing specific information regarding an actual dispute, while elsewhere we have worked to preserve the confidentiality of participants and events. Second, the Common Ground conference was not an effort focused at resolution of a specific dispute among a clearly defined set of parties; it was a conference voluntarily bringing together people involved in a conflict much larger in scope than their personal involvement.

Our focus is on how the facilitators organized this event and the lessons that may be drawn from their experience. Mary Jacksteidt and Adrienne Kaufmann, co-directors of the Network, are experienced facilitators and mediators. They facilitated the steering committee that formed the Network in 1993, and they have conducted workshops and dialogues about abortion in dozens of cities around the country. I first met them in the early days of the Network. As a member of the steering committee, I have come to greatly respect their capacity to manage an extremely challenging project. The larger organization, Search for Common Ground, brings special expertise to the process. It has involved itself in highly contentious, volatile situations all over the world, from Russia to the Middle East to the Balkans to southern Africa. Therefore, in describing facilitators in this context, we are discussing knowledgeable, seasoned staff.

In organizing the conference, the Network identified several types of sessions. There would be facilitated dialogue sessions offered throughout the conference for small groups of activists with no previous experience in dialogue about abortion. A single extended colloquy would be offered, as well, for those seeking deeper discussion over two days. However, most of the conference contained skills sessions around issues of how to develop or maintain local efforts at dialogue and group formation. Issue sessions focused on insights that had been gained through the first few years of such trials. There were also opportunities for various local groups to share their stories with those from around the country. Finally, there were plenary sessions built around specific issues, such as concerns facing the media when covering the abortion issue.

As an intense, value-based dispute, the abortion issue offered many opportunities for explosive rhetoric that could undermine the goals of the conference. The organizers needed to take several steps to improve the likelihood that their best intentions would result in success. First, they established the conference ground rules and made it clear they must be honored as a condition of attendance. As participants arrived, they were asked to attend brief conference orientation sessions in which the ground rules were reinforced, people were introduced to one another, and support resources were identified. Second, they limited participation to a manageable size, insuring their capacity to facilitate the meetings. In accepting applications to attend, the Network asked participants to identify themselves as pro-life, pro-choice, or facilitator/other, thereby building a list that attempted to balance representation of these groups.

Third, the Network recruited facilitators for the many workshops and dialogue sessions that would occur. They asked all presenters to create opportunities for facilitated small group discussions within each workshop and worked with presenters to do so. Facilitators were oriented to their roles at an initial training session the first evening of the conference, and opportunities were created to address their concerns throughout the conference. Fourth, a conference "trouble shooter" was identified. Her role was to either facilitate resolution of disputes that arose or find another person to do so. Finally, careful attention was paid to ensure that participants were supported to view this conference as a first, not a last, effort. If people could take home possible action agendas for local groups, or could develop together a new plan for more concerted action together, that was a desirable outcome. The organizers, though, viewed themselves as facilitators and remained flexible about emerging needs and agendas. This flexibility proved important, as an impetus for future action clearly developed in the conference.

These details, combined with other strategies that we have observed elsewhere in this book, resulted in a highly productive and successful experience. The conference offers an excellent example of facilitation in a public setting, replete with highly political actors and expectations. As such, the Network for Life and Choice provides inspiration to those of us dealing with less complex conflicts.

The Inherited Staff Conflict

Jose ran the research division of a computer software company that, after years of strong growth, was now experiencing layoffs and flat earnings. He invited a facilitator to conduct a staff retreat on team building. It seemed, according to the director, that people in the research division had difficulty working well together. He offered that he had been in his position for two years, and that his predecessor was much more outgoing and charismatic . . . perhaps the group required inspiration that he could not offer? Maybe morale was low because of fear of layoffs? He was a good researcher, Jose offered, but had no previous experience as a manager. The facilitator agreed to organize the meeting, provided he could speak with staff members individually to receive their input on the agenda.

Through these individual discussions, the facilitator gained a clear understanding of a conflict that was preventing the group from being an effective team. Apparently, the department had been run for many years by Marion, a strong-willed director who had built their department into the largest in the company. Through her leadership, they had developed a national reputation as a topnotch research division, thrusting their company into the forefront of a highly competitive field. Then Marion had a falling out with management, people reported, resulting in her leaving to take a leadership position elsewhere. People were unclear as to why Marion had gone, filled with misinformation gleaned from rumors and hearsay. Top managers had never informed them of what had happened, only that Jose would now be promoted to run the division. It was clear that people had never had an adequate opportunity to resolve these historic issues.

The research division had many current concerns with which to fill an agenda. They needed to improve communication with other divisions about pending projects. They needed to organize workload efficiently, given no prospects for increased staff, plus they had to take control over scheduling issues that were now causing great stress. How could they address these current concerns without acknowledging their internal conflicts? And what were their expectations of Jose as their leader?

The facilitator offered a tentative agenda for the retreat through a written summary from the needs assessment:

RESEARCH DIVISION RETREAT AGENDA
8:30 a.m.–4:00 p.m.

8:30– 9:00 a.m.: Check-in/Hopes and hesitations for this meeting/Ground rules
9:00–10:15: Outcomes Identification Exercise—What do we expect of one another in our work together?
> Break
10:30–Noon: Problem Solving: How might we best organize our workload? What schedule best meets these expectations? How do we communicate about problems in these areas.
1:00–1:15 p.m.: Check-in/How is it going so far? Any changes needed?
1:15–2:30: Problem Solving—what are our needs regarding leadership in the department? Specifically, what do we need from Jose? What does Jose need from us?
> Break
2:45–3:30: Synthesis: Next steps—Tasks to be assigned—Agenda for next staff meeting
3:30–4:00: Check out—How well did this meeting meet our needs?

Although he sent the tentative agenda to all members, the facilitator received no feedback from the group prior to the meeting. He then called Jose, who only said that the agenda appeared to offer a good point of departure for the session.

As the meeting began, all were asked to share their feelings about the meeting and the proposed agenda. A couple of people made brief comments, impressive in their lack of passion. After all had spoken in this manner, the facilitator made the observation: "In my discussions with you prior to the meeting, I had come to understand that people felt very strongly about a number of issues. While there were hesitations expressed about discussing these issues, for fear they were out of your control or in the past, there was still passion in your voices. Today, I see none of this passion. What's going on here?"

Jose took the initiative to respond. "You see, there are two people who are not here today. They were laid off on Friday. People are pretty sad and angry about it. I think some people blame me for not protecting those positions. The idea of focusing on the future, and how to get work done, feels really bogus to all of us, including me. And you know what? I feel like I have failed!"

After a brief silence, others began to speak. There was great frustration about the layoffs, and everyone feared he or she could be next. While there was some anger toward Jose, they generally recognized his powerlessness to impact such decisions. From there, the group discussed how things had changed in the past two years. Although Marion had been successful, she was not especially liked by her staff; Jose was more widely respected as a caring, honest leader of the group. While Marion had never allowed cuts in the research division, the times in which she operated were different. She excelled in start-up phases and had little patience for maintaining a group or managing it through difficult times. That was why she had left; she had been told of impending cuts and, offered an opportunity to start another venture at a higher salary, had taken it.

The group continued this discussion for over two hours, with everyone participating. There were occasional breaks in the group conversation in which individuals spoke directly to each other about perceived concerns and conflicts. These frequently resulted in tears and, at conclusion, hugs. Finally, near noon, the facilitator suggested breaking for lunch. During lunch, he summarized the agreements he now understood and other issues that appeared to be outstanding. The remaining issues closely resembled the problem-solving issues initially identified on the agenda.

The afternoon session began with the facilitator summarizing agreements and offering the problem-solving topics as afternoon agenda items. Remarkably, people now seemed upbeat and energized. They gratefully affirmed the summaries and moved to address their substantive issues. Within two hours they had completed a strategic plan, assigned tasks and clarified roles for the upcoming year. In check-out, various group members acknowledged the burdens of guilt, blame, fear, and stress that had accumulated over time. They thanked Jose for his patient support and encouraged one another to persevere with their plan of action. All left with hopes that, while these ideas might not be perfect, they would lead to real improvements.

The group had expressed the hope that the facilitator would meet with them again, to further develop their skills in communication and team effectiveness. Unfortunately, this did not occur. While the research division staffers now worked more effectively together, they could not escape the stressors placed upon them by the larger company. Gradually, over time, some left the group for other positions. The facilitator spoke occasionally with Jose, who would always express the desire for continued training that never occurred. Jose persevered and no longer blamed himself. He now realized that the company did not prize certain issues he felt were important to address, but he wanted to remain until the financial situation might allow smoother sailing. Training money was so scarce and, given the lack of crisis, had fallen from priority with management.

This case study is instructive in several respects. First, it demonstrates the power of longstanding misunderstandings or feuds as factors inhibiting a group's ability to work well. The conflicts within the group were subtly debilitating it, resulting in malaise. This was not a conflict characterized by much fighting. It had quietly transformed the environment into one where people had withdrawn from one another. Second, this case shows the importance of facilitator flexibility. The initial agenda was simply not going to meet the needs of the group. Once the problem had been named by Jose, the floodgates were opened to a genuine outpouring of participant feelings. Only after this had occurred could the agenda become their focus. Interestingly, their expert capacity to address such issues now marshaled itself quite efficiently.

A third insight comes from the type of leadership presented here. The facilitator needed to name the problem within the process, while the director needed to name the substantive issue. Once the group shifted to problem solving, the facilitator could step aside and allow them to exercise their natural roles with one another. He could then offer leadership by synthesizing these insights and moving the group out of the emotional discussion into the substantive discussion. Knowing when to make such shifts is a key element of the art of facilitation.

Finally, this case study demonstrates some of the realistic limits of the process. Although the research division was able to make great strides, there was no follow-up to build upon these insights. Most companies react to crises, and lose their appetite for training and group development when the crisis disappears. Middle managers such as Jose are limited in their power to move such issues to a wider forum. Furthermore, they fear their own jobs may be lost if they are too vigorous in such matters while the company is experiencing difficult times. Paradoxically, Jose and his staff could have been better served by developing a sound model of an effective team within their department and encouraging its replication elsewhere. The research division could have become a model team for the company, thus influencing the larger company to make changes. In this manner, not only would their colleagues have appreciated how the research division had improved, but the overall efficiency of management might have resulted in bigger profits and increased job security. Regrettably, the facilitator was never extended an invitation to influence the situation in that direction.

NOTES

1. There are distinct differences between the concepts of needs, interests, and concerns in conflict resolution literature. For further information regarding these distinctions, refer to: Heitler 1990; Fisher and Ury 1981; Folger and Poole 1984. While we recognize these differences, the terms are used interchangeably in our discussion here.

2. I wish to acknowledge Susan Heitler's analysis (Heitler 1990), as well as that of my partner, Dr. Lisa Webne-Behrman, in developing this interpretation of the "Prisoner's Dilemma."

3. The term "BATNA" was first developed by Roger Fisher and William Ury at the Harvard Negotiation Project.

4. For further insights regarding energy as a transforming force in conflict, see Thomas Crum, *The Magic of Conflict* (1978), and Dudley Weeks, *The Eight Essential Steps to Conflict Resolution* (1992).

Chapter 6

Facilitating Consensus

Consensus decision making, whereby all group members reach a decision together, is an important option within the facilitated meeting. The general act of consensus building reflects a commitment to the values of facilitation: democracy, equality, and honesty. However, while all facilitated groups seek to build consensus, they are not bound to use it as a decision-making rule. Distinctions regarding such choices, as well as clarification of the conditions required for reaching consensus, are articulated in this chapter.

GROUP CONDITIONS NEEDED TO SUPPORT CONSENSUS

The process of achieving consensus evolves from an affirming environment and from clear ground rules that support the goals of the group. Members must perceive the meeting to be a safe place, where they may freely engage in dialogue without fear of ridicule. They must have definite procedures through which they derive their authority within the larger organization and understand whatever constraints are realistically placed upon them. In order for their deliberations to have meaning, they must possess legitimate power to act on their own behalf and sufficient freedom from external limitations.

The need for these conditions is illustrated by a current trend in organizational life: Self-Directed Work Teams. Self-Directed Work Teams, or SDWTs, have been established in many companies in order to bring true decision-making power to the grass roots level of participation. SDWTs increase effectiveness, bring decisions closer to points of implementation, and encourage employee participation in the workplace. They are frequently interdepartmental, bringing together people that normally have separate reporting structures. The groups are often informed that they should operate by consensus whenever possible, resolve their own issues, and set their own goals and priorities.

In practice, however, SDWTs usually lack the authentic power required to build consensus, since: (a) individuals continue to report to and be evaluated by traditional supervisors within the hierarchy; (b) budgets, schedules, and other significant work factors are controlled outside the team; (c) members of SDWTs frequently have multiple assignments and, therefore, simultaneous allegiances to a variety of projects in conflict with one another; and (d) companies focus primarily on outcomes and results, rather than process and learning, in evaluating the success of a particular project. In fact, evaluation criteria are often set externally, rather than by the group. This undermines group ownership of the solutions to problems.

These factors conspire to undermine credible consensus within groups and lead to a sense of frustration, helplessness, and resentment. In the old hierarchical system, workers knew what they were accountable for, while in the new system, there is great uncertainty and stress. As a consequence, many workers resist reform efforts, especially in organizations in which there is a history of distrust and manipulation. Thus, in order for work teams to credibly utilize consensus, the following conditions need to be present:

1. An affirming environment supported by clear, mutually accepted ground rules for procedure.
2. Freedom from external structures, so that authentic power may reside within the group.
3. Equality of access to information within the group, so that all may effectively participate in problem solving and decision making.
4. A genuine commitment among participants to process (vs. product).
5. A dedication to shared understanding, including a flexibility to shift positions in light of new insights.

These conditions are a checklist for facilitators in assessing a group's potential for operating unanimously. Any missing conditions must be addressed before engaging in the problem-solving process. This provides an opportunity for group members to acknowledge any limitations placed on them and also serves as a starting point for dialogue with management. If constraints are imagined, management has the responsibility to dispel them; if they are real, management should come to terms with their impact on the efficacy of the group.

STRATEGIES FOR BUILDING CONSENSUS

Several of the strategies discussed in previous chapters are important to the consensus-building process. For example, the use of active listening, both by the facilitator and group members, is a key skill. Taking what we refer to as a "listening stance" into the problem-solving process is crucial to the establishment of the required environment. The various approaches to problem solving, including IDEAL, Mind Mapping, and Future Problem Solving, should be within the facilitator's tool box for creating consensus. Groups should have a variety of problem-solving approaches at their disposal, for dealing with different types of issues. Finally, being prepared to move from large to small groups and back again can be critical to fostering effective discussion. In combination, all of these strategies help facilitate consensus.

To build consensus, it is often helpful to begin by having small groups develop recommendations for consideration by the large group. Then ambassadors of the various subgroups meet in conference to negotiate through differences. This is generally followed by a report to the large group for final approval. The facilitator, negotiating for the process, may take a very active role in suggesting such procedures. However, substantive decisions and recommendations emerge only from group members.

The PEACE/6 Model for Collaborative Negotiation outlined in Chapter Five is especially relevant to consensus building. It enables the group to focus on underlying concerns, rather than initial positions, as the key source of solutions. Furthermore, it promotes flexibility and objectivity in decision making, while respecting the substantive interests of the participants. Groups are often unnecessarily limited by majority rule decision making. However, the process of consensus can yield optimal solutions.

THE ROLE OF POLLING IN GROUPS

A critical tool for groups seeking consensus is the use of polling, or taking the impression of group members on any given issue. Contrary to myths about consensus, polling is an accepted component of the process. In its definition lies its distinction from voting: while voting reflects a decisive position, polling indicates a temporary attitude on an issue. A group may poll its members in order to understand the strength of support (or opposition) to a proposed solution. For example, if a staff is trying to establish a new scheduling policy, some may advocate it passionately, while others may express reservations. If the facilitator polls the group, it can be determined whether further discussion is truly required. If there are reservations, it will be understood whether they are strong enough to block consensus.

Two simple methods of polling are frequently utilized. One approach asks people to go "thumbs up," "thumbs down," or "level hand." The down position reflects opposition, the up position demonstrates support, and the level position shows a willingness to allow others to decide (i.e., "I can live with it."). Another approach uses "five fingers and a fist," where a five reflects strong support, three indicates modest support, one shows a willingness to "live with it," and only a fist blocks consensus. We prefer using the latter method, for it gives a clearer picture to the group of levels of support. It also offers an opportunity to build a stronger solution once an acceptable level has been achieved and communicated. Polling is not used to end discussion, but to clarify and focus further dialogue. This reduces misunderstanding, affirms areas of agreement in times of impasse, and improves the efficiency of the consensus-building process.

THE IMPORTANCE OF BLOCKING IN GROUPS

The expression of dissent within the facilitated meeting is related to the genuine expression of power that goes with it. This power is often best understood through the judicious use of blocking a decision of the group. The ability to exercise this veto is at once a threat and an opportunity to express confidence and trust. Those using the block must be prepared to expend further effort to resolve impasse, while those being blocked (usually the majority) must treat the veto with respect. As mentioned earlier in the discussion of impasse, blocking can offer unique opportunities for group members to look inward and gain an improved sense of trust from working through this dilemma.

Critics of consensus often point to the use of blocking as a time consuming, inefficient obstacle to success. If it is used as a subversive behavior to undermine a group's progress, it can be highly frustrating to other members. Filibusters and reconsiderations fall into this category. However, legitimate blocking can be a powerful channel to voice concerns. It actually improves the effectiveness of the group, bringing issues and uncertainties to the table that may strengthen both the quality of the decision and the group's resolve to implement it. Often boards and committees "efficiently" pass decisions, only to find resistance being expressed by those who were reluctant to express it during the meeting. It has been our experience that, when properly facilitated, blocking in consensus can be highly efficient in the long run, even if apparently cumbersome in the short term.

OTHER DECISION-MAKING OPTIONS WITHIN DEMOCRATIC GROUPS

As implied earlier in this chapter, a distinction may be drawn between consensus building and consensus decision making. It is possible to work toward consensus but not have decisions made by unanimous approval, so long as group members agree to follow alternative procedures. A summary of these decision-making options follows.

Advisory Opinions

Frequently, groups offer their advice to others who ultimately make a decision on an issue. This advice may reflect areas of consensus that have unanimous consent. They may also indicate areas of disagreement, in which the primary contending arguments are represented. Finally, areas where no opinions are offered may be part of the report forwarded to the decision-making group.

Temporary Use of Voting

Democratic groups may hold consensus as a goal, rather than an operational reality, in dealing with certain classes of issues. They may identify items, a priori, that they choose to resolve by majority rule, two-thirds vote, or other margins of approval. They may also name conditions under which they choose to suspend rules for consensus after a certain period of time. As long as the group agrees to such ground rules democratically, the facilitator may help them decide through voting.

Technocratic Decision Making

An efficient use of members' talents may be to decide by technocracy, or by the decisions of experts in a particular area. If an organization has members who specialize in select issues, it often makes sense to empower them to make certain decisions without the approval of the rest of the staff. For example, financial decisions under a spending threshold may be too trivial to bring to the board or entire staff for approval. Operational decisions within functional areas may be best decided by those who must live with them on a day-to-day basis. However, a larger overseeing group must retain involvement and integrity if the system is to remain democratic. Be wary of isolating subgroups too far from their shared responsibility in the overall management of the organization. Otherwise, the credibility of other decisions made by the full group may be undermined.

Classes of Membership

Another option may be to designate certain classes of membership that participate in various types of decisions. While subgroups in a technocracy are formed based on expertise, they may also be related to ownership or standing within the group. For example, a cooperative may only allow full members the right to participate or block in the consensus-reaching process. Others (e.g., customers, community members) may have an opportunity to speak at meetings but not to make decisions. Classes of membership could entitle certain senior members to participate in company decisions, using a stock threshold to determine who participates in the consensus process. Still others would retain a voice in the problem-solving process. Within a team-oriented business, some participants could be designated team members, with expectations related to decision making, while others might be resources to the group, who have an advisory role.

These options are presented to broaden the facilitator's set of tools, as well as to allow groups the opportunity to consider alternatives to consensus decision making. These may be especially useful to groups that are new to consensus, or come from a more autocratic orientation. These alternative decision-making options may ease the transition to democratic management.

THE IMPORTANCE OF EVALUATION

An essential element of the facilitated meeting is the evaluation of the meeting by participants. Evaluation is inherently a subjective process, relying upon the value-laden perceptions of the group's members to provide perspective. However, the combined responses of participants can lend some systematic and, perhaps, objective feedback regarding the process and outcomes of the group's problem solving.   For groups deciding by consensus, this is especially important.

Just as "check-in" is an important ritual, "check-out" can be a significant component of the meeting. This closing phase of the meeting (previously discussed in Chapter Three) provides time for discussing the benefits and costs of the meeting which has just transpired. It also provides an opportunity for closure and clarification of delegated tasks to occur between meetings.

We have a tendency to focus on outcomes when performing evaluation of our work. *What were the results of our work on the project? How many people benefited? Did we achieve our goals?* These are examples of outcome-based evaluation questions. These may be compared to process-oriented evaluation questions, such as, *How did we feel about the process of the meeting? Did people fully participate? Is there a sense that all input was treated with respect? Did we use our time efficiently?* Answering these types of questions during check-out helps the group learn about the practice of effective meetings at a time when the meeting itself is fresh in everyone's mind. It also provides feedback on the meeting by people who may have been more quiet or selective in their vocal participation. Finally, it legitimizes the possibility that different members may have different perceptions of the meeting's process, even if all have a sense of satisfaction about its outcomes (or the other way around). A related factor is the importance of using internal, rather than external, criteria for evaluation. For the group to determine its own criteria for success, and to evaluate their process on that basis, helps inspire a sense of ownership among group participants.

The evaluative phase of the meeting allows the group an occasion for celebration. So much energy is spent in meetings on task, as it should be. But the chance to celebrate the completion of the tasks is especially valuable in stressful, conflictive situations. The energy charge that results from this celebration is contagious, and members may be able to recall it in future times of impasse and disillusionment.

Consensus is a robust approach to decision making that offers a chance for excellent results. It must be approached with care and support for creating conditions of success. This includes attention to evaluation of the process, through which the group may improve its skills. Over time, commitment to regular assessment can improve group efficiency and allow members increasing opportunity to enjoy the benefits of consensus.

CASE STUDIES IN FACILITATING CONSENSUS

Reaching Large Group Consensus—A Facilitator's Role

Members of a high school teaching staff were having difficulty determining priorities for their school. Among the sixty in the group, fifteen were members of a governance council that ostensibly met with the principal on a monthly basis to resolve such issues. However, in practice, the council members felt undermined. They looked on the principal as reluctant to give them real control and on the larger staff as a group that constantly questioned their actions. As a result, they had brought certain key concerns about future school governance to the larger staff. The principal retained an external facilitator to guide the group through this process.

The facilitator, after consultation with the principal and several members of the council, conducted two initial sessions with the entire governance council. During these discussions, she was able to encourage the group to clarify its desired relationship with the principal and the staff. It was especially helpful to bring out resentment and discord that had accumulated through the years. Once they accomplished this, the group had relatively little difficulty articulating their expectations of one another. In addition, the facilitator helped the group focus on communication and conflict resolution steps that could prove useful in the future. The group then adopted ground rules to support them in their meetings.

The next stage, however, was more complex. The council sought a broader staff consensus regarding their role in the school, as well as an overall staff commitment to new ways of making decisions. Although a majority decision would be legally acceptable, the council wanted full group ownership. Given the historical lack of trust among the staff, any semblance of a *fait accompli* in the council's decision making would undermine the opportunity to build consensus. The facilitator needed a process that would be fully inclusive and participatory.

She began by introducing the purpose of the meeting and clarifying both her role and the ground rules she preferred for the conduct of the meeting. After forming small groups for check-in, she asked those groups to clarify the situation: *What were some of the needs of the staff at this time? What were some strengths they brought to the process? What were some barriers that undermined their process of working together?*

After having the small groups discuss these questions, she asked each group to share one or two ideas that may be helpful to the larger staff. Such ideas, she said, would have to reflect a consensus within the small group. All ideas were recorded on flip chart paper posted in the front of the room. Finally, before convening the large group, she asked each small group to evaluate the quality of its discussion.

As the various groups reported to the staff, a number of ideas emerged that were consistent across groups. Overall, people sought similar things from one another: they wanted to be treated with respect; to be included in significant decisions, while empowering the council to resolve most areas; to be informed of changes in a timely manner by the principal; and to be involved in meetings that made decisions in an efficient manner. It was through this process that various council members had been able to share the results of their discussions with the larger staff. All were relieved to observe widespread consistency between council perceptions and those of their colleagues. The principal was pleased, as well, for this meeting was now clarifying which areas the staff wished would remain at his discretion and which ones should come to either council or the large staff for approval.

After a break, the facilitator summarized and recorded perceived areas of consensus among the staff. After presenting each item, she sought questions, comments, and language revisions in order to craft the statement more accurately. Finally, after covering all points, she asked people to return to small groups for further discussion: *How did they feel about these guidelines? Were there reservations about any items? Were other issues, important in the previous small group discussion, omitted from the emerging consensus?*

After ten-minute discussions in small groups, the facilitator convened the large group. She sought reservations or concerns that remained, but received only feedback of joy and relief. People realized that they were experiencing a process they could replicate whenever necessary, and that the skills and procedures being employed to solve these issues could improve the efficiency of their staff and council meetings. The only revisions made were cosmetic, as people shared affirming enthusiasm throughout their reports. After hearing from all groups, the facilitator thanked them for their hard work and their courage in seeking to work together after so much frustration in the past. She double checked to be certain everyone was satisfied with the consensus and adjourned the meeting.

This case study is instructive as an illustration of large group consensus decision making. The entire staff needed to reach consensus and needed clarity about who was making certain decisions. They also wanted to address the psychological concern that trust was required in giving the council power to govern the school. Although the council could have legitimately just assumed power, their efforts to build consensus with the entire staff improved chances for long-term success. In our approach to large group consensus building, agreement is reached through a series of empowering stages: First, ground rules set the tone for the meeting. Second, the use of small groups as problem-identification and problem-solving units increases participation. Third, the small groups offer a forum for practicing consensus building and evaluating group process. This practice is necessary among groups that lack familiarity with the consensus process, or where there is any history of conflict and distrust. In this case, both elements dictated the preferred use of small group decision making as an interim step in the process.

A fourth empowering technique used in this case was to return the tentative agreement to those same small groups, checking for agreement and relating the final decisions to initial discussions of concerns. This greatly improved both the quality of the solution and the likelihood of ownership in implementation. Finally, the facilitator utilized the earlier work of the council as an important, yet not binding, piece of work. Their involvement dovetailed with that of the larger staff. Because they had thought about the issues so thoroughly, their expertise shared with the large group improved its efficiency. Furthermore, their initial experiences with the consensus process modeled an approach that others could more readily follow. It's one thing for a facilitator to demonstrate active listening and a collaborative approach to problem solving, but for your colleagues and leaders to do so is especially compelling.

In addition to these empowering stages, the facilitator utilized her position as a synthesizing set of eyes and ears. She brought together ideas that came from the eight small groups and presented them in a coherent manner. Along the way, she checked for clarification and, as needed, revisions that arose from honest review of the concepts. Finally, she demonstrated patience that, paradoxically, improved the speed and efficiency of the group. A staff of sixty people was able to resolve some important issues within the scope of a three-hour meeting.

Modifying Consensus Within an Overall Decision-Making Structure: Horizon House

Horizon House was a highly regarded human service agency specializing in helping people with disabilities find meaningful work in the community. Established in the mid-1970s in an era of experimentation, the founders had always operated by consensus. Now, after nearly two decades in business, the current staff felt trapped by their legacy. Consensus didn't work, they said. It was slow, cumbersome. The majority felt they were often held hostage by an individual staff member who was "just a bit uncomfortable" with a decision, often leading many to acquiesce in order to reach consensus. Finally, they reported, their meetings were hopelessly bogged down, often for hours. The agenda was filled, with both items that had to be resolved and others carried over from one agenda to another.

The facilitator learned of Horizon House's staff dilemma from its director, Susan. Susan had been with the agency for three years. While she was pleased with the quality of work coming from the staff, their meetings were depressing her. She respected the tradition of consensus brought to the group by senior staff who had been there for twenty years. However, she felt compelled to find consensus at times when she would rather have made an independent decision. She also wanted the staff to learn more about their decision-making options and go through a problem-solving process by which changes could be made. They had all agreed, she said, to hold a full-day retreat in which to resolve these issues.

The facilitator sought individual written input from the twelve staff members (including Susan) in order to better understand their needs for the meeting. A few responded, but most answers were never received. Of those that came, all indicated the same frustration with meetings and the inability of the group to reach consensus. They also identified Susan as somewhat controlling and impatient. Another staff member, Roger, was viewed by some as "burned out," always blocking progress through his negative attitude.

From these responses, the facilitator developed a tentative agenda. He thought it made most sense to initially offer the group what it had requested: a brief educational session on consensus, alternative decision-making approaches, and the conditions required to achieve consensus (as presented in this chapter). After this training component, he would facilitate a group discussion of options in decision making for Horizon House. As the retreat began, he offered this agenda to the group, who accepted it as a good place to start. Other introductory comments made by group members were about kids, the weather, upcoming vacation plans, and so on. People were clearly uneasy about discussing difficult topics and were relying on the facilitator to lead them into this territory.

As the educational session unfolded, skeptical questions began to emerge from the group: "You mean that we don't have to use consensus all the time? But if we stop in some cases, won't some people abuse that power to force changes through the group? What do you do if an individual constantly blocks consensus, just because 'it doesn't feel right' to him? Can you shift to majority rule just to get on with other matters?"

These types of questions were starting to bring out legitimate concerns within the group about their mutual commitment to true democratic functioning. They indicated to the facilitator a need to stop instructing and start facilitating dialogue. He told the group of this concern and asked them to consider their best direction for the meeting during a ten minute break.

During the break, several people approached the facilitator. Each had concerns about a meeting in which old grudges and festering misunderstandings would be brought forth. They all preferred to move back to the initial agenda, approach their decisions dispassionately, and have a reasonable day together away from the office. This was all getting too uncomfortable for them.

Upon returning to the group meeting, the facilitator opened by seeking direction from the group. All were silent, except Susan, who asked that they return to the planned agenda. The facilitator then framed the dilemma: If you sit back and receive information now, there may not be adequate time to use the information to make good decisions. If it is important to you that you decide on changes today, we must discuss people's hesitations about the consensus process, explore people's fears about change, and arrive at solutions based on this dialogue.

At this point, the facilitator sat back, waiting for people to respond to his statement. He had assertively negotiated for the process and challenged the group to enter an uncomfortable place with him. Interestingly, it was Roger who first accepted this challenge. He started talking about his fears of change, saying that he felt his only leverage was to block decisions that he thought were poorly considered. Others then offered their frustrations, citing Roger for his inflexibility and Susan for her impatience. They also expressed appreciation to each of them for their passionate dedication to the disabled and to Horizon House. Gradually, all members of the group shared feelings that ranged from frustration to concern, some of which had been simmering for many years.

After a time, the facilitator summarized their concerns and asked them to focus on the future: *In conducting staff meetings, what ground rules would work effectively for you?* He asked them to forget their traditional approaches and offer, in an idealized sense, what they wanted to do. Once freed from both their procedural constraints and their emotional baggage, the group offered many ideas. After recording this brainstorm for about twenty minutes, the facilitator asked people to review the ideas that had been offered: *Are there any ideas on this list that any of you would reject? Are there others you now recognize have been omitted?* He then introduced the idea of using five fingers and a hand (discussed earlier in this chapter) as a way to poll a group for a level of consensus, an interim stage of decision making. Returning to the items on the chart a few minutes later, the group had little difficulty finding agreement. Still, there were a few items in which some members were only mildly positive; these solutions were then improved by the group, as appropriate.

Among the decisions made that day was the agreement to maintain consensus as a tool for certain types of issues, and move to consensus of subgroups as an alternative. This made more sense in light of the fact that, while they were only a dozen people, their involvement was divided into individual and small group projects in which there were definite stakeholders. By giving subgroups the power to make some determinations on their own, Horizon House staff were freed from the unrealistic expectation, developed over time, that all decisions required full staff consensus. While the decisions of small groups would continue to be reported to the larger staff, they would only be open to further deliberation if serious concerns were raised regarding their impact on the entire organization.

The Horizon House staff also empowered Susan, as director, to make more decisions independently. She could make certain expenditures, hire temporary staff, and submit grant applications without involving the full staff. A budget committee was established to develop the budget, for large group approval, and a personnel committee was similarly organized. In bringing these issues to the staff for approval, these committees would require a two-thirds majority approval. Consensus would no longer apply to all decisions.

Finally, the group also identified an agenda committee to formulate agendas for staff meetings. They were encouraged to review carried-over items and determine which ones could be assigned to a subcommittee, shifted to e-mail, or dropped completely.

This case study serves as a good example of how a group can modify a previous commitment to consensus decision making while retaining its philosophical value of democratic management. By utilizing consensus more efficiently, in subgroups closer to the actual point of impact, Horizon House increased its capacity to operate effectively. By categorizing decisions by type of action required (subgroup consensus, full staff consensus, or two-thirds majority approval), the staff were released from baggage that had bogged them down for years. If the types of modifications instituted by Horizon House are approached with an eye toward future review and further improvement, they can rescue a group that has fallen into the abyss of too much participation.

The facilitator stance in this case was assertive and instructive. He articulated concerns from the start, when members of the group were reluctant to do so, but he resisted the urge to wrest responsibility from the group for its own agenda. By flexibly moving away from the instructional, consultant mode to facilitate dialogue, he opened up channels of communication that had been clogged with fear and what we call "gunk."

However, there was a very real risk taken by the facilitator in this situation. Horizon House staff could have easily resented his move to have them engage in the discussion and projected their frustrations with one another toward the facilitator. We have seen this from time to time over the years: A group, in denial of its internal difficulties, will occasionally focus pent up anger at the facilitator. At such times, it remains important not to be defensive. A facilitator should reflect on what is now being said and seek clarification from the group about: (a) how widespread the feelings are; and (b) whether it would be worthwhile having someone else facilitate the group at this point. This issue not only affects external facilitators, as described here, but internal group members who may be assuming the facilitator role. It is crucial, at such times, not to become engaged in new efforts to derail problem solving by focusing on the qualifications of the facilitator to run the meeting. The group's issues have been its own and must remain its own.

Another risk is demonstrated by the Horizon House case. It is the danger that faces an organization that, once committed to consensus, now retreats from it. By giving greater power to Susan, the staff now chanced a more autocratic approach. By identifying categories of issues where consensus was no longer required, they now jeopardized involvement in decision making about important concerns. In moving to department-based decisions, they risked being excluded from possibly contentious, yet vital, discussions.

In fact, we have seen such steps serve as the initial actions of groups that move to traditional hierarchy. Several organizations we have worked with over the years have moved away from consensual, collective management, which they championed in their earlier years. They argue that consensus was inefficient, that our current competitive environment makes consensus a luxury they cannot afford, and that talented managers are not trained in this model and are uncomfortable with it. These arguments, while making sense in the context of their individual experiences, miss some crucial points I have tried to communicate throughout this book. By focusing on effective process, which can be time consuming in the short run, organizations can ultimately increase long-term efficiency. This is a move that is profitable to companies, as both the quality of decisions reached improves and experienced employees are retained. Utilizing trained facilitators enhances the capacity of an organization to develop effective work teams and make sound decisions, and an outside consultant can help executives and staff overcome their initial discomfort with participatory management. This generally results in invigorated leadership and greater staff commitment. When consensus is discarded, these companies now tend to suffer maladies of traditional businesses: staff alienation, high turnover, poor communication, and unproductive meetings that cost the company in meaningful ways.

CCR—An Ongoing Commitment to Consensus

For many years, the Center for Conflict Resolution (CCR) in Madison, Wisconsin, served as a think tank for the development of ideas related to participatory management and consensus. As discussed in Chapter Eight, we are indebted to CCR for providing the foundation for much of our current work at Collaborative Initiative, and I am personally grateful for my experience there in the early 1980s. It is from that experience that I now draw to describe an organization's ongoing commitment to consensus through internal facilitation.

CCR staff meetings occurred every other Tuesday night. Members came from a variety of backgrounds, including business, law, education, social work, and communications, and all held jobs outside of their work with CCR. Most worked for CCR between five and ten hours per week, with a few working close to full time. Group size ranged from six to fifteen members, plus an assortment of volunteers and interns who came for short periods of time. Because CCR was a nonprofit organization, many members volunteered hours for which they were never compensated. They shared a genuine sense of commitment to alternative dispute resolution and the development of democratic process.

We felt strongly that our own process must mirror the advice we gave others in responding to their needs. Therefore, our staff meetings were internally co-facilitated, with an agenda formed by all members contributing items. We also valued check-in as our only opportunity to understand each other fully, beyond our work roles, and placed it at the start of every meeting. This meeting phase often took on added meaning; as members underwent personal and professional crises, check-in offered a safe space in which to discuss these experiences. Occasionally, such issues were so significant that they resulted in additional staff meetings being scheduled to address the business that now had to be postponed. While this may appear unproductive, in fact it increased our sense of trust in one another and made us more focused and productive in addressing our work.

The responsibility for co-facilitation rotated among members. At times, the facilitators were chosen because people needed to gain experience in the role. On other occasions, it fell to people because they were the least involved in the upcoming agenda. Sometimes, people facilitated together as a way to gain experience working as a team. The meetings followed many elements of the process outlined in this book. Whenever an item arose where the facilitator needed to participate in discussion, she or he would "pass the clipboard" to a co-facilitator or to another member who volunteered. This process worked so smoothly and automatically that over time we developed simple nonverbal signals that conveyed this need. It would occur seamlessly, with scarcely a break in the discussion.

The tests of true consensus came at almost every meeting. There always seemed to be an item that divided us, whether it related to managing our finances, admitting new members, allocating responsibilities, or pricing our products and services. There were certain issues, such as how people were compensated for their work or who was taken on as a client, that seemed to be always resolved in the same way, in the manner of the founders and earlier CCR members. As time changed and new people became involved, this became a source of conflict within the group. This led to a critical series of meetings that form this case study.

In the 1970s, CCR's client base was comprised primarily of schools, nonprofits, collectives, and nontraditional organizations. In the 1980s, we began receiving calls from larger businesses and saw an emerging market for our services. Some staff felt strongly that we should continue to concentrate on those who seemed philosophically attuned with us, our traditional constituency. They argued that we should market more to these groups, offer free workshops to educate and involve our local community, and publish new materials to meet their needs. Others contended that our traditional client base was small and financially unable to support us. We needed to branch into new, more lucrative areas to support low-cost services we might offer to poorly funded community groups. Besides, by reaching out to big business, more democratic practices might reach much larger numbers of people. The traditionalists and the reformers were both passionate in their beliefs, and the discussion went to the heart of people's commitment to CCR. There was a real danger that, if a decision were made by majority rule or rhetorical debate, some would no longer feel that the organization represented their interests. A consensus was required.

To resolve the matter, we devised a three-step process. First, there was a meeting at which all were encouraged to share ideas, clarify concerns, and listen. Effort was made, by design, to reach a decision at this meeting. There was also agreement that this meeting would be tightly facilitated, that is, the ground rules would be vigilantly monitored by the facilitators and all group members, and time limits on holding the floor would be enforced. Second, three small groups would meet after the first meeting. Each group had balanced representation of traditionalist and reformer viewpoints, plus a member of another small group serving as their facilitator. That way each group had a more neutral, external facilitator, while the facilitators were guaranteed a subjective voice in their own small groups. In these subgroup meetings, people tried to problem-solve and offer tentative resolutions to the large group. They were asked to identify: (a) areas of consensus: (b) persistent areas of disagreement, with predominant sentiments; and (c) other areas of interest and concern.

The third phase was to bring these various ideas together in a full staff discussion. This meeting was devoted to debate of the small-group recommendations in order to reach consensus regarding the future of the organization. Each of the small group facilitators assumed reporting responsibilities in the initial phase of this meeting, in which virtually everyone felt included and respected. Although there were times when feelings were hurt or meanings misunderstood, the group was amazingly efficient at resolving the issues. It was decided that CCR would seek new client groups through direct marketing to large companies where we had some initial contacts. In addition, we would network with human resource managers and train directors to reach new companies. Finally, we would offer a series of low-cost workshops in Madison, involving CCR alumni as well as current staff, intended to appeal to our traditional constituency. Finally, we agreed to make two important structural changes: (1) moving to a departmental framework that increased efficiency of operations; and (2) holding a retreat in which we could chart a vision of CCR to guide the organization for the next three years. During the next several months, all of these decisions were implemented successfully. They provided a new framework that grounded the staff for several years.

In reviewing this case study, the outcomes are less important than the process. CCR recognized that it had a contentious issue that could be a turning point for the organization. All businesses face such dilemmas, and it is crucial to recognize them as they occur. They are not problems to be avoided; rather, they are crises that offer profound opportunities for growth, learning, and increased commitment to the company.

The process CCR devised allowed them to fully utilize their internal resources and talents. By patiently setting aside a longer meeting time (at least three hours) to talk without the pressure to decide, they created genuine opportunities to empower the staff to ultimately make a considered decision. By forming subgroups with representatives of adversarial positions and investing these groups with responsibility for problem solving, most of the basis for consensus had emerged prior to the final meeting. By giving facilitators other small groups where they could participate, these facilitators were freed to focus on the process, rather than substance, when called upon to do so. An alternative would have been to retain external facilitators, but this case illustrates the capacity of an organization to resolve such matters internally, both a cost savings and an important training experience.

Finally, this process afforded the current members an opportunity to remove expectations of their "ancestors" with dignity and respect. They were able to reach their own conclusions about the purpose of CCR and were then freed to devise their own organizational structure and vision to guide the future. By inviting past staff to participate in the workshop series (which successfully revived local relationships between CCR and traditional client groups), the current group acknowledged their gratitude and utilized their predecessors' skills in a meaningful way. It also afforded informal opportunities for the alumni to recognize how CCR had grown and prospered and how the organization was now in capable hands. These relationships with past staff, managers, board members, and others are often neglected in our busy world of the here and now. Yet they can often form faceless ghosts that haunt us; by creating positive opportunities to involve staff from different generations together, such anxieties may be laid to rest.

Chapter 7

Facilitating
Team Development

DEFINING A TEAM

Facilitators are often used in team development, helping group members function as a cohesive and effective work group. A team is defined here as "any group of people who need each other to accomplish a result," a simple definition that has been understood for at least four hundred years (Senge et al. 1994). However, there is more to this definition than is immediately apparent, for successful teams are extremely challenging to develop. An effective team can be distinguished from other groups by several characteristics:

1. Members perceive a shared goal or purpose.
2. Members are concerned with balancing personal and group needs in achieving this purpose.
3. There are clearly understood roles and functions within the team.
4. There is attention to nurturing effective communication among all members.
5. The team fosters interdependent relationships, required to achieve its goals.
6. The team is evaluated as a unit rather than as a collection of individuals.

Facilitators are called upon to: (a) help develop and clarify team goals; (b) foster effective communication regarding strategies to achieve goals; (c) educate team members in the skills and procedures of effective team problem solving, often including consensus decision-making; and (d) help teams resolve conflicts that have impeded their effectiveness. This chapter will provide an overview regarding how facilitators approach these diverse tasks, utilizing skills that have been developed in previous portions of this book.

As the saying goes, "There is no I in team." But there is a tenuous balance between "me" and "we" in this concept. The facilitator understands this tension and empowers team members to make their own determinations about how to resolve it. By endorsing the characteristics of an effective team, the facilitator helps team members communicate with one another successfully, not merely to meet the task functions of the group, but also to maintain a cohesive, affirming environment. By so doing, the team is truly able to develop the interdependent relationships required of a democratic work group.

FACTORS CONTRIBUTING TO TEAM EFFECTIVENESS

Mark Alexander of the University of Toronto has distilled several factors contributing to team effectiveness (Alexander 1985). We have adapted these elements and developed the Team Effectiveness Assessment Model (TEAM) for surveying team members regarding group performance. The TEAM Survey is offered in the Activities section of this chapter. We often present these factors as a training tool within team-building workshops and find that they offer a useful starting point for groups seeking to understand both their strengths and their weaknesses. They are offered here to provide an overview of the challenges facing teams:

1. Shared Goals and Objectives—Explicit, clearly stated goals guide the work of the team. Specific, measurable objectives are developed by team members for achieving these goals within designated time frames. The team's goals reflect an understanding of the overall organization's goals and philosophy.
2. Utilization of Resources—Through an affirming environment, members are encouraged to share their insights, talents, and skills. Differing work styles are brought out and blended, rather than ridiculed. Members are encouraged to know one another beyond their formal roles, potentially bringing other talents to the team's activities.
3. Trust and Mutual Respect—Team members demonstrate respect for one another and trust each other within the context of their work. They can count on each other for support, follow through on promises, and deal directly with each other in expressing concerns.
4. Conflict Resolution—The team brings forward matters of conflict as a normal function of its development. In managing conflicts, members negotiate credible and durable solutions. Issues of concern are regarded with respect, including emotional concerns that may be crucial to unlocking other issues.
5. Shared Leadership—Effective participation by all members in leading various tasks and assignments fosters a broad sense of ownership for team goals. There are numerous opportunities for growth, both personal and professional, that encourage risk taking. Members feel they are doing meaningful work, rather than merely serving to rubber stamp the decisions of others.
6. Control and Procedures—Members of effective teams clearly understand the purpose of their meetings. Agendas, schedules, and other procedures are developed in a prescribed manner, with shared authority for creating them. The facilitator role, whether internal or external, promotes democratic participation in meetings, even in hierarchal organizations.

7. Effective Interpersonal Communication—Communication is valued and supported throughout the team, not merely along the formal chain of command. Members practice active listening, assertive communication, and collaborative problem solving, fostering openness about issues facing the group.
8. Clear Decision-Making Approaches—The mechanism for resolving problems must also be clear. The team may decide by consensus, majority rule, or some other means, as appropriate, but all must understand where authority rests in each particular situation.
9. Experimentation and Creativity—The effective team encourages new ideas and welcomes offbeat approaches to problems. Team members move beyond the boundaries of established processes in order to experiment with new ways of seeing and doing, rather than responding, "Oh, we tried that once and it didn't work."
10. Evaluation of Process—Finally, the effective team is continually concerned with effective group process, and sets time aside for this purpose. Both as a routine element of ongoing meetings (e.g.,"check-out") and as a scheduled time that occurs less regularly, team members critique themselves, work to improve the quality of their meetings and their project management, and provide insights about new approaches that may be helpful for addressing future situations.

A concise list of these factors is given in Figure 7.1. The implications of these factors for the team's facilitator are several. In an ongoing group, the team benefits from a designated facilitator who is primarily concerned with helping them excel in each of these areas. It means formally selecting such a person (or persons) and valuing the facilitator role. This also means that the larger organization that houses the team must endorse this position.

Figure 7.1
Ten Factors Contributing to Team Effectiveness

1. Shared goals and objectives
2. Utilization of resources
3. Trust and mutual respect
4. Conflict resolution
5. Shared leadership
6. Control and procedures
7. Effective interpersonal communication
8. Clear decision-making approaches
9. Experimentation and creativity
10. Evaluation of process

CHARACTERISTICS OF A HEALTHY ORGANIZATION

Alexander's factors for team effectiveness are closely related to Rosen and Berger's research with the Healthy Companies Foundation (Rosen and Berger 1991). After analyzing hundreds of organizations throughout the world, Rosen and Berger concluded that eight strategies could help develop "people, productivity and profits." (See Figure 7.2.) These strategies help us distinguish between "healthy" and "unhealthy" organizations, according to Rosen and Berger:

1. The organization fosters the presence of a respectful work environment, characterized by an atmosphere that encourages people to communicate with one another honestly, taking risks to clearly convey needs and identify problems. Key elements include trust, appreciation, communication, and ethics. This strategy is summarized by Rosen and Berger: "The power of respect is greater than the power of money."
2. Leadership is shared throughout the organization: "Wise leaders know how to follow." The healthy company is characterized by empowering (vs. controlling) leadership, where participatory management and team approaches are encouraged. Top managers seek input from subordinates and integrate such ideas into the direction of the company.
3. Change is embraced as a natural opportunity, to be managed. Rather than reacting in a crisis mode to transitions, staff in healthy organizations seek to manage change. There is a proactive orientation to the evolution of the company and its clients' needs. People collaborate to respond to challenges, rather than place blame or "hold the course" until things settle down to be "like the good old days."
4. The company cultivates lifelong learning opportunities for all staff. There is a genuine commitment to training all staff, not just managers, in the core competencies of the workplace. These skills include: (a) the ability to learn; (b) technical knowledge; (c) aptitude in dealing with people; (d) emotional literacy; (e) intuitive abilities; and (f) personal management.
5. The company promotes the health of its workforce. In viewing the resources of workers holistically, the healthy company supports prevention efforts, exercise programs, smoking cessation, back care, substance abuse treatment, mental health counseling, stress management, and the like. It often includes the provision of Employee Assistance Programs, either internally or through contract services.
6. The company seeks to eliminate "sick" jobs. All staff work together to understand the nature of work within the organization. Managers seek to eliminate or revise those jobs that add unhealthy stress, demoralize staff, are characterized by redundancy, and so on. They promote worker safety, including the curing of "sick" buildings. Efforts are made to personalize and privatize work spaces, as much as possible.
7. The healthy company celebrates differences in its workforce. The company recruits and supports a diverse workforce, going beyond meeting quotas to welcome a mosaic of talents and perspectives. Staff are provided opportunities to manage prejudices (culture, age, gender, lifestyle, etc.) as a tool for learning how to celebrate these differences.
8. There is a genuine effort made to balance work and family as partners for life. Rosen and Berger recognized that myths regarding work and family priorities need to be exploded. Traditional gender roles (e.g., women at home, men as breadwinners) don't fairly describe the current makeup of our workforce. The healthy company supports staff in seeking a balance between work and home priorities, supports multiple life paths (including nontraditional career choices), and helps workers retain power in making important life choices.

Figure 7.2
Characteristics of a Healthy Organization

1. A respectful work environment is fostered.
2. Leadership is shared.
3. Change is embraced as an opportunity.
4. Lifelong learning opportunities are cultivated for all staff.
5. Health of the workforce is promoted.
6. "Sick" jobs are eliminated.
7. Diversity in the workforce is celebrated.
8. Effort is made to help staff balance work and family.

STRATEGIES FOR ACHIEVING HEALTHY TEAMS

In reviewing Alexander's and Rosen and Berger's lists, we see clear philosophical support for the values of facilitation. These principles, combined with several pragmatic strategies outlined here, may offer the facilitator a variety of approaches to use in supporting team development. First, members should be clear about the goals and purpose of their group. Team members must, therefore, clarify their individual visions of the team's purpose and contribute them to a collective understanding. Visions should be daring, far-sighted, and idealistic starting points for pragmatic discussion (Block 1989). By sharing them, team members understand more about their values, their biases, their perceived stumbling blocks and resources, and their initial impressions of the steps required for accomplishing their goals. An activity that we use for facilitating such discussion, the Team Visioning Exercise, is included at the end of this chapter.

Second, the team facilitator encourages effective communication among all team members, regardless of formal roles or hierarchal relationships. This can only be accomplished through the use of techniques previously discussed herein: active listening, internal development of ground rules, open sharing of concerns and conflicts, and deliberate, methodical problem solving. While this may seem obvious by now, many work teams focus so exclusively on task that communication functions are viewed as unnecessary luxuries. From our perspective, they are the foundation on which effective team problem solving is based.[1]

Third, the team needs to develop clear procedures by which it understands its accomplishments and shares its learning with others. Meeting minutes, research, progress notes, and so forth must be gathered and organized to provide a "team memory." In this way, as membership changes and recall fades, the team is able to maintain documentation of its best practices. In a workplace where many project teams start and end within a single year, and where members may belong to several teams simultaneously, the facilitator's assistance in formulating this team memory is especially critical.

Fourth, the team's sense of interdependence must be fostered, rather than allowed to occur (or not) by happenstance. When organizations make a transition to the team approach, they often retain the baggage of old organizational forms and practices, such as department-specific hierarchies, controlled lines of communication, individualized reporting and evaluation structures, and bureaucratic problem solving. Teams, on the other hand, require interdependent relationships; referencing our initial definition, they are groups in which members *depend on one another to accomplish their purpose.* This means that the facilitator needs to help team members clarify their new roles and relationships, some of which may be open to interpretation or conflict. Members must transcend turf battles that normally occur within the traditional, competitive organization and form collaborative relationships in which their individual goals are considered in light of the collective need.

This dynamic is frequently accepted in the world of athletics. For example, Phil Jackson, coach of the Chicago Bulls basketball team, balances a variety of immensely talented, often egocentric individuals within the larger team structure. Jackson endeavors to help each man understand his niche within that team and retains individuals who espouse this philosophy. The result is not just one great season, but an evolving organization that passes its insights on to many players. It has also resulted in several NBA championships (Jackson 1995).

This leads us to a fifth key strategy for the team facilitator: fostering evaluation of the team as a unit rather than as a collection of individuals. In the workplace, this need is frequently undermined by individual salary schedules, formalized performance reviews, and minimal empowerment of team members to assess their own accomplishments. As discussed in Chapter Four, democratic groups must set the criteria by which they evaluate their own successes or failures, rather than depend upon external validation of their work. The team facilitator helps the group through this process by posing key questions: *What is our purpose? What strategies have we adopted for achieving it? What roles are we as individuals playing in performing these tasks? How will we know if we are succeeding or failing in our jobs? How will we inform one another of these evaluations? How will we communicate to others, external to our group, that these are the bases of our evaluation? How may we encourage dialogue with stakeholders about possible conflicts between their evaluative criteria and ours?*

Finally, the facilitator should consider the team's need for recognition. Team members need opportunities to mark milestones in their history together, as well as a chance to acknowledge accomplishments and even to celebrate. All too often, the work environment is geared toward recognizing failure or paying token homage to lifetime achievements. Teams are dynamic, highly productive groups that frequently require redefinition and adjustments. Therefore, opportunities for recognition should be more frequent, a balance between internally and externally based rewards. For example, the team may hold a small celebration each quarter, to acknowledge special contributions over that time period. The company might also recognize all teams in a larger event, as part of an annual employee appreciation program.

All groups eventually reach an adjournment stage. Given the mature relationships that often exist, this can be highly emotional. Since members will naturally move to new groups and locations, they will understandably mourn the loss of the comfort of their former group. The facilitator should help all members note this turning point, thank those who are leaving, and help those who remain to come to terms with their new needs and roles. Rather than unduly focusing on such transitions and bogging down the group, as is sometimes feared, this strategy actually energizes the group and helps members move forward in a more efficient manner (Bridges 1991). It also helps individuals take what they have learned with them to improve their new teams.

In summary, these six strategies (see Figure 7.3) help to create healthy organizations in which teams can excel. The facilitator provides important keys to unlocking team potential. As we endeavor to create learning organizations, where teams play in increasingly central role, the proper facilitation of such groups is a highly valued skill.

Figure 7.3
Strategies for Achieving Healthy Teams

1. Develop a collective understanding of the goals and purpose of the group.
2. Encourage effective communication among all team members.
3. Establish and document clear procedures; collect and organize data to provide a "team memory."
4. Foster interdependence.
5. Promote evaluation of the team as a group, rather than as a collection of individuals.
6. Recognize the needs and celebrate the accomplishments of the group.

SYNTHESIS: DEVELOPING EFFECTIVE TEAMS

The factors and strategies described so far in this chapter conspire to form a concise model of the effective team, represented pictorially in Figure 7.4. By helping group members strive for the elements outlined by Alexander and by Rosen and Berger, utilizing the strategies we have offered here, team facilitators can offer valuable assistance to their groups.

This model is best understood as an interactive whole, rather than a set of discrete, independent variables. Much as a house relies upon a firm foundation, the effective team relies on a clear vision upon which to build its success. This vision must be balanced, holistic, and far-reaching, so it can support an affirming environment, strong group process, facilitative leadership, a balance of personal and group needs, and an optimal problem-solving capacity (the rooms of the house). It accomplishes this through attention to the specific needs of each space. In summary, the overall capability of a team is a product of our attention to all of its dimensions, rather than narrow excellence in a few.

Figure 7.4
Team Building Blocks

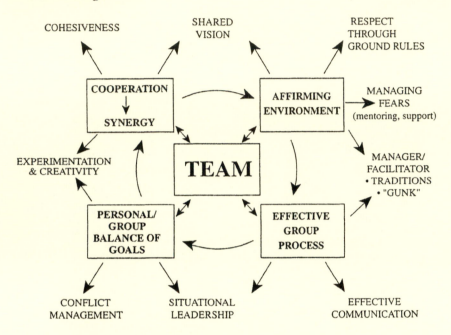

CASE STUDIES IN TEAM FACILITATION

The Inside/Outside Facilitator

Several years ago, I was asked to facilitate a task force at a college where I was employed. In this case, I served as an "inside/outside" facilitator, internal to the organization but external to the group. As the task force formed, I met individually with several team members to clarify both their understanding of the team's purpose and my role as facilitator. From these discussions, I learned that while most members came to the team willingly, some felt they had been assigned or were otherwise obligated to attend. I also learned that these people, many of whom were quite influential within the college, held deep fears about the possible damage to their reputations (and power) that could come from team failure. Clearly, their participation would be limited, unless they received assurances that their reputations would be protected.

As we approached our initial meeting, therefore, I focused on team development functions in our agenda. We established ground rules, including elements of confidentiality, we shared some initial anxieties (interestingly, people were quite candid about these fears), and we collectively realized that we were unclear about our mission. This led to a meeting with our sponsor, the dean who had launched our task force, in which I facilitated a frank dialogue about the purpose of the group. The result was a clear sense of member allegiance to the team, an in-depth understanding of our scope and parameters, and a firm commitment to the group by the dean. At that point, we were able to rally our resources and complete our project in a timely manner.

This case study reinforces the value of pre-negotiation as a phase of the meeting process. It permitted me to ascertain the true agenda of the group and to help them form a team that could meet it. It also demonstrates the importance of being flexible about content, allowing groups to explore process first. Finally, it confirms the need for a facilitator who can negotiate for process and resolve conflicts that arise in the initial development of a group. This task force could have been easily derailed by anxiety and a mistaken sense of disempowerment. Instead, by addressing these concerns directly and bringing the right people to the table, it was able to fulfill its purpose quite well.

The Facilitator as Stakeholder: Learning to Trust as an Internal Facilitator

Another case comes from a time when I started a university student service program. In that situation, I was an internal facilitator, also empowered with the authority of executive director. I wanted us to operate with consensus, yet I was also a stakeholder with specific, personal responsibility for our success. There were external sources of funding, often with differing criteria for success, and we were a new operation with little understanding of what our start-up operation could accomplish. As I assembled our management team, I sought individuals who could both succeed in their specific turf responsibilities and participate as active members of a team. But I also had to share my power, which was, at times, quite uncomfortable. I had my own fear of failure and the belief that I could do certain things more efficiently on my own, rather than collectively. I had to address my own hesitations about trusting the process before we could forge any agreements.

In this case, there were certainly failures. However, we generally exceeded all expectations of our sponsors, built a highly reputable organization (that has endured for over twenty years), survived political battles that would have cut our funding significantly, and established a model of democratic management that has remained a hallmark of the agency. As facilitator/executive director, I employed several of the strategies described earlier: I fostered an affirming environment, based on trust and credible follow-through; we collectively developed internal criteria for success, leaving a subgroup to negotiate with our board and sponsors about external demands; we established clear, yet flexible, roles and relationships within the organization that allowed team members to cross-train into new positions and mentor successors; we communicated formally and informally on a regular basis; and we regularly evaluated our process, as well as our performance, developing innovative computer-aided research techniques. As our agency grew and branched out into new service areas, our management team kept process as its central concern. I learned to trust. The more I facilitated, rather than controlled, the more effectively I managed the operation. It remains a lasting example that I recall in trying times.

The External Facilitator: A Precarious Position

A third case study demonstrates the evolving, sometimes precarious role of the external facilitator. In this example, two organizations were considering a possible merger. They were concerned that, allowed to continue separately, neither would fulfill its potential, and either might fail to survive. We began with pre-negotiation, from which it was learned that significant trepidation existed on both sides. One group worried about being swallowed and controlled by the other, larger group. Its members also expressed concerns about how their operations and services were valued by the other group. The larger group feared inefficiency on the part of the smaller organization and didn't understand their function. Both groups shared the concern that, after all of the dialogue, no action would be taken and the matter would be unresolved. This would be worse than never starting to talk, some felt, although all agreed that the status quo was unacceptable.

As a result of pre-negotiation, I shared my insights with each organization. Interestingly, one group felt that my statement of the concerns and tasks now before them was accurate, while the other group felt I was inaccurate and, even worse, had exacerbated the differences between the organizations and poisoned the atmosphere. However, in our initial meetings, this anger toward me was channeled into an affirmation of positive intentions on both sides. Through an initial agenda of discovery and trust building (which was resisted by more task-oriented members) the divisions between organizations were reduced and a sense of camaraderie emerged. Over time, I encouraged the groups to act increasingly as one team, fostering direct communication and problem solving, rather than relying either on me or on the traditional separate channels of communication. In the end, the group members agreed to principles of merger and adopted a timetable for its accomplishment, with specific milestones along the way. Once they developed internal resources for continuing the process, the external facilitator was no longer required.

This case study, besides depicting the delicate role of the facilitator, illustrates the importance of our strategies. The group had to develop its own clear goals and purpose in order to form a team. They had to devise procedures by which they could accomplish this, and they needed to practice effective communication in order to transcend prejudices that preceded their direct contact and permeated their organizations. As a team, they recognized that they were ambassadors for others, as well, and found security in working with their constituencies. Work teams often represent others who are not directly at the table, including people who perceive antagonism and protectionism as more palatable than collaboration. The facilitator does not solve such problems, but merely helps team members identify their interests. Once they understand how they feel about these concerns, they may come to terms with them.

Work teams provide a wealth of opportunities for the practice of facilitated meeting processes. Although the examples cited here involve white-collar management situations, the strategies are equally applicable to assembly-line teams or community project groups. The facilitator has an ongoing role to educate team members about process and help them inform one another about content. Contentious situations may then be managed by those responsible for them, and all members gain windows of understanding that may be transferred to other situations.

ACTIVITIES IN TEAM DEVELOPMENT

Team Effectiveness Assessment Model (TEAM)

Derived from the ten factors for team effectiveness outlined earlier, the Team Effectiveness Assessment Model (TEAM) allows group members to evaluate their team's performance at a specific point in time. It serves as an excellent springboard for robust discussion from which participants may focus problem-solving efforts. TEAM is advantageous because it is efficient (it takes only a few minutes to complete), multidimensional, and self-scoring. Instructions are as follows:

1. Pass out copies of the accompanying TEAM form to all participants. Have them read its instructions and complete the form, indicating levels of agreement or disagreement with each statement. Ask them to be sure to focus on a *specific team* in giving their responses (if they are members of multiple teams, they may take the survey again).
2. After about five minutes, ask participants to break into small groups of four to six members. They should share their responses to each question, round robin, with one another. Note: If this is a training exercise, with representatives of different teams participating, the insights from discussion are still worthwhile. However, TEAM is most powerful if used with intact teams. If preferred, you may leave an entire larger group intact for sharing responses in this stage. However, it is likely to move more slowly and, in most cases, to reduce participation. We strongly recommend small groups for the initial sharing of responses.
3. After about twenty minutes (which is barely enough time for most groups), ask group members to evaluate the process in which they were just engaged: Were all members heard, respected, and understood? Did they feel they were honestly able to share their criticisms of the team? Was it a productive discussion? This type of feedback is an important element of the learning process and related trust building.
4. Reconvene as a large group. Ask each small group to contribute any insights that were gained from their discussion. Specifically, attempt to identify:

a. Which factors did most agree were strengths of the team?
b. Which factors did most agree were weaknesses?
c. On which factors were there differing assessments of team performance?
d. What are the implications of these perceptions for improving team performance?

Team Effectiveness Assessment Model (TEAM)

Frequently team members have varying perceptions of their group's effectiveness. TEAM allows you to evaluate your group's performance in ten important areas and compare your views with others on your team. Please take a few minutes to respond to each question. If you are a member of several teams, answer all questions as they pertain to one particular group. Then, with others in your group, share perspectives and scores. As a result, we hope you gain insights into areas of strength and weakness, as well as understand next steps that may help your group.

1. Goals and objectives are clearly understood and agreed upon by team members.

                5-----------------4----------------3--------------2--------------1
Strongly Agree   Strongly Disagree

2. Member resources are fully recognized, respected, and utilized in the group.

                5-----------------4----------------3--------------2--------------1
Strongly Agree   Strongly Disagree

3. There is a high degree of trust that exists among members of the team.

                5-----------------4----------------3--------------2--------------1
Strongly Agree   Strongly Disagree

4. As conflicts arise within the group, team members deal with them honestly and effectively.

                5-----------------4----------------3--------------2--------------1
Strongly agree   Strongly Disagree

5. There is full participation in leadership, including sharing leadership roles.

```
      5----------------4---------------3--------------2--------------1
Strongly Agree                                Strongly Disagree
```

6. There are clear and effective procedures to guide team functioning (e.g., agendas, ground rules).

```
      5----------------4---------------3--------------2--------------1
Strongly Agree                                Strongly Disagree
```

7. Communication among team members is open and effective, across roles and functions.

```
      5----------------4---------------3--------------2--------------1
Strongly Agree                                Strongly Disagree
```

8. The team has established procedures that are understood and accepted for making decisions.

```
      5----------------4---------------3--------------2--------------1
Strongly Agree                                Strongly Disagree
```

9. The team encourages creativity and experiments with innovative ways of solving problems.

```
      5----------------4---------------3--------------2--------------1
Strongly Agree                                Strongly Disagree
```

10. The group regularly sets time aside to evaluate its functioning and process.

```
      5----------------4---------------3--------------2--------------1
```

After responding to each question, add the total score: _____. This indicates your overall assessment of team performance at this time. Although responses are subjective, total scores are roughly indicative of various levels of satisfaction, as follows:

43–50:   Indicates a high level of satisfaction with team
          performance at this time.
35–42:   Indicates generally strong levels of satisfaction at
          this time.
27–34:   Indicates moderate levels of satisfaction, with
          perhaps some areas of concern that require
          attention from the group.
19–26:   Indicates several areas of concern that require
          attention from the group.
10–18:   Indicates strong feelings of concern regarding
          team performance. Serious attention should be
          given these areas of concern.

The entire process can generally be accomplished in about an hour. From the results, the team gains a baseline of data indicating its current level of performance, as assessed by its members. It may prove worthwhile to have members complete the TEAM survey at a future date, following any interventions to improve group functioning. In this way, TEAM can serve as a simple yardstick for evaluating the group's effectiveness

Team Visioning Exercise

Among the challenges facing a team, the concept of team vision has received much attention. It is crucial for team members to develop and articulate personal visions, share them, and derive a common picture of their purpose as a group. This exercise helps groups accomplish this task. We wish to acknowledge Alice Phelan, a fellow mediator and facilitator, for sharing this exercise with us in 1989. It is presented here in a form that lends itself to team development, but it may also be utilized by individuals seeking to clarify their visions of work or home environments. Instructions are as follows:

1. Have team members spend some time learning about and discussing the concept of visioning prior to this exercise. A good reading would be *The Empowered Manager* (Block 1989), "What Is a Vision and Why Is It Important?" on pages 102–115.
2. Ask participants to relax, perhaps even close their eyes. Then ask them to try to visualize their *idealized workplace*, within the parameters of their current situation.
3. Offer questions that encourage them to develop these visualizations: *What does this place look like? How does it feel to be there? What are people doing in this environment? What does it sound (or smell) like?*
4. Ask participants to focus on their team within this idealized workplace: *What is the team doing? Who is involved and what role is each person playing? How does it feel to be part of this team?*

Team Visioning Exercise Form

Vision:				
Goals that flow from this vision				
Influential resources of actors to meet goals				
Barriers (personal, interpersonal and/or structural)				
Next steps/ something that can help				

5. Ask participants to jot down ideas that flow from these visualizations. This is personal writing, not for public sharing, and may be in any form they desire. Allow ten minutes for the development of these ideas.
6. Ask people to form pairs (or triads) within which they should share their personal visions, identifying both the idealized workplace and the team as a part of that ideal. In these discussions, they should listen to each other and seek clarification, but defer judgment.
7. Bring people together as a large group. Ask them to share their visions, including their initial thoughts on the role of the team within that vision. (This discussion can also provide a useful tool for relating vision to the assessments in the TEAM survey, discussed earlier.) Allow at least forty minutes for this discussion. As appropriate, you may defer the following steps to the next meeting.
8. As a large group, complete the accompanying Team Visioning Exercise Form. All members should be encouraged to participate. In the top box, the group develops a statement that represents their vision of the idealized workplace. Since this may be derived from a number of differing personal statements, it is important not to compromise this statement as a mediocre attempt to build consensus. As necessary, use other strategies we have offered regarding conflict resolution and consensus building. In this way, the emerging vision statement is meaningful and useful for answering later questions.
9. The group should proceed to answer all questions on the Team Visioning Exercise Form. The time to be allotted varies greatly among groups.
10. After completing the exercise, the group should, as usual, evaluate its process. As appropriate, the group should determine next steps to be taken and assign members to accomplish them.

This exercise often has a profound effect on people, for it dares them to think in terms they might otherwise not entertain. By developing a collective vision and relating this vision to personal desires, all members are encouraged to share ownership in the product of their efforts. Even if the vision only serves as a reminder of an ideal they cannot realistically achieve, it still functions as a navigation point that guides their efforts and highlights common work goals.

Outcomes Identification Exercise

This is an exercise we learned a number of years ago and have used in many situations. It is an especially effective tool to use with groups that have been in conflict, for it helps them focus on areas of strength and shared expectations, as well as specific differences. For all teams, it is a useful tool for helping members articulate their expectations of one another, so they may clarify areas that require further attention. Instructions are as follows:

1. Pass out the Outcomes Identification Exercise Form to all participants. Explain that the purpose of the exercise is to help team members clarify and communicate their expectations to one another. Furthermore, remind the group of the various types of needs (substantive, procedural, and psychological) that may exist within the team.
2. Ask each participant to follow Step #1 on the worksheet and respond individually to the question: "What are some outcomes that I desire at my workplace?" Brainstorm a

list of possible responses. Give people about three to five minutes to list responses. Encourage them to list as many responses as possible.

3. Form small groups of four to six members, and have them each appoint a recorder. Follow Step #2 on the worksheet: in each group, have members share responses from Step #1 round robin, while the group recorder writes them on a list. Tell participants that if one of their answers has been mentioned by someone else, they should skip it and choose a different response from the list. If all responses on a personal list have already been named, people may pass. Allow ten to fifteen minutes for this step.

4. Occasionally, we have people completely share their lists before moving on to the next step. Usually, though, it is more effective to go round robin two or three times. The goal of this step is to generate a list of about a dozen items, which then serves in the next phase of discussion.

5. Participants now move to Step #3 on the worksheet, in which they develop affirming statements regarding themselves and one another. In facilitating this step, encourage people to fully develop their statements orally, even if they are unable to do so in writing. As before, they should share their statements round robin, within small groups. Allow ten to fifteen minutes for this step.

6. As appropriate, have small groups decide by consensus which desired outcomes are the most important to them. They may select one, two, or three items from their collective list, or develop a new statement. In some situations, this step may be unnecessary. It generally takes about five minutes.

7. Evaluate the process within small groups, in about ten minutes. Ask members to consider:

   a. What have you learned as a result of generating this list?

   b. How did it feel when you heard others articulate their desired outcomes?

   c. How did it feel when you developed the affirming statements about colleagues? when you heard someone else refer to you? when you "bragged" about your own work toward a desired outcome?

8. Reconvene as a large group. Have recorders share the small group lists with the larger group. At this point, the group may go in one of several directions:

   a. You might seek insights regarding the lists that were generated. Generally, there is a high degree of overlap, and the lists are dominated by procedural and psychological needs, rather than substantive ones. Generally, most of the priority items are within the control and power of the team to manage, rather than that of external sources (e.g., management, funding sources, customers, etc.).

   b. You might ask the group to clarify which desired outcomes are already being achieved within the team. This is a chance to affirm success within the group.

   c. You might ask which items appear to be most important to achieve now, given the gap between the status quo and desired outcomes. These items may now form an agenda for a future problem-solving session.

Generally, we find the Outcomes Identification Exercise serves as a simple, yet powerful, means of uncovering aspirations that have gone unexpressed within the group. It also provides a level playing field for their expression, through small group idea sharing. Finally, by focusing on the positive, it reminds team members of the importance of such an outlook.

Outcomes Identification Form

1. Individually, respond to the question: "What are some outcomes that I desire at my workplace?" Brainstorm a list of possible responses (3–5 minutes).

2. Round robin, share responses with the group. Each person shares one idea at a time, until all are satisfied that the main ideas have been covered. The group should appoint a recorder for this task.

3. Each participant then takes an item from the collective list and completes the following two statements:

"An outcome I am working to achieve is _____.
                          (a desired outcome from the collective list)
I am proud of my work in this area because _____
_____."

"I know that _____ is working to
                 (another team member)
achieve_____.
             (another item from the list)

I feel this is important because _____
_____."

Try to elaborate on these statements, so they are completely understood by others in your group. For example, you might state: "An outcome I am working to achieve is a cooperative work environment. I am proud of my work in this area because it has resulted in a sensitive and respectful atmosphere, where people can be themselves and share ideas honestly." "I know that Lisa is working to promote greater accountability within the team. This is important because it encourages all of us to report concerns and accomplishments honestly to one another, and it keeps problems from festering until they get too large to manage."

4. As appropriate, you may find these statements are worth sharing with others not in your small group. Take some time to let someone else know how much you appreciate what he or she contributes to the team.

NOTE

1. Additional insights regarding their application to team development are more fully developed in other texts: Peter Senge et al., *The Fifth Discipline Fieldbook*, 1994; and Peter Block, *The Empowered Manager*, 1989.

Chapter 8

Stages of Group Development: Impacts Upon the Facilitator

The facilitated meeting described earlier in this book provides a useful approach to the formation of a group. The initial work to set the tone and establish ground rules gradually gives way to an ongoing procedure through which the group meets, discusses and decides issues, and develops relationships over time. In high functioning groups, the meeting is viewed as a vital opportunity to meet with colleagues, be productive, and feel professionally stimulated. Group members are excited about participating, contributing significant energy to team efforts that provide professional and personal satisfaction.

This chapter focuses on the facilitator role in promoting the development of such groups. Using our understanding of the phases of group development, we will examine the varying roles of the facilitator during each stage. We will identify milestones to consider in applying the art of facilitation to the process, as well as provide insights regarding the styles of leadership most appropriate to each challenge. Using a comparative case study involving two facilitated groups with different strategies, we will apply principles developed throughout the book to broaden our understanding of group process.

THE GROUP OVER TIME: PHASES OF DEVELOPMENT

There is considerable debate among social scientists about the natural phases of a small group's development. Much of this debate centers around perceived differences in small group purpose, and the impact of related goals upon its phases of development. Several theories arose in the 1950s and 1960s that attempted to explain small group behavior, resulting in useful contributions to our understanding of how facilitated groups work (Cartwright and Zander 1968).

In his book on small group behavior, Marvin Shaw (1976) summarizes the contributions of these various theories to our understanding of groups. They are offered here to provide a theoretical context for our pending discussion of the role of the facilitator in the evolving group. They are related to other issues raised throughout this book, as well.

Field theory holds that behavior is the result of a field of interdependent forces. Proposed and developed by Kurt Lewin some fifty years ago, this approach examines group behavior as part of a system of interrelated events. It has proven useful as a foundation for understanding social systems, such as families and organizations, and the behavior of conflictive groups in such systems (Lewin 1948, 1951).

Interaction theory views the group as a system of interacting individuals. It commonly includes three elements: activity, interaction, and sentiment, focusing upon the relationships among these elements. It is useful for understanding communication patterns within groups and how people behave in natural (versus experimental) patterns of communication.

Systems theory is quite similar to interaction theory and has superseded it in popularity in the past twenty years. They differ in that systems theory examines interactive elements within the system, such as positions and roles, with emphasis on group inputs and outputs. By focusing on the contributions to the "box" that contains the small group, we are able to learn more about how many of its experiences are environmentally influenced, if not determined. While this minimizes the impact of some interactions that a facilitator may manage, it speaks strongly to the potential power of group membership, pre-negotiation, arrangement of the meeting environment, and other factors addressed in the forming stages of development. It also supports the view that attending to the adjournment factors, noted later in this chapter, can enhance the impact of the group on the larger system.

The sociometric orientation emphasizes interpersonal choices among group members. The morale and performance of the group depend on these relationships. It supports the importance of the affirming environment and the establishment of ground rules and other procedures that enhance group process. The stronger and more positive the relationships among members, the more likely the group may engage in positive, goal-oriented behaviors.

The psychoanalytic orientation derives from Freudian psychology. It is concerned with motivational and defensive processes of the individual as related to group life. The general psychology orientation attempts to extend theoretical analysis of individual behavior to group behavior. Essentially, both of these approaches seek to deny the uniqueness of group experience, versus individual behavior, in explaining the evolution of groups. While they have stimulated a great deal of research, they have yielded little empirical evidence to support such assertions. Groups do tend to follow patterns that result from interactive effects, whether from individuals or systemic forces, that result in our need for unique understandings of the group experience.

These various theories of group behavior have contributed incrementally to our understanding of the role of the facilitator. However, it fell to Hersey and Blanchard, starting in the early 1980s, to provide the missing elements that offered catalysts to our work. Their development of situational leadership theory (Hersey and Blanchard 1988) revolutionized businesses, for it offered a framework of leadership and management that transcended the static views of the day. Their situational approach allowed us to recognize that the management of employees, groups, and organizations must respond flexibly, depending on the situation. Thus, they laid the foundation for what we have developed as the facilitative approach to management.

For example, Hersey and Blanchard theorized that managers of new employees were required to use a "telling" approach to leadership. They should provide specific information about tasks, simple steps for accomplishing those tasks, and clear understanding about how those tasks related to one another and the company. The new "stage one" employee has little concept of the big picture and shouldn't be free to make decisions in areas where he or she is not yet qualified. In a traditional management model, this style would be seen as autocratic, but in Hersey and Blanchard's view, it is an approach that provides necessary context and security for an employee in an unfamiliar place. In contrast, the "stage four" employee requires a mentoring style of leadership. This staff member, who performs his or her functions at a high level, uses the manager as a sounding board for ideas and runs with them independently. The manager provides new challenges and opportunities for growth, raising critical questions and helping the employee connect with other staff who can serve as resources for solving specific problems. Here, the supervisory relationship is dramatically different from the other scenario, as is the style of leadership to be employed. The manager offers collaborative leadership that is fully inclusive and highly democratic. The needs of the employee and the manager are now met through this participatory approach.

These distinctions in leadership style resonate with changes in style necessarily offered by the facilitator of an evolving group. As we will discuss in the pages that follow, styles of facilitation and priorities of leadership tasks change through the development of the group. As the group evolves, and its needs evolve, it requires somewhat differing stances from the facilitator. These orientations, in turn, lead to checklists of tasks to be accomplished, which call upon the facilitator to use the range of tools we have discussed throughout this book. It is here that the "art of facilitation" is truly applied.

Phase One: Forming

Forming is the initial phase of a group's existence. During this period, members orient themselves to the needs and purpose of the group. They relate these needs to their own as members, clarifying personal levels of commitment to the group. During this phase, group leaders emerge, either through direct ascendency of conveners or through delegation of such authority by the organizers and sponsors of the group. This is a crucial stage in the life of the group: If well facilitated, it can result in moving efficiently to establishing norms and purpose for the group. If poorly led, the group's struggle for identity and purpose can significantly derail it, setting the tone for frustration and conflict.

For example, product development teams were organized at two competing companies, ABC Corporation and XYZ, Ltd. ABC and XYZ manufacture specialized paper products, including bathroom tissue, paper towels, and facial tissue. In this highly competitive industry, the two companies had determined that there was an unmet need to provide highly absorbent, disposable towels to athletes, to be used in conjunction with workouts and sporting events. They envisioned a market that included elite athletes, coaches, and training centers at its core, with expansion to occasional, recreational users and families. Each company's management recognized the need for expediently developing a product for this market, and each company organized a team to attack the problem.

The managers at ABC brought together representatives from several departments to work on this important team, recognizing the value of a variety of perspectives on the project. They had identified a group of talented individuals at ABC, people who could creatively undertake this challenge and bring the product to market within eighteen months. They included people who could design the product, determine its best manufacturing process, develop an effective cost and pricing structure and, ultimately, market and sell the product. The team was to be chaired by Rachel, vice president for marketing.

Prior to the group's initial meeting, Rachel prepared a carefully considered agenda, posted on a flip chart, as well as a packet of meeting materials. Each team member also had a fifteen-minute, face-to-face discussion with Rachel, in which she clarified the purpose of the team, provided reading materials as background preparation, and underscored her appreciation of the members' willingness to participate. She used these individual discussions to listen to prospective members, too, as they described what they needed from her as group facilitator. In addition, Rachel arranged for the group to meet in a comfortable room at an area conference center. Participants entered a space that was relaxing, away from the distractions of their offices, yet organized to support the work at hand.

Across town at XYZ, top managers also organized their product development team. A memo was sent to each department, from which individuals were sent to the initial meeting of the team. Michael, an engineer with special expertise in the design and manufacture of high absorbency materials, was notified that he would be team leader for the project. As with all other XYZ project teams, participation on this team was required, regardless of other current commitments, unless one received permission from a supervisor to be excused from the project.

Michael sent a notice to all members via e-mail regarding the first meeting. In his note, he asked people to bring their calendars, since it was always so difficult to schedule times that most people could attend. As participants arrived at Conference Room B in the basement of XYZ's office building, they came without a clear sense of the purpose of the group or an understanding of their roles in its effective management. Michael started the meeting by providing a brief history of XYZ's involvement in the athletic market. He outlined some of the challenges to be faced in developing materials that are both appropriate to serious athletes and affordable to recreational users. He concluded his remarks by saying that he wasn't sure they could really produce what management wanted in a cost-effective way, but that "it isn't our problem to figure out the pricing of this thing, just to make it useful."

Discussion was then opened to all. A few people complained that they were too busy to take on this project, yet they felt no power to change management's priorities. A few others speculated that other people should be part of the team, but these ideas didn't lead to any particular resolution. In the end, Michael agreed to "get more information so we can start moving on this thing," and people spent the final fifteen minutes of the meeting looking for a common time to meet again. However, since some people had already left early, it was unclear whether the next meeting would work with everyone's schedule.

Meanwhile, Rachel had convened ABC's group for its initial meeting. She started by having people check in, each discussing his or her feelings about being a member of this group. Most were enthusiastic about participating, but all expressed fears that it could overwhelm their other workloads. Rachel added this concern to the agenda, noting that assignments between meetings needed to reflect the capacity of group members to accomplish those tasks. After check-in, Rachel offered ground rules for the conduct of meetings. These were readily accepted, but a few members offered additional ideas that went beyond those points that Rachel had considered. The group reached consensus that it would meet biweekly for two hours, keeping this initial meeting time as one that worked well most of the time. While the conference center was nice, they agreed to meet at the ABC training room, which was adequate for their needs and more convenient for a midday meeting. Still, they appreciated being able to get away to this location for their initial meeting, and agreed to do this again once every three months. They agreed to produce meeting minutes, both for their own benefit and to keep management appraised of their progress. They would rotate the recorder role among members for now, but decided to review how this was working after two or three meetings. If necessary, they could seek secretarial assistance to help in this area.

Rachel then focused on the purpose of the group and ABC's capacity to achieve its goal: *What issues do we need to address so we might produce a super absorbent, disposable towel for serious athletes?* The team brainstormed responses to this question for about thirty minutes. After a break, they categorized their responses into marketing, financial, manufacturing, and distribution questions. Small group task forces were then established to explore responses to these issues and report on them in upcoming meetings, within a sensible chronological sequence. It was agreed that the group would focus on one set of issues per meeting, but that each task force would appoint a representative who would communicate regularly with Rachel.

The team then evaluated its initial meeting, at which time the members praised

Rachel for her fine work as team leader. They left the meeting with a review of the tasks at hand, clarification of their next meeting time and location, and a positive sense they were headed in the right direction. The group was now well along the formative phase of development.

In examining the two cases of ABC and XYZ, we see clearly the relative impact of strong facilitation in the forming phase of the group. The XYZ group has left its first meeting with little sense of commitment and only a vague idea of its scope and purpose. Individuals are not yet *members* of this group, only participants in a meeting they have been told to attend. Although they may yet accomplish the task set before them, their work is hampered by an ambiguous mission statement, vague and reluctant leadership from Michael, and a general lack of teamwork skills.

The ABC team, however, is already a *group*. Its members truly see themselves and one another as members of a team, committed to its common purpose and dependent upon one another to achieve it (see definition of team in Chapter 7). Rachel, as a facilitative team leader, has played a significant role in bringing the group to this point: She met individually with members prior to the meeting, helped them prepare to participate effectively, and affirmed their importance to the group. She arranged for a meeting space that underscored her respect for the group and her recognition of their need for an environment that would support their work. She conducted the meeting in a manner that encouraged full, specific participation around meaningful questions, and genuinely empowered members to take leadership over tasks facing the group. She simplified jobs, such as agenda formation, establishing ground rules, and determining meeting times, by offering initial ideas in these areas. Moreover, she stayed flexible when concerns and new ideas were offered, modifying her tentative plans as the group took ownership of the process. Finally, she provided useful opportunities to group members to evaluate the meeting and summarize tasks that would occur between meetings. Her listening, respectful stance modeled a style of behavior that others both appreciated and emulated.

Phase Two: Norming

Norming is the phase in which a group establishes its norms and procedures for effective group functioning, including: (a) ground rules for the conduct of meetings; (b) expectations, roles, and responsibilities for the accomplishment of the group's business; (c) organization of tasks and strategies through which these functions are executed; and (d) the relationship of these group norms to the larger cultural expectations and attributes of the organization. In this phase, the group begins to experience the identity it established in the previous phase. There is fine-tuning and elaboration of the group identity that was idealistically expressed in the formative stage of development. Such experiences are crucial to the continued growth and development of the group, for they allow the group to develop skills it will need to solve problems and resolve conflicts to be experienced in accomplishing its goals. By articulating norms as they are established and experienced, the facilitator helps group members understand the meaning of democratic participation. As such, the group can acknowledge the meaning of their experiences, incorporate this learning into their ongoing skills and bring resulting insights into future meetings.

While the facilitator needs to be assertive around the organizing functions of the forming phase of development, she or he needs to share ownership of these responsibilities in the norming stage. Otherwise, the group can easily fall into a pattern of facilitator dependency, in which non-democratic norms would be established within the group. Such habits can be difficult to change once they are incorporated into group norms and, since they conform to traditional expectations of leaders, are especially likely sources of conflict within the group. Thus, a more collaborative style of leadership must be modeled by the facilitator in the expression and codification of group norms. Although this may appear less efficient in the near term, this style will ultimately improve group efficiency over time. As well, it will provide early tests of the group's skills and commitment that will be useful to managing the conflicts it will inevitably experience.

Returning to our groups at ABC and XYZ, we find the groups are experienced the norming phase of development in different ways. An examination of the second meeting of each group tells much of the story. XYZ's product development team met again about three weeks after its initial session. Although all departments were represented, four new group members replaced four others who were unable to personally attend. This information surprised Michael, the team leader, as well as other group members; no notification had been received from either the absent members or their replacements prior to the meeting. However, this is normal at XYZ, where people are involved in many teams like this one and attend "too many meetings."

To his credit, Michael began this meeting by reviewing the mission of the group. He attempted to bring new people up to speed by reviewing, in some detail, information shared at the last meeting. He then sought questions and comments from group members, which resulted in a tangential discussion about last year's emphasis on marketing a new line of pocket-sized tissues for business customers. During this discussion, which actively involved Michael and two other group members while the others were silent, an observer could have witnessed side conversations about other work and at least two people pulling out pocket organizers to jot down unrelated thoughts on other projects and tasks. One member even took out his cell phone and went to a corner of the room to place a call.

After about ten minutes, Joyce from marketing objected to the direction the meeting had now taken, saying she was extremely busy and that she didn't see how this discussion of last year's tissue campaign was informing the group. Michael responded defensively that he thought it was quite relevant, for it instructed them about mistakes they should not make again. Joyce inferred that he was blaming her, and the marketing department, for shortfalls in pocket tissue sales. The rest of the group fell silent in the presence of this conflict. After a few moments of uneasiness, Petra, a sales associate, suggested that this meeting needed to get focused on finding solutions to the problem the group had been given. Petra offered a few questions she thought had to be answered if XYZ was going to produce a specialized product for athletes: "Why are people going to use this product? Why should they buy such a product from XYZ, who has little previous penetration into the athletic equipment market? How had management thought of marketing this product, and at what price? Are we creating a totally new product here, which requires new technology and additional time to develop, or is this the repackaging of materials for which we have previous expertise?"

At that point, a few other members supported the importance of the concerns Petra had raised. Michael stated that he didn't know much about most of these questions, but he did have a response to the inquiry about technology. He then launched into an explanation of the technology that was being applied here, including how his lab had won awards for developing this material two years ago. His point, that XYZ was simply applying existing technology to the design and production of a new product, was lost to the members of the group. A glazed appearance settled over most group members, and they began to trickle slowly out of the meeting.

After the meeting, a few members approached Petra. They thanked her for raising the issues she had brought to the group and wished the group could address some of those questions. She responded that she was only trying to help, but it appeared that Michael was unaware of how to manage a group well. Some observed they had been in other groups with Michael before, and that he had a tendency to share his knowledge to the detriment of the meeting. He knows a lot, they said, but he sometimes offered this information at the expense of others sharing what they needed to share. They asked Petra to meet with Michael before the next meeting to express their concerns, but Petra responded with great reluctance. She was only a sales associate, and she was afraid of making waves with Michael. They all walked away shaking their heads in frustration.

ABC's product development team had a very different type of second meeting. Rachel brought the group together with a quick update on some happenings in the company over the past two weeks. Apparently, the CEO had read their initial minutes and had e-mailed Rachel that he really liked the direction they were now setting for themselves. She wanted to pass this word to people as encouragement. She had each member briefly check in to the meeting before getting to the agenda for the day. From these introductions, the group learned that two people were feeling distracted by other work and one person had a terminally ill parent who was requiring a great deal of energy. It was noted that these three people would not be able to take on special assignments over the next two weeks. A few members whose parents had died were able to briefly acknowledge the pain and difficulty of such an event for the man who was now dealing with it.

From here, a task force within the group delved into an issue earmarked for discussion at the previous meeting. They began by reviewing highlights of information they had provided members in advance. Rachel then facilitated discussion about the task force's suggestions, through which the larger group was able to reach consensus on a few basic items and offer guidance to the task force for further work. As this discussion concluded, Rachel asked the representatives of the remaining three task forces to share progress reports, as well as any questions they now needed to be considered by the group. In conclusion, the group affirmed the value of this meeting and clarified the agenda, time, and location for its next session in two weeks.

The contrast between XYZ and ABC is reflected in the meeting norms that have been adopted. The XYZ team is floundering, settling into a pattern of reticence and indirect communication. The group's leader, Michael, is dominating discussion. In response to criticism, he is becoming defensive. Because of built-up frustrations, members are withdrawing their energies from the group or, as in Petra's case, looking for safe ways to participate and get the job done.

For the ABC team, Rachel has set a tone of participation and involvement that is extremely affirming and motivational. Members have taken initiatives to communicate directly with one another, both during and between meetings. They arrive prepared to work, yet still set aside a few minutes in each meeting to understand more about one another personally. There is flexibility being demonstrated, from the facilitator and from the members, regarding the individual professional and personal needs of members. The result is that norms of respect, democratic participation, and consensual problem solving are now being established.

It is important to recognize that the norming phase does not begin or end with the second meeting of the group. It begins early in the first meeting, as the team leader attempts to facilitate the process. Members quickly establish patterns of communication, participation, power use, and decision making within groups. Although it is useful to note a distinct phase that reflects the formalization of such norms, it is important to recognize they are being established within the group from its inception. Indeed, many norms within small groups are inherited from other groups. For example, if a company's meetings are typically characterized by people arriving late, bringing other work, or sitting back to wait for the team leader to tell them what to do, these norms are usually carried to new groups as expectations. If the forming and norming stages are facilitated in a manner that reinforces such standards of behavior, they are likely to become quickly entrenched. Members will continue to see such behavior as "the way things have always been around here and the way they always will be." There will be little sense of power accrued, either within leadership or membership, to change such expectations.

If the facilitator takes the initiative to change such patterns by modeling open communication, for example, people may thrive on the experience. Once these new patterns are established, this unusual experience provides an opportunity to change the expectations brought to other settings. It is extremely challenging to change the dominant culture of an organization, however. Therefore, these reforms need cultivation and encouragement in the other phases of the group if they are to have any hope of transference as a new model for the company.

Phase Three: Storming

The next phase of group development, storming, reflects the inevitable challenge of conflict management within small groups. How the facilitator responds to the expression of conflict frames an important turning point in the evolution of the group. It is a moment of truth from which either optimal functioning or hopeless fragmentation will likely follow.

The storming phase can be surprising to many participants, for it frequently occurs quickly and after a period of relative harmony. In this phase, members begin to express disagreements over a proposed course of action or decision of the group. This expression may take one of several forms (see conflict styles discussed in Chapter Five), ranging from angry, aggressive arguing to passive withdrawal from participation in the group. On occasion, the conflict may not be recognized as such; people might simply say, "Fine. We can do it your way if you like." Beneath the surface, the storm is brewing for them and for the group.

In the storming phase of a group's life, the facilitator must separate him or herself from the content and emotion of the conflict and become a guardian of the process. More than in previous phases, facilitators must be extremely wary of their own biases, prejudices, and beliefs, for they may jeopardize credibility to be neutral in the face of disagreement within the group. This danger is especially evident in cases where the facilitator is a subject of direct disagreement (as in the earlier situation between Michael and Joyce). In such circumstances, it is astute to seek a co-facilitator who may assist while you advocate for your stake in the discussion. This threat to neutrality is also present in more subtle ways, as a group considers a course of action that you question, or certain members behave in ways you find repulsive (shouting, name-calling, etc.). In short, managing the process in the storming phase requires a special strength in leadership to help the group through a rocky set of transitions (Bridges 1991; Taft 1987).

As we further examine our product development teams at ABC and XYZ, their approaches to the storming phase are instructive. As we saw in the previous discussion, XYZ has already experienced some conflict, and their initial responses to the expression of disagreement have gone poorly. At the next meetings, the group began to focus on the problems at hand, essentially addressing the questions raised by Petra at the second session. Michael and the others participated more comfortably within their traditional roles at XYZ, with marketing advice coming from Joyce, sales advice from Petra, and technical advice from Michael. Others offered information as it was sought from the group. The meetings become routine and fairly functional, as the group began to build a plan for the manufacture and distribution of a new disposable athletic towel. On the surface, this was a normal team at XYZ, with a few people assuming most responsibilities and some others offering occasional input. People appeared to be relatively comfortable with this approach, for it didn't tax their energies greatly and seemed to be accomplishing its purpose.

However, during their fourth meeting, cracks in the peace became more noticeable. Joyce offered a marketing plan for the product, which she named

"Sweat Soaks," to the group. A few people chuckled and liked the name, as well as her plans for marketing it, but others said the name was unappealing and confusing with "sweat socks," a very different type of product. A few jokes were then made at Joyce's expense. She didn't find them to be humorous, and became noticeably upset and tight-lipped. Michael, as team leader, made a brief comment about how marketing often came up with ideas "the rest of us find strange" and attempted to move the discussion to another subject. Joyce responded, however, that this group needed to decide what it wanted her to do: "Do you want me to develop this campaign, or don't you? I'm not going to waste my staff's time and energy on this product if you think it won't sell. If you don't like Sweat Soaks, does anybody have a better name for the product!!??"

The meeting room was now tense. The longstanding discomfort of the group had expressed itself in an impasse over an important issue. Whether or not Michael's comments had triggered Joyce's response was secondary. Whether her ultimatum was fair or not was of little consequence. The group was now at a turning point in its development, hindered by its inability in previous sessions to establish positive norms and skills for managing conflicts. Michael offered that nobody questioned Joyce's staff or its abilities and that her campaign should proceed as she was planning it. If anyone could come up with a better product name, they should let Joyce know. Otherwise, he suggested, they would use the "Sweat Soaks" name unless someone in top management told them not to. Hearing no disagreement with Michael's advice, Joyce agreed to proceed. The group adjourned with no further comment.

The storming phase of the ABC product development team was experienced in a very different way. During its next meeting, the marketing task force presented its ideas regarding the product. They weren't sure what it should be called, but presented three working names to the group for discussion: "Dry Out," "Sweat Banned," and "Super Dry." After some fun-filled discussion that included some additional ideas being offered, the group reached the consensus that "Super Dry" had the most potential and asked the marketing group to move forward with that name.

The discussion then turned to how to market the product, and there were very strong feelings about this issue. Some felt the product should be marketed initially to elite athletes through their teams, with highly leveraged sales agreements, as a way to gain initial exposure in a key client group. Others felt there should be a broader marketing approach, appealing to recreational users through athletic magazines, fitness centers, television and other media. Some raised concerns about whether it was appropriate for this team to address this issue at all, while others resented the idea that such control should just go to marketing. There was no need for a team if they were going to revert to traditional roles, they asserted.

As this passionate, fairly heated discussion began to unfold, Rachel recognized it as a legitimate conflict facing the team. This was the first real conflict in the group, she stated, and she wanted to affirm their ground rules in this discussion. She summarized the concerns being expressed: "Is this an appropriate issue for our team to address? If so, do we need any additional information in order to participate in an informed way in a decision outside our normal expertise? If not, how do we feel about delegating this issue to a department? What are the implications of this decision for other issues we might address?" Rachel framed the issue appropriately, both in terms of how the group would need to address it today and as a concern with implications for the future.

From here, various group members took turns sharing their reactions to the questions posed by Rachel. She made a point of restating each person's perspective before moving to the next member, seeking clarification where others felt it was needed. After about twenty minutes, she called for a ten minute break. During this time, she asked people to consider what had been said and to consider how to proceed. When the group returned, Rachel affirmed how important this discussion was for the group. She added encouragement for how they were dealing with their disagreement, to which several others added brief nods of support.

The group was able to reach consensus that such matters were of concern to them, and that one of the distinctions between the traditional mode of making decisions and the team approach was embodied in this issue. The group would have to develop marketing knowledge in order to answer the questions before it. Similarly, in order to reach a meaningful consensus about any other issues, the team would need additional information in those areas. They delayed any marketing decisions until they could receive needed information, and all task forces were asked to consider the types of expertise that might be required for their groups to make informed decisions. As the team ended its meeting, they concluded that this had been the best meeting of the group thus far.

As we see from these examples, the norms and skills developed in prior phases of the group play a critical role in setting the stage for the storming phase. As the group encounters real dilemmas, in which disagreement and conflict are realistic components, it must be able to manage storming effectively. If the earlier experiences have not resulted in the development of tools to handle such crises, as in the XYZ team, the group will lack the capacity to respond effectively. On the other hand, if the group's previous work has resulted in a strong sense of efficacy and a foundation of respectful communication, this ground work will support them in addressing important issues of disagreement. This foundation was readily apparent in the ABC team.

From these examples, we see further demonstration of Rachel's strong facilitation skills. She recognized that the group was entering a crisis, and she responded with powerful, facilitative leadership on the issue. She did not exercise this power by grabbing authority from the group; rather she used her influence to empower the group by reminding its members of their own capacity to succeed. Her credible affirmations of their efforts, coupled with her ability to name the problem and frame the issue concisely, helped the group navigate its way through a powerful storm. As well, her ability to use the issue as an instructive opportunity to prepare for future issues helped them find solutions that became more far-reaching and useful.

Phase Four: Performing

The fourth stage of group development eludes many work groups, for they disband without ever achieving it and experiencing it together. Performing is the phase when all members of the group are operating as a team in its best sense (see earlier discussion of teams in Chapter Seven), interacting in a synergistic manner to bring their resources toward a common goal. The performing group exists in a state similar to that described by the situational leadership model as it relates to a stage four employee; these are people who set their own agenda, who are personally driven to achieve and who utilize leadership as a guide within the big picture of the organization (Hersey and Blanchard 1988). Most of us have experienced groups in the performing stage at various times throughout our lives: the championship sports team; the theater company in a successful show; the church or synagogue group committee that always gets things done well; and the work group that goes above and beyond in attacking a company project.

The facilitator for a group in the performing stage has a vastly different job than during the forming stage. Earlier, the facilitator was required specifically to orient members to their task together. Now, they understand their mission fully and eagerly engage in its accomplishment. While previously the facilitator was needed to establish and enforce ground rules, now the group needs little reminder that it has ground rules, because they are completely internalized. Indeed, in a fourth-stage group, it may be difficult for an observer to distinguish the facilitator from other group members. A group in the performing stage resembles someone who has successfully learned to drive an automobile. At first the new driver is at a level conscious incompetence: he is incompetent as a driver, and every step of the process is a conscious decision—turn the wheel, clutch, downshift, apply the brake, and so forth. However, through practice the driver finally reaches a level of unconscious competence. He now knows how to operate a vehicle, and he continuously makes unconscious, automatic decisions about driving that enable him to simultaneously maneuver the car, listen to the radio, and carry on a conversation with fellow passengers. No longer is every move a deliberate, exhausting choice.

Still, the performing group requires the facilitator's leadership in several important areas. First, the group must remain on track with its goals, time lines, resources, and parameters in decision making. The facilitator reminds members of these issues and, as warranted, leads problem-solving discussions that resolve these matters. Second, the successful group has a natural tendency to want to exceed its immediate purpose, or to expand work in a way that diverts energy from its primary concern. For example, if a group has just successfully designed a fund-raising campaign, through which its members have made wonderful contacts for future sales, they may want to send those contacts information about their other products. To do so, however, would distract them from the immediate fund-raising campaign at a time when their full energy is required. The facilitator needs to serve as "agent of reality" to remind them of the real consequences of decisions to move in other directions. He or she must reign in that energy and keep it focused.

Finally, the facilitator of a group in the performing stage must begin to prepare for the conclusion of work. As we will present in our discussion of adjournment, bringing the group to closure can be among the great challenges of facilitation. Preparation must begin while the group is in high gear, especially if the group must report its work to others or leave a record of its accomplishments for others to follow.

As we examine our two groups, we see very different stances by the facilitators at this stage. Over at XYZ, Michael has struggled to have the group complete its work on schedule. He stayed late at the office, doing many tasks himself. He became impatient with Joyce, whose marketing plan for "Sweat Soaks" seems similar to several other past campaigns. At this point, Michael just wanted the committee to make its final report and get the project approved for manufacturing. It is also true that Michael had recently been asked to chair another committee, so he felt like he was juggling too much. There wasn't time for meetings, with so much work to do, so Michael didn't call any for two months.

Finally, after most of the work had come together, all members were sent a copy of the draft final report for their review and comment. A few e-mailed remarks relating to their own expertise, but few suggestions were offered. Michael decided to submit the final report with few changes from the previous draft. As he did so, he sent all members a note of thanks for their contribution. He recognized they had competing work priorities but were still able to stay on task, and he appreciated their professionalism. Since everyone was so busy, he said, there would not be a need for any additional meetings.

Meanwhile, the ABC team had entered the performing phase of development. Their group primarily met through task force meetings, internally facilitated with support from Rachel. The larger team continued to meet biweekly, at which time members checked in, reviewed their immediate tasks, and moved to their small groups effortlessly. Occasionally, Rachel was late due to conflicts in her schedule, but the meetings simply began without her. Everyone knew the rules, shared in their observance, and followed through on their commitment to the group. After forty-minute task force meetings, the larger group convened to report on progress, raise issues of concern to the whole, coordinate strategies, and relate their current work to their goals and time line. At the conclusion of each meeting, members briefly checked out and clarified tasks to be accomplished between meetings.

Over the next three months, the task of developing and marketing "Super Dry" sport towels evolved into reality. Throughout the process, Rachel kept her superiors informed and excited about the work of her committee. Occasionally, she even encouraged them to attend committee meetings, so they could show their support for the team and observe its functioning firsthand. As a result, it became clear that "Super Dry" had the approval of ABC management, and that the resources required to produce, market, and distribute the product were online and available. The group prepared to complete its work six weeks ahead of schedule.

Phase Five: Adjourning

The final phase of a group comes to it with the same certainty as death and taxes. The adjourning stage marks the closure of the group, whether formal disbandment or noting the conclusion of a particular class of membership. It is a highly emotional phase in the group's history, approached alternatively with excitement, relief, or frustration by various members. In some cases, this level of emotion contributes to a desire to avoid dealing with adjournment altogether.

The facilitator has several critical functions in this phase. First, it often falls to the facilitator to recognize this phase as adjourning and articulate this to the group. Second, it becomes important to clarify what information needs to be shared by this group with others, and the facilitator plays a key role in identifying and organizing this collective knowledge so it may be tapped in the future. Third, the group's members need an opportunity to evaluate their experiences with the group, in relation to both to outcomes and process. Evaluation should be related to the needs of membership identified in the group's formative phase. This evaluation also allows members to consider what they have learned from their work together and how it may benefit them in other groups. Finally, the group often requires an explicit opportunity to adjourn and say good bye to its members. If the group is to be reconstituted with new members (such as an ongoing board of directors or a public school committee), it may make sense to hold a special joint session of the two groups to bridge the old group with the new. Either way, the need to acknowledge the adjournment is important, and this phase requires the close attention of facilitators.

We have already witnessed elements of how XYZ approached the adjourning phase of its project team. Members were busy with other projects, so Michael courteously sent them the final report and thanked them for their work. Because there was little sense of group ownership of the project, although there was certainly individual commitment to completion of the task, there was little perceived need to meet again. However, Michael and his superiors at XYZ ignored some of the opportunities offered by a closing meeting. A final meeting could have resulted in a broader sense of commitment to the final product that still needed to be manufactured and sold. The meeting could have been instructive, both for Michael as the facilitator and for the various group members, if it uncovered areas of satisfaction and frustration with the group's process. From this evaluation, the group could have issued a set of comments to XYZ management that might have resulted in an improved product design process in the future. Since there was no meeting, and no alternative mechanism for the members to communicate as a group, the raising of any outstanding concerns was left to the individual.

All too often, we witness companies like XYZ. They go about their business in this manner year after year, with little regard for the costs of this approach. Because staff grow accustomed to this process as the norm ("It's the way we do things around here—I don't know why"), they become resigned to accepting it as the way things need to be in the future. Only when a crisis forces a company to examine its internal process, because it is now obvious that something is wrong, does it become possible to make changes. Even in such circumstances, however, leadership is often so accustomed to the old way of doing things that they find it challenging to take the risk involved in change. Such companies remain entrenched in mediocrity.

ABC's approach to adjournment was quite different. After the team presented its final project to the president and the board, they went to lunch together and celebrated their accomplishment. Then Rachel asked that they return the following week to the conference center where they had initially met, for one final meeting of the group. For that meeting, she asked people to bring information they felt would be important to include in their final project file, even if it might seem idiosyncratic. She also asked people to take a few minutes to consider what type of group might be required to shepherd the manufacture and distribution of "Super Dry" for the company.

As members came to their final meeting, several remarked at how appropriate it was to return to the conference center. They recalled how they had felt at their first meeting, including anxieties about becoming involved in this group. They remembered some of their early struggles with the project, how overwhelming it had felt, and how the establishment of task forces had been so helpful. Someone recalled the conflict over the marketing issue, from which they had recognized that a team was significantly different from a traditional group in its scope and approach. Finally, members complimented one another and Rachel for various contributions made over the past several months.

A few people brought mementoes of their work together, including notes taken during heated discussions, various materials that had been compared before deciding on the best approach for their product, sketches of logos for alternative marketing campaigns, and other items that triggered memories of their experience. They agreed which items needed to be saved for the permanent record and which could be discarded; a few people eagerly asked for some of the discarded items for their personal collections.

Rachel asked members to go around one final time, asking them to consider *one lesson being taken from this experience to future project groups at ABC.* This focus question resulted in a variety of ideas, which led to informal suggestions from other members about how people might incorporate what they had learned elsewhere. For example, one member said that she now felt that all project teams should hold initial meetings away from ABC, but she didn't know how to make that happen. Another member thought that such a space and its cost could be incorporated into a project budget. Rachel knew how to have this idea pursued, and offered to work with the two members concerned to see if it might be accomplished. On another matter, one member recalled that Rachel had met with each of them briefly prior to the initial meeting. This had made a significant difference in his commitment, he said, and he thought he would now do this in groups he led.

Several people wished the group could remain together, although it could not realistically form the ongoing project monitoring team. The group reached an informal consensus that they wanted Rachel to head this new team, and offered a few names of people within the company whose expertise would be valuable in this process. Rachel invited all members of the group to contact her about the ongoing progress of the "Super Dry" product, stating that she hoped to remain involved in the next group in some capacity. As the group adjourned, several members commented informally about how they would see each other in meetings on different projects. Although this project team had reached its conclusion, workplace colleagues continue to interact with one another in a variety of settings. The relationships, and what has been learned through them, continue in a number of situations over long periods of time. Recognizing the importance and duration of these connections frames the value of this respectful, careful approach to the adjourning phase of the facilitated group.

CHECKLISTS FOR FACILITATORS: CRUCIAL MILESTONES IN THE PROCESS

As we outlined the five phases of group development, a number of tasks were identified that facilitators should complete. These tasks may be organized around critical points in the experience of the group, milestones that bridge the group among the phases of its life. By viewing these tasks as checklists to be completed, a facilitator may stay focused on the appropriate needs of the group at a particular time. In addition, such checklists may assist a facilitator in better understanding which phase of development is truly being experienced by that group.

Milestone A: Before the Initial Meeting

The group has yet to form as a group. Members scarcely perceive themselves as members of a collective effort and have widely varying senses of commitment to the project. Therefore, this is an important time for the facilitator.

Communicate with as many members as possible, preferably on an individual basis, prior to the first meeting. Clarify the purpose of the group, hopes and hesitations that members bring, and the resources and parameters of the group. Define your role as facilitator.

Encourage member communication with the group's leader or convener, if other than the facilitator. This will assist in resolving confusions or concerns brought to the initial meeting.

Prior to the first meeting, send readings or other materials that members need in order to be prepared to participate. Such information should directly relate to the needs of the formative stage, and not overwhelm people with unrealistic or unnecessary work.

Clarify the meeting location, and be sure it meets the needs of the group for its initial meeting. Table space, comfortable chairs, lighting, breakout spaces, food, beverages, and the like should be considered.

Develop an initial agenda for the meeting. As appropriate, send this agenda to members in advance of the meeting. Solicit feedback regarding the agenda prior to the meeting.

Provide materials and supplies at the meeting that people will need to perform their work. Paper, pens, tape, and so on can play an important role in the success of this initial effort.

Arrive early enough to check the room properly, make changes that may be required, and perform meeting and greeting functions at the start of the meeting.

Milestone B: After the First Meeting

The first meeting has taken the group through its formative stage, and has likely begun to establish procedural norms to be followed in the future. The group will likely emerge from this meeting with a clarified sense of mission and purpose. There will be work to be done, and people may need assistance in accomplishing this work. There will be others, who may not have attended the first meeting, who will now need to be brought into the group's process in a seamless and effective manner. They will require communication, either from the facilitator or a designated group member, so they understand the group's decisions and clarify their own stakes in membership.

Summarize notes from the initial meeting and distribute them to members in a timely manner. If another member has served as recorder, the facilitator should coordinate efforts with this person. Meeting notes serve as an excellent reminder of the accomplishments of the group. They also reinforce the idea that certain people are members of this group; it is a new identity that requires concrete reinforcement in black and white. By personalizing distribution with an accompanying note, the facilitator can also highlight tasks this individual needs to accomplish (e.g., "See #2") or decisions made that were especially important to that person. (A sample set of meeting notes appears in the appendix.)

Summarize tasks to be accomplished and the persons responsible. This list should accompany the minutes for review by each member. Where the responsibility or time line for achieving certain goals is ambiguous, the facilitator should state this for all to review at the next meeting.

Follow up personally with group members who did not attend the initial meeting. For various reasons, some members may have been absent. It is crucial that they continue to see themselves as members of this emerging group, with an important role valued by those who attended. The facilitator should either directly contact these members or be sure this is done by another member who has taken such responsibility. The meeting date, time and location should be clearly communicated to such persons with as much lead time as possible. The group may have identified potential new members at its meeting, and these people should be contacted with similar care.

Work with task forces or subgroups to meet needs of the larger group. Often, subcommittees flounder in the time between meetings, uncertain either of what they need to do or of how to do it. The facilitator should check with these teams, and work with them as needed, so they experience success. At times, they may require additional information that the facilitator can help them acquire.

Distribute a list of members and interested others to the group prior to the next meeting. This list can prove quite useful as members attempt to contact one another for work outside of meetings. It also reinforces members' perception that they are, indeed, a group. By including interested others in this listing, the stake of the group in the larger organization or community is also recognized and supported.

Circulate a tentative agenda for upcoming meetings so members can review it, offer additional items, and prepare for those meetings. Once again, the facilitator's goal with a democratically managed group is to have all members perform their roles at their best. By providing an agenda in advance, the facilitator reinforces this responsibility and makes it possible to fulfill it. All too often, people complain, "We don't know what this meeting will be about," reducing their sense of efficacy and control of the agenda. By establishing this precedent after the initial meeting, the facilitator helps foster the expectation that such communication will be routine.

Milestone C: During the Storming Phase

As the group proceeds with its work, it is natural that it will encounter the storming phase, where conflict dominates the group. As discussed earlier, these conflicts may or may not manifest themselves as heated discussions. Rather, an air of uneasiness may subtly surround the group. Indeed, the storming phase may be marked by less discussion of issues and concerns, making it difficult to understand what problems exist and how they may be addressed.

Become an astute leader in the management of impasse. As noted in our previous discussion of impasse, there are several strategies a facilitator may employ to assist the group. Offering leadership in discussing feelings, reframing issues, looking at alternatives, and developing flexible solutions is a critical function of the facilitator in this period.

Between meetings, meet with key stakeholders in the conflicts facing the group. If possible, the facilitator should meet (or speak by telephone) with group members whose talents and energy will be critical at moving the group out of the storming phase. Through such caucus discussions, help members clarify their needs, their options, and their fears about the situation. Encourage them to bring ideas for problem solving to the next meeting.

Between meetings, speak with moderates who may be less visible stakeholders in these issues. As we observed in the discussion about multi-party disputes, there are often moderates in the dispute who tend to speak less. Their needs and concerns must be understood, and these moderates frequently need to be encouraged to participate. If not supported, these people (who so often hold the key to solutions because they are not entrenched in positions) disengage from the group and shift their energies elsewhere.

Beware the "rescuers" seeking quick fixes to complex issues! The group is likely experiencing great discomfort in this phase. Thus, many members will readily and indiscriminately gravitate to solutions (anything!) to relieve this discomfort. The facilitator must patiently remain comfortable with the uncomfortable at this point, checking for genuine agreements and durable solutions to problems.

Validate the struggle facing the group. This is a time often marked by blame and despair. It is important for the facilitator to support the group and normalize the storming phase as an important time that the group must face in order to accomplish its mission. Some members may also make the choice to leave the group, which then offers an opportunity for those who remain to understand their own feelings about the impact of such decisions.

As the group solves its critical issues, celebrate this accomplishment as a rite of passage. Since we tend to view conflict as a bad occurrence, its resolution is viewed as something that should also be hurried. Facilitators should acknowledge the meaning of the event that just occurred, including an evaluation of both outcomes and process.

As noted earlier, storming marks a turning point in the evolution of a group. It provides a crucial opportunity for growth that enables the group to enter the performing phase, with its high levels of productivity. If poorly handled, however, storming will give way to group dissolution, and a premature transition to adjournment.

Milestone D: Facilitating Adjournment

The facilitator may be the first member to recognize that the group is coming entering the adjourning phase. It is important for this phase to be explicitly named and identified for the group, for only through its appreciation may the group fully benefit from its experience. The facilitator approaches adjournment with respect for the variety of feelings that may be present, as well as an understanding of the substantive tasks that must be accomplished before the group disbands.

Notify the group that it appears to be preparing to adjourn. In certain cases, this understanding requires no clarification, as all members know far in advance that they will be ending their work on a certain date. Surprisingly, however, many groups are unaware that their work will be ending, or that a certain meeting will be the last one. Identifying such a time as a normal group phase may not occur to most members.

Talk about how it feels to be adjourning. Once again, there are widely differing perceptions of this time in the history of the group. It is important to our collective learning that we identify these feelings, discuss what we take away from the experience, and take the opportunity to acknowledge the contributions of the group to our organization.

Clarify which items need to remain in the team memory for future reference. As the group disbands, it should take stock of the information that must remain accessible to others. Just because a task force adjourns, for example, does not mean that the work ends; it is frequently carried on by others who will need access to information, records, decisions, research data, and other knowledge stored in the team memory. Clarifying the scope of this information and who is responsible for organizing it requires facilitator leadership, especially since most members will be making the transition to life beyond the group.

Celebrate!! The group has accomplished some wonderful things, had important discussions, and touched the lives of its participants. This may be celebrated in a variety of ways: presentation to others (i.e., conference, report, performance); a party; a debriefing meeting after a presentation to others; a gift exchange in which people thank one another for specific contributions; or a closing ceremony to conclude work together (e.g., we often have our extended classes conclude with the creation of a collage together).

By formally identifying this time, all have an opportunity to acknowledge its meaning and bring closure to the group. The facilitator who exercises leadership in this phase performs an important service, both to the group and the larger organization.

CONCLUSION

In this chapter, we have attempted to provide a longitudinal framework for applying the skills of the group facilitator. Earlier, we provided an outline of steps to be followed in the facilitated meeting. At that time, we noted that such steps vary among settings, and we have provided insights regarding how these settings vary over the life of the group. The phases of group development outlined here should also be understood as a general framework in which there is great individual variety: Some groups experience little storming, for example, yet prove to be quite productive. Some groups spend little time formally establishing ground rules, while others struggle with this exercise for lengthy periods of time. Some groups are characterized by members with little interest in process, while others may become obsessed with it to the point where they neglect reaching productive outcomes and closure.

The art of facilitation derives from recognizing this variety. We seek to apply the skills and strategies we have presented in a way that best meets the needs of a group at a particular point in time. Along the way, we develop new insights about group behavior. From this knowledge we refine our approaches and our understandings. As more organizations introduce facilitated groups and practice these skills, this knowledge base will widen further and inform us all.

Chapter 9

Facilitation and Its Philosophical Traditions: Personal Reflections

The concept of facilitation, as used in this book, owes its existence to several diverse ideologies, including Quakerism, Reconstructionist Judaism, participatory management, democratic educational reform, and Gandhi's pacifist movement. These philosophical traditions are given a brief overview in this chapter, to illuminate our current approach to facilitation within an historical context. Although there are other doctrines that influence facilitation today, the schools of thought mentioned herein have had the most marked effect on our work.

SPIRITUAL COMMUNITIES

Spirituality and Social Action: The Quaker Movement

The Quakers provide a three-hundred-year-old model of a spiritual community that operates democratically, making decisions by consensus. The Quaker movement, which sprang from theories of George Fox in seventeenth-century England, was an important influence in the development of American colonial government (Trueblood 1966). Its members held governorships in several colonies, crowned by Pennsylvania, the great experiment in Quaker leadership. However, it is on the day-to-day process of Quaker life that we must focus, for it is from the principles and organization of the Quaker meeting that we derive a true appreciation of democratic process.

The principles of the Quaker meeting include: (1) a firm commitment to ground rules of respect, demonstrated through active listening; (2) personal representation and ownership of viewpoints; (3) non-hierarchical, cooperative approaches to problem solving; and (4) decision making by consensus. These ideas bridge the Quakers' spiritual and social concerns with the ideas of nonviolence and social justice.

As noted by David Elton Trueblood, these values are applied in the organization of the monthly meeting:

In the characteristic business meeting of Quakers all over the world, the decisions are made without voting, and without adherence to ordinary parliamentary rules of order. The hope is that the clerk will be a sensitive person who can find the "sense of the meeting" without a show of hands. He is supposed to try to search for essential unanimity and to judge by "weight," rather than by mere numbers. When there is a clear division, the usual practice is to postpone a decision for at least a month or to settle into a time of worship and prayer. Frequently, the effect of such waiting verges on the miraculous. It does not always succeed, but it succeeds so often that there is no serious doubt concerning the wisdom of the method. One beneficent effect is the avoidance of 51–49 decisions which almost always leave a residue of bitterness. The Quaker method of reaching decisions is slow and outwardly inefficient, but the results are often healing. That it has not always been faithfully followed is evidenced by the few unhappy divisions which Quakers have experienced in the course of more than three centuries. (Trueblood 1966)

Quaker philosopher and political reformer Mary Parker Follett, in her pioneering work *Creative Experience*, drew directly from this tradition. She proposed that America meet the challenges of democracy through reforming the public meeting:

Thinkers about democracy then have passed the stage of merely perfecting mechanisms of voting and representation; their aim is to train minds to act together constructively. The democratic problem is now recognized as the problem of how to get collective action that is socially valid, that is satisfying by the criteria of enhanced living; the problem of how to maintain vigor and creativeness in the thinking of everybody, not merely of chosen spirits. (Follett 1924)

Follett described the steps of this process. First, it is important to collect good information from those with expertise on the subject at hand. Second, it falls upon all of us to shed light on the question from our own experience. Third, we should seek to unite our various experiences, "one with the other and with the material provided by the expert" (Follett 1924). Follett's prescription for democratic participation resulted in the development of the collaborative problem-solving approach we espouse here. Her methodology succinctly describes the dialogue process we attempt to facilitate in our meetings, both in public settings and in more private work places.

Reconstructionist Judaism

In 1922, Rabbi Mordecai Kaplan founded the Society for the Advancement of Judaism (SAJ) in New York City. From its modest beginnings at the SAJ synagogue, the Reconstructionist movement grew to represent a fourth major branch of Jewish theology (the others being Orthodox, Conservative, and Reformed Judaism). It is an approach that seeks to understand scripture in contemporary terms and to unite the experience of the present with the wisdom of the past (Alpert and Straub 1985; Goldsmith, Scult, and Seltzer 1990).

Reconstructionist congregations have significantly redefined the processes of worship and decision making as a result of this philosophy. The rabbi is seen as a resource, sharing insights from scripture to inform decisions of the group. Services and meetings are generally led by a lay facilitator, concerned primarily with promoting full participation, respectful dialogue, and consensus. Through such attention to process, the Reconstructionist congregation reexamines dogma, questions historic interpretations, and develops new rituals that guide today's spiritual practice. In addition, they explore the relationship of contemporary Jews to broader society and develop social action programs and educational workshops as a bridge to non-Jewish communities.

Like the Quaker movement, Reconstructionist Judaism offers a comprehensive outlook for guiding a spiritual community. Both philosophies draw upon the firm conviction that if we facilitate process well, excellent outcomes will follow. They exhibit patience and respect for the membership's collective ability to seek wisdom. Furthermore, they tie their spiritual communities with society, dedicating themselves to justice, tolerance, and understanding.

PARTICIPATORY MANAGEMENT

In a radically different vein, the tenets of facilitation also stem from participatory management theory. Emerging only in the last twenty years, it offers a philosophy of leadership that fosters openness and collaboration in the workplace. Reforms in decision-making procedures, the generation of flat organization structures, the rise of self-directed work teams, and the creation of the work group facilitator are central elements of the participatory management philosophy.

Throughout the 1970s and 1980s, the Center for Conflict Resolution (CCR) in Madison, Wisconsin, laid vital groundwork for participatory management by promoting democratic, consensual approaches to business. Founded in 1974 to offer counseling to draft resisters, CCR went on to provide consulting to large corporations, academic institutions, and government agencies. CCR members developed models of what they dubbed "democratic management" which advocated collaborative approaches to conflict resolution, the use of consensus decision making in management, utilization of collective organization forms in business, and most importantly, the development of the facilitator role. (Auvine et al. 1997; Avery et al. 1981)   These ideas formed a foundation for my experiences at CCR (1981–1984) and have continued to influence our work at Collaborative Initiative in subsequent years.

Without the work done by CCR and other similar organizations, Ford Motor Company may have never weathered its major transition in the early 1980s. Ford's economic free fall, which precipitated widespread budget cuts and layoffs, necessitated a complete overhaul of the company. This, in turn, required management to develop new collaborative ways of working with employees.

Management started from the ground up, creating the Employee Involvement (EI) program, through which even line workers could have a voice in how their workplace operated.   These problem-solving groups, usually organized around one or two key logistical issues, spawned a complementary managerial program: Participative Management (PM). The prime function of the PM component was to teach managers how to guide workers with the new EI system in place—no easy task given the initial resistance of traditionalists who preferred the status quo.

The results of this intensive retooling were phenomenal for Ford: increased market share, fewer repairs, smoother union negotiations, greater employee satisfaction, and a vastly improved public image. While not a panacea for every corporate ailment, the EI/PM process nonetheless gave Ford the edge it needed to withstand a long-needed economic transition, and eventually became part of the transition itself. It has served as an example for numerous other businesses (Rosen and Berger 1991).

Rosen cites other examples of companies that have benefited from aspects of participatory management: Chaparral Steel in Texas, where informal meetings are often held in hallways or mills so the president can see and hear employees in their own work milieu; Quad/Graphics in Wisconsin, a printing company with no employees but partners that direct the business through peer groups; and Boston's Beth Israel Hospital, which has placed its entire staff on work teams (Rosen and Berger 1991). During the past decade, participatory management has become such an implicit aspect of corporate culture that it is for many companies no longer a radical, threatening idea. The challenge to leaders today is to ensure that employee empowerment remains an actuality and not just another business buzzword.

DEMOCRATIC EDUCATIONAL REFORM

Theories of democratic educational reform, based on the prolific writings of John Dewey, Paolo Freire, and John Holt, have directly influenced my own approach to facilitation. Throughout his long and productive life, John Dewey articulated an approach to learning that wed theory and experience. He theorized that a facilitative teacher can help create an environment that structures experiences for learners, who then assimilate what they are taught on an individual basis. As a result, students would be motivated to learn how to learn and to take part in the larger world around them. For Dewey, this ability to participate effectively in society was a core skill required for democracy.

Dewey's ideas were proliferated by other educational theorists. They included, most notably, Maria Montessori, whose Montessori schools resulted in teaching approaches and techniques that were influential in the later reforms of the 1960s and 1970s. The 1960s movement to make education relevant to students, for example, drew heavily on Dewey for its pedagogical inspiration.

Other key influences came from the writings of Brazilian reformer Paulo Freire. In his *Pedagogy of the Oppressed* (1971) and subsequent writings, Freire expounded his theories involving conflict at the heart of the struggle to learn. His experiments with "conscientiazion," consciousness-raising dialogue groups, have had direct impact on approaches to both teaching and facilitation. He was firmly committed to empowering learners to define their own agendas, drawing upon their political and social experiences to do so. He applied his techniques to a wide range of settings, including literacy campaigns in South America, labor organizing in Toronto, and the development of a post-colonial government in the small African nation of Guinea-Bissau. His work on dialogue has profoundly affected the art of facilitation.

John Holt, a Boston educator whose writings eventually spawned the modern home schooling movement in the United States, was also a contributor in this area. Holt began his teaching in the 1950s using traditional methods. He soon discovered, however, that these approaches failed to resonate with most children. Consequently, he questioned much of what was passing as education in public schools. Through his landmark books, *How Children Fail* (1964) and *How Children Learn* (1967), Holt set the stage for a series of critiques of public schooling by other observers. [1]

As Holt's encounters with education continued, he raised serious questions about the ultimate efficacy of reform within schools (Holt 1972). This led him to embrace alternative models, such as the community learning exchange and family-based education, as being more constructive environments for learning. According to his definition, the model facilitative instructor shares expertise where appropriate, as does a librarian, who operates as a receptive resource rather than one who structures learning. He also encouraged the involvement of a variety of teachers in children's lives, to be practical role models rather than figures in isolated, fragmented experiences.

NONVIOLENCE AND SOCIAL CHANGE

Theories of non-violent social change have resulted in conflict management strategies that are at the center of the facilitator role. The crusades of Mohandas Gandhi, starting with the South African railway campaign and culminating in the struggle for Indian independence, embraced a set of principles that have direct bearing on us today: nonviolent resistence, listening to one's enemy, and managing conflict.

Gandhi's life and work are well-documented elsewhere (Bondurant 1958; Woodcock 1971), but his philosophy is most succinctly captured in two of his own works. His autobiography, *My Experiments with Truth* (1957) traces Gandhi's formative experiences, including his adoption of the principles of *ahimsa* that guided his personal discipline and spiritual life. From this work, we gain an appreciation for the experiences and struggles that led to his personalization of nonviolent philosophy. We also witness, through his experiences as a young adult, the formation of his commitment to social justice. In his collection of essays, *Non-Violent Resistance* (1951), Gandhi outlines the philosophy of *satyagraha*, what he dubs the "truth-force" that guided his approach to political action. Gandhi's regard for any adversary as a "fellow seeker of truth," rather than his enemy, was a profound departure from traditional pathways to political change. His patience and discipline were taught to millions of his followers in India and abroad.

The American civil rights struggle drew directly from Gandhi's strategies, starting with the Freedom Riders, who sought desegregation of trains and buses in the South during the 1940s and 1950s and were morally committed to nonviolence. Combined with legal initiatives of the NAACP and others, they successfully overturned Jim Crow laws that regulated transportation. By the time Dr. Martin Luther King, Jr., rallied hundreds of thousands to the civil rights cause in the 1960s, this tradition was well established. It continues today in organizations such as Amnesty International, Plowshares International, Search for Common Ground, Southern Poverty Law Center, and others who advocate for human rights through nonviolence.

In summary, these four traditions of facilitated spiritual communities, participatory business management, democratic educational reform, and nonviolent social change form the foundation for our conceptual framework. The facilitator role that I define in this book is steeped in these traditions. It is also consistent with more recent efforts to reform corporations and organizations to be more open and inclusive. As such, it is an approach that invites the reader to seek additional resources. It causes one to reflect upon one's own philosophical roots, as well.

NOTE

1. Throughout the 1960s and 1970s, numerous efforts were made to promote democratic approaches to teaching and learning. Specific experiments, such as those in New York, Chicago, Boston, and Ann Arbor, directly influenced the experiences of many teachers and

students. Ivan Illich and Jonathan Kozol were foremost among theorists in this area, in addition to John Holt. Kozol continues to share his philosophy through prolific writings and public speaking engagements.

Appendix A

Situational Conflict Styles Assessment Exercise

Read the scenarios below, then respond to the questions that follow, keeping in mind how *you* would respond in each specific role within each conflict. Please give honest, realistic answers to each question.

Situation 1a

You and a colleague are jointly responsible for developing a presentation. S/he has a very different way of approaching the project, waiting until the last minute, leaving much more to "see what the situation brings." You prefer to attend to details, practice the presentation several times, etc., but your meetings are being canceled due to conflicts in his/her schedule. When the presentation day arrives, everything is a disaster! Equipment is set up wrong, handouts are missing, and in the middle of the presentation, s/he digresses with a story that uses up time you needed to make some key points. As you are leaving, s/he says, "Well, this could have gone better. But I think people liked it."

1. What *behavioral response* would you most likely have to this conflict?

    _____ A. You glare angrily at your colleague and loudly declare that the entire presentation was a failure and that it was all his/her fault. Then you go directly to your immediate supervisor, blaming your colleague for the disastrous presentation and refuse to work with him/her ever again.

    _____ B. You nod in agreement with your colleague, while inside you wish you had the nerve to tell him/her that you think it could have gone much better and that you are concerned about working with him/her again in the future.

_____ C. You busy yourself with clean up and leave quickly, saying you have another appointment. You try to escape seeing that colleague whenever possible in the future.

_____ D. You voice your disagreement, but acknowledge the fact that if you work together again, s/he will likely handle it in a similar fashion. Therefore, you would split any future responsibilities exactly in half.

_____ E. You disagree with your colleague, telling him/her you are worried about how other people in the department perceive your ability to handle responsibility. You discuss his/her busy schedule and agree that on your next project together, you'll swap child care to help him/her deal with stress and get things done on time.

2. What types of *emotional responses* would you feel in this situation? (check all that apply)

_____ anger	_____ confusion	_____ shame
_____ sadness	_____ happiness	_____ fear
_____ other:		

3. What type of thoughts (*cognitive responses*) go through your mind in this situation?

4. What *physical responses* would you have to this situation? (check all that apply)

_____ sweaty palms	_____ tunnel vision
_____ excitement	_____ elation
_____ anxiety	_____ nausea
_____ rapid breathing	_____ tension:

___ forehead	___ cheeks
___ neck	___ arms
___ back	___ legs
___ other:	

_____ other:

5. Given your overall response to the situation, what do you find to be helpful?

6. What needs to be changed or improved?

Situation 1b

You and a colleague are responsible for developing a presentation. S/he has a very different style of approaching the project, planning everything down to the last detail and insisting that everything be written down on index cards. You prefer to have a general idea of how the presentation will go, but want to leave room for audience participation, including a question and answer period. The request for this presentation came only two weeks ago, and with three children at home, it has been difficult for you to squeeze in meetings with your colleague on top of the regular work day. Yesterday you had to miss a meeting because your babysitter canceled at the last minute. When the presentation day arrives, there are some equipment mix-ups and several handouts are missing, but the audience doesn't seem to mind. Towards the end, one attendee asks a particularly thought-provoking question, which necessitates a fairly lengthy response from you. Before you know it, it's time to finish up—where did the time go? You leave the presentation feeling that, although everything didn't go exactly as planned, there was genuine interest in the material and appreciation of your knowledge. As you are leaving, you say to your colleague, "Well, this could have gone better. But I think people liked it." S/he stares at you, shocked. "This was a disaster," s/he says, " I can't believe you wasted so much time on that last question. They'll never come back again!"

1. What *behavioral response* would you most likely have to this conflict?

_____ A. You feel your blood rising and say loudly: "The only part of the presentation they didn't like was yours. Well, you won't have to work with me again, anyway." That same day, you go to your immediate supervisor and demand to be removed from future projects with this colleague. Who needs to work with such a control freak?

_____ B. You shake your head, feigning agreement with your colleague, while inside you wish you had the nerve to tell him/her that you really thought the presentation went okay. Furthermore, you thought it was totally appropriate to spend so much time answering audience questions.

_____C. You busy yourself with clean up and leave quickly, saying you have another appointment. You try to escape seeing that colleague whenever possible in the future.

_____ D. You assert your disagreement with your colleague. You suggest that in the future, you split the presentation exactly in half. S/he can control the first half of the agenda, while you take the second. This will ensure him/her all the time needed to get his/her points in, in whatever manner s/he chooses.

_____ E. You assert your disagreement with your colleague and indicate your interest in maintaining a healthy work relationship with him/her. You learn that s/he is concerned about others' perceptions of his/her ability to handle a heavy workload, especially since s/he has made incredible efforts at improving his/her organizational skills. You empathize, telling him/her about your child care dilemmas. You agree to try to be more organized next time, and s/he offers to help by swapping child care in the future. You both tell your supervisor that you need more lead time for future presentations.

2. What types of *emotional responses* would you feel in this situation? (check all that apply)

_____ anger	_____ confusion	_____ shame
_____ sadness	_____ happiness	_____ fear
_____ other:		

3. What type of thoughts (*cognitive responses*) go through your mind in this situation?

4. What *physical responses* would you have to this situation? (check all that apply)

_____ sweaty palms	_____ tunnel vision
_____ excitement	_____ elation
_____ anxiety	_____ nausea
_____ rapid breathing	_____ tension:

___ forehead	___ cheeks
___ neck	___ arms
___ back	___ legs
___ other:	

_____ other:

5. Given your overall response to the situation, what do you find to be helpful?

6. What needs to be changed or improved?

Situation 2a

You have Johnny Jones as a student in your class this semester, and he is not doing very well. He is often late and unprepared, and he doesn't seem especially interested in class. You arrange a meeting with his father. Mr. Jones, initially pleased to hear of your concerns, later becomes defensive. His voice growing louder, he says that you make unreasonable expectations of your students. Kids

Johnny's age have other things on their minds, he contends. You are at fault for not being more flexible or helpful when Johnny has struggled.

1. What *behavioral response* would you most likely have to this conflict?

_____ A. You tell Mr. Jones that you are not being unreasonable. Other kids in the class manage to get their work done, despite outside interests. Rules are rules, and you can't make exceptions for one student. If Johnny doesn't get his act together, you will have no choice but to fail him.

_____ B. You listen to Mr. Jones rant and rave for half an hour, which makes you late for an important meeting. At the end of the conversation, you tell Mr. Jones that you will "see what you can do," but after you leave, you still have no idea how to help Johnny do better in class.

_____ C. You cut your conversation with Mr. Jones short, saying you have to get to a meeting soon. You tell him you will have to talk about it at another time but do not schedule anything with him or make any definite plans for dealing with Johnny in the future.

_____ D. You assert that you do not feel you are being unreasonable. Mr. Jones agrees to get Johnny to school on time and make sure he is completing all of his homework assignments. Several weeks later, you find Johnny is abiding by the rules, but only doing the bare minimum with no real enthusiasm for learning. You feel compelled to agree when his father says, "You can lead a horse to water, but you can't make him drink."

_____ E. You arrange a meeting in person with both Johnny and his father. At the meeting, you and Johnny come to an agreement that if, with his father's guidance, he can make it to school on time and complete his homework assignments to the best of his ability, you will work out a more interesting reading list for the class. You will even include publications with articles about some of Johnny's favorite activities, such as mountain biking and skateboarding. You make sure both Johnny and Mr. Jones are aware that a lifelong enjoyment of reading and open lines of communication are far more important to you than simply enforcing rules.

2. What types of *emotional responses* would you feel in this situation? (check all that apply)

_____ anger _____ confusion _____ shame
_____ sadness _____ happiness _____ fear
_____ other:

3. What type of thoughts (*cognitive responses*) go through your mind in this situation?

4. What *physical responses* would you have to this situation? (check all that apply)

_____ sweaty palms	_____ tunnel vision
_____ excitement	_____ elation
_____ anxiety	_____ nausea
_____ rapid breathing	_____ tension:

___ forehead	___ cheeks
___ neck	___ arms
___ back	___ legs
___ other:	

_____ other:

5. Given your overall response to the situation, what do you find to be helpful?

6. What needs to be changed or improved?

Situation 2b

Your son Johnny is a student in Ms. Smith's sophomore English class, and you know he is not doing very well. You are a divorced, single parent with sole custody of Johnny. You usually work third shift and sometimes don't come home from work until after Johnny has left for school in the morning. When he comes home from school, you are usually still asleep. He is frequently on his own and has to cook his own meals, but you can't afford to leave your job. You are actually a little proud of how self-sufficient Johnny has become over the last few years, especially when he helps out by going to the grocery store or cleaning the apartment. Recently Johnny brought home a note from Ms. Smith, which said he is in danger of failing, due to tardiness, incomplete assignments, and a bad attitude in class. You appreciate her concerns, but when you meet with her, you feel a growing resentment over her lack of flexibility and helpfulness. She doesn't have any idea how much of a struggle it has been for you to raise Johnny alone or for Johnny to grow up in a broken home. She offers only criticisms of Johnny, who is really a great kid. When she asks your opinion, you volunteer that you think she is placing unreasonable expectations on her students. She takes offense at this comment and says, "If Johnny wants to succeed in the real world, he's going to have to meet high expectations. The other kids are able to get their work done and participate in extracurricular activities. Johnny is just going to have to keep up."

1. What *behavioral response* would you most likely have to this conflict?

_____ A. You yell that Johnny has been out in the real world more than most of the other kids in the class. What he needs is a better teacher who understands kids. You leave the meeting angry and go directly to the principal's office, where you insist that Johnny be transferred to another English class.

_____ B. You listen to the teacher, nodding your head in agreement, but you are convinced that she needs a better grasp of the situation. You are afraid that if you voice any further disagreement, Johnny's grade will suffer, so you leave the meeting resigned that there is nothing to be done.

_____ C. You cut your meeting with the teacher short, saying you have to get to work. You tell her you'll have to talk about it later, but you don't schedule anything or make plans for the future.

_____ D. You disagree with Ms. Smith, but promise you will make sure Johnny gets to school on time and completes all his homework. You can't however, make him love school. As long as he's not talking out of turn or smart mouthing the teacher, there's not much you can do about his attitude.

_____ E. You assert your disagreement and ask if you can arrange a meeting that includes Johnny, since his needs are an important factor. At the next meeting, you allow Johnny to explain the difficulties he has getting to school on time and getting his work done. You make arrangements to have a tutor help him twice a week, until you can get moved from third to first shift. You learn that Ms. Smith is more concerned with helping Johnny to enjoy reading than with enforcing rules, and you successfully encourage her to add some bicycling and skateboarding periodicals to her reading list, to motivate Johnny to read more.

2. What types of *emotional responses* would you feel in this situation? (check all that apply)

_____ anger   _____ confusion   _____ shame
_____ sadness   _____ happiness   _____ fear
_____ other:

3. What type of thoughts (*cognitive responses*) go through your mind in this situation?

4. What *physical responses* would you have to this situation? (check all that apply)

_____ sweaty palms   _____ tunnel vision

_____ excitement   _____ elation
_____ anxiety   _____ nausea
_____ rapid breathing   _____ tension:

___ forehead   ___ cheeks
___ neck   ___ arms
___ back   ___ legs
___ other:

_____ other:

5. Given your overall response to the situation, what do you find to be helpful?

6. What needs to be changed or improved?

Situation 3a

You are an administrator who feels overloaded with projects and paperwork. You work hard to keep things balanced, trying to provide your secretary with clear information and adequate lead time. But you are often unavailable, tied up in meetings. You recently gave him a report to type that you need today, as part of a large project to be done with other administrators. But when you arrived at the office this morning, you saw the report sitting on his desk, in a stack of work to be done, not looking anywhere near completion. Shortly before 10:00 a.m., he tells you he has a 2:00 dental appointment.

1. What *behavioral response* would you most likely have to this conflict?

_____ A. You take the report from his pile and announce you are taking over the project. At the meeting, you present what you can, then approach your supervisor about having your secretary transferred to another department. The day after the meeting, you blame him for your poor performance in from of the other administrators and threaten him with the loss of his job. At this stage, you don't want to hear any more of his excuses.

_____ B. You take the report from his pile and with a sigh of resignation, tell him he is no longer responsible for it. You spend the next four hours in your office, completing the report yourself, even though it means missing two other meetings and canceling lunch with a colleague.

_____ C. You shrug your shoulders and shut yourself in the office all morning. At noon, you decide to make an excuse not to attend the administrators' meeting. You ask your secretary to file the report when he is finished with it, but you don't ever read it.

_____ D. You ask your secretary about the status of the report. When he responds that he has worked on part of it, but it's not yet finished, you agree to complete a portion of it yourself, so he can make his dental appointment. You are still concerned about his completing future projects on time.

_____ E. You ask your secretary to take a break over coffee to go over the day's agenda. You learn he is confused about completing the report, because you have also given him some statistics to run by the end of the day. You learn, too, that the dental appointment is an emergency to correct a broken filling. You agree to devise a system for assigning priorities to future deadlines. In the meantime, you give him permission to give top priority to the administrators' report, so it will be finished by the time he needs to leave for his dental appointment.

2. What types of *emotional responses* would you feel in this situation? (check all that apply)

_____ anger	_____ confusion	_____ shame
_____ sadness	_____ happiness	_____ fear
_____ other:		

3. What type of thoughts (*cognitive responses*) go through your mind in this situation?

4. What *physical responses* would you have to this situation? (check all that apply)

_____ sweaty palms	_____ tunnel vision
_____ excitement	_____ elation
_____ anxiety	_____ nausea
_____ rapid breathing	_____ tension:

___ forehead	___ cheeks
___ neck	___ arms
___ back	___ legs
___ other:	

_____ other:

5. Given your overall response to the situation, what do you find to be helpful?

6. What needs to be changed or improved?

Situation 3b

You are the secretary to an overworked administrator. She is often unavailable, due to a heavy meeting schedule, but you try to keep up and meet all of her deadlines. She recently gave you a report to prepare for an administrators' meeting today, but you have a stack of statistics to compile by the end of the day. To make matters worse, you broke a filling in your tooth yesterday, and you can't get in to see the dentist until 2:00. You leave a memo on your boss' desk to that effect. As the morning wears on, you find the pain from the tooth evermore distracting, but you keep plugging away at the statistics, knowing that you also need to complete the report by the end of the day. Later that morning, your boss spies the incomplete report on your desk and takes it without saying anything, leaving right away for a meeting. When she returns at noon, she announces you'll have to cancel your dental appointment in order to finish the report.

1. What *behavioral response* would you most likely have to this conflict?

_____ A. You refuse to cancel the appointment and tell her she's impossible to work for. You tell her you have to go to the men's room, but actually you go to your supervisor's office and complain that your boss is denying you important medical leave. You threaten to file a grievance with your union, unless something is done about your boss. The best solution would be to transfer to a more reasonable administrator.

_____ B. Even though your tooth is throbbing, and you don't think it's fair that your boss took the report away without asking, you cancel the appointment and stay until the report is finished.

_____ C. You wait until your boss is at lunch, then take the rest of the day off sick, calling in a temp to finish the report.

_____ D. You call your dentist's office and get your appointment postponed until later in the day, so you can complete the report. You are rushing around so much that you never find out why your boss took the report from you in the first place.

_____ E. You tell your boss you could both use a break to go over the list of assignments for the day. You learn that not only did she forget that she gave you the statistics to complete, but she didn't read all of your memo about the dental appointment and had no idea it was an emergency. She's really concerned about getting the administrators' report done, which is why she took it off your desk in the first place; she thought she could finish it herself, but her noon meeting ran late. Together you come up with a system for prioritizing your future workload.

You offer to move your dental appointment to later that afternoon, so that both the report and the statistics can be completed on time.

2. What types of *emotional responses* would you feel in this situation? (check all that apply)

_____ anger   _____ confusion   _____ shame
_____ sadness   _____ happiness   _____ fear
_____ other:

3. What type of thoughts (*cognitive responses*) go through your mind in this situation?

4. What *physical responses* would you have to this situation? (check all that apply)

_____ sweaty palms   _____ tunnel vision
_____ excitement   _____ elation
_____ anxiety   _____ nausea
_____ rapid breathing   _____ tension:

                   ___ forehead   ___ cheeks
                   ___ neck   ___ arms
                   ___ back   ___ legs
                   ___ other:

_____ other:

5. Given your overall response to the situation, what do you find to be helpful?

6. What needs to be changed or improved?

Conflict Styles Key

Use the key below to assess your personal conflict style. Bear in mind that each different type of situation may evoke a different conflict style. This assessment may help you realize what kind of situations provoke conflict styles that are less productive and allow you to think about alternative responses.

Every time you answered A to question 1, you are using a *competing* conflict style. You move directly to meet your needs in the situation, with less regard for the needs of others. This conflict style is often characterized by aggressive communication and little listening. (Win/Lose)

Every time your answered B to question 1, you are using a style that is *accommodating*.

You yield to the needs of the other person or group, feeling that they are more important in the situation. Often characterized by submissive communication, accommodating conflict styles generally do not allow the other person to be aware of your concerns. (Lose/Win)

Every time you answered C to question 1, your are using a *withdrawing* conflict style (also called *avoiding*). You avoid bringing up possible differences, or perhaps deny that a conflict even exists. There is often limited communication or avoidance of contact, the issues fester unresolved. (Lose/Lose)

Every time your answered D to question 1, you are using a conflict style that is *compromising*. You assert your position, but are willing to trade off possible solutions through negotiation with the other party. Communication is assertive and respectful, though limited by presenting positions. (Win Some/Lose Some)

Every time you answered E to question 1, your are using a *collaborating* conflict style. You assert your needs and interests clearly and specifically, while hearing and respecting those of the other person. You try to consider the big picture and maximize relationships, as well as substantive issues. (Win/Win*)

Your other responses to the scenarios (emotional, cognitive, and physical), as assessed in questions 2 through 6, are also related to your personal conflict style. These types of responses, however, are not attributable to just one conflict style. For example, you may experience sweaty palms or tension, no matter what conflict style you are using, even if you are engaging in collaborative negotiation. Competing in conflict may evoke happiness in one person and fear in another. You may feel elation in a competitive situation, but so may someone engaged in collaboration. Being aware of these responses, many of which are our most basic "fight or flight" reactions, and how they relate to our overt behavior is a key element in dealing productively with conflict.

* In this situation, the *outcome* may not necessarily be Win/Win. What is important is the agreement to engage in a *process* to try to resolve the conflict, in which *underlying issues* from all parties can be explored. The Win/Win aspect is derived from the fact that each participant's interests or needs (rather than just positions) are discussed. That in its own right makes no one a loser.

Appendix B

Role Plays

WORKPLACE BUDGET CUTS

Scenario

Recently, the president has informed your management group that due to significant cuts in the 1998–1999 budget, two staff positions need to be eliminated, saving the company approximately $100,000. Four departments have been identified for probable staff reduction. The departments include: Training and Human Resources, Marketing and Promotion, and Finance and Sales. Each department is comprised of a department director and two to four staff members. Each of the identified departments serves the entire company.

Management has requested that the heads of each of the earmarked departments meet to negotiate the staff downsizing. Therefore, the department heads must come together to determine where and how staff cuts will occur.

Director of Training and Human Resources Department

You have been with the company for twenty-five years. You thoroughly enjoy your position and are extremely committed to the staff who work within your department, as well as to the staff throughout the company. You have helped to create a topnotch training program and take great pride in the state award the department won this past year for its Basic Skills Education Program, an innovative approach to retaining a diverse labor force. You have been through this budget cut business before and are frustrated with what seems like lack of support from the board for your program. Five years ago you lost two staff members to budget cuts. You were able to adjust; however, if any more staff are removed from the department you don't see how it can continue in a worthwhile manner. You are really considering submitting your resignation if your program is reduced any further.

Director of Marketing and Promotion Department

You have been with the company for five years. You started as a sales rep and moved into this position when the marketing and promotion department was formally established, only two years ago. As director of the marketing department, you continue your sales duties part-time because you enjoy it and earn extra money from commissions. You are shocked that your program has been earmarked for possible budget cuts. The program is so very new and has received a great deal of support from clients, board members, and involved staff. The president, however, has seemed tentative about the program and you have always, at least to yourself, questioned the company's commitment to the modern marketing concept. Quite frankly, you're frustrated with the amount of money that goes into the Basic Skills Education program, under training and human resources, often at the expense of many bright staff who aren't receiving the opportunities and challenges they deserve.

Director of the Finance Department

You have been with the company for ten years, always working with the finance department, having become its director six years ago. You see this program as providing an innovative approach to financial management, fostering full participation among staff in building effective budgets and taking ownership over all aspects of the financial picture. The program not only works with staff, but also with the client. Since customers receive accurate cost information from all company contacts, there are fewer surprises and greater trust in the integrity of the information. This has resulted in a significant improvement in accounts receivable in the past year, and the opportunities for improved cash flow have been growing. You anticipate needing additional assistance in the upcoming fiscal year to meet the demand for services.

Director of Sales Department

You have been with the company for fifteen years, and you are committed to creating a well-rounded and outstanding sales department. You are proud of the variety of men and women who have thrived under your mentoring and leadership, moving on to other companies. Over the last couple of years your department has earned a name for itself in the sales area, generating major revenue for the company and becoming a tremendous source of spirit and pride. You've discussed your concerns regarding the possible budget cuts with several members of the chamber of commerce as well as key colleagues in the community. Many in the company would be quite upset if the sales budget were cut and would not hesitate to gain support by whatever means possible.

MOSS ON OUR BACKS: A SCHOOL AND COMMUNITY CONFLICT

Scenario

A group of parents have come together out of frustration with the "lack of discipline" at Sunnyside School. Calling themselves "Make Our School Safe" (MOSS), these parents have begun to show up at school unannounced, confronting misbehaving children on the playground, criticizing teachers for lack of toughness and, ultimately, calling for the resignation of the principal for his "lack of backbone." In response to this parental movement, another group of parents has formed, "Caring for Children" (CFC). They feel that the school has made great strides in recent years, since a more child-centered curriculum was introduced to the students. They feel that only a few disruptive students are responsible, and that the MOSS group has overreacted and undermined the integrity of the teachers.

Previously, there has been a Parent Forum at which MOSS and CFC members ended up hurling epithets at each other. The principal, under attack by the MOSS group, has welcomed the support of the CFC's. But he is concerned that their approach inappropriately blames kids; he wants a more integrated approach to the problem of school violence, involving social services, additional training for staff in conflict resolution, and a better playground supervision program during recess and other transition times. The superintendent, in the meantime, has been very noncommittal; he doesn't want to alienate MOSS or CFC parents. So he has asked you to facilitate the upcoming Parent Forum.

MOSS Representative

This school is out of control! Teachers aren't firm enough with kids, and the principal is more concerned with being nice than in promoting discipline and order. All of these "special needs" children are taking too much time away from my children receiving an education. This district should set up a separate program for those kids, bring expectations back to school, and get a new principal who can stand up to these CFC liberals.

CFC Representative

MOSS represents a significant danger to the needs of all children, and they must be stopped now! Rarely do I get involved in such things, and frankly, I'm afraid that I will be shouted down in the forum. But the principal has made such great changes in these past two years and should be supported. There was a caring, positive environment at Sunnyside again—at least until MOSS got on our backs!

Principal

I've worked hard to create a positive environment at Sunnyside in my two years here. My staff is behind me, but these MOSS parents bring a real negative energy to our work. I appreciate their concerns: they want a safe school where kids can learn, and I agree. But "back to basics" is a phrase of a bygone era. We have kids here whose basic needs are very different, and we must promote caring and respect. I wish the superintendent would show some leadership and support me strongly, but what can you expect? Why bother?

Teacher

This principal is the best person we've had here in my fifteen years at Sunnyside. In the past two years, we've received great support in learning how to respond to disruptive kids, introduced new curricula that really prepare kids for middle school, and developed a strong corps of new teachers. There are a few old-guard staff who don't want change, but most of us support the new approach. MOSS must be eliminated. Why can't parents just let us do our jobs?!

THE GREAT SMOKE OUT

Scenario

Gazette Press has published a morning newspaper for nearly fifty years. Like most manufacturing companies, Gazette Press has undergone profound changes in personnel policies in the past few years. Recently, management has decided to prohibit smoking on plant grounds, a move that has generated controversy among workers of all ranks and departments. A smoking policy task force was formed to determine how best to implement and monitor the new policy.

You have been asked to facilitate the task force for Gazette Press. The task force has been formed to: (1) develop policies for monitoring implementation of the no-smoking rule; (2) develop educational programs for clients, staff, and others using the facilities to assist with implementation; and (3) establish a dispute settlement system for resolving conflicts that arise. Recognizing that most disputes are resolved informally, rather than through prosecution, the company president wants your task force to recommend policies that can be self-regulated by staff.

The task force, appointed by the president, includes the managing editor, the human resources director, one representative from each department, an intern, and the Employee Assistance Program (EAP) coordinator for the company.

You have been brought in as a facilitator at the request of the president, who has given you this overview of the task force. You have been given access to administrative support and research and three months to complete your work within a tight budget. This is a moderate-sized company, with modest wages, but it attracts good staff by offering interesting work, advancement opportunities, and high quality of life in the community.

Advertising Rep

You don't want to be here; there are many other things you could do with your time this summer. This a stupid rule that takes an educational and social problem and makes you a law enforcement officer. If you can get this group to refocus on the educational mission of the newspaper, rather than sanctions, it will be worthwhile. But you suspect there is another political agenda here.

Human Relations Director

It is critical that people change their attitudes about smoking (and drinking, for that matter). Our children are being taught by their parents that smoking and drinking are okay. We need policies that include positive incentives for responsible behavior and punitive consequences for negative behavior that endangers the rest of us. As a reformed smoker, you know how tough these habits are to break, and you have little sympathy for staff who want a smoking lounge in the building.

Production Rep

You have been asked to serve because, as a smoker, you have been outspoken in your opposition to the new rule. You would rather see the task force fight to change the rule, as it is too restrictive on the rights of smokers. However, you are willing to try to find a policy that accommodates the needs of people in your situation. You agree that staff should not smoke on plant grounds, except in designated areas, but you think there should be many more areas developed than this anti-smoking task force will support. That guy from human resources in always trying to foist his ideas on the rest of you!

Circulation Rep

You work in an area where hardly any staff smoke, and the only building users who want to smoke are occasional clients at meetings. You don't understand why people are so upset about the policy; it's for the good of everyone's health. You want to be sure that a prevention component in included in this policy. This is a chance to fund educational programs for nonsmokers, before they make bad choices.

Intern

You developed a peer helper program at the university last year and, while most students think it's a joke, it has made a real difference for those who have participated. You think that staff will be most responsive to hearing "don't smoke" messages from other staff and want a strong educational program established. A good public relations campaign could make all the difference in how everyone perceives the new policy. You are really excited about this task force.

Managing Editor

You volunteered at the last staff meeting to join this task force, because it is very important that a realistic policy be developed. Too often people get caught up in idealistic concepts, not dealing with the real world. People who want to smoke will smoke; we need to be realistic about that. Let's not get into trouble because a few liberals in the capital get carried away. You've smoked for twenty years with no ill effect. Your teenager smokes at home, and it's okay with you. This task force had better not spin its wheels with do-good ideas that will waste the company's money (you're a shareholder, too)!

Accounting Rep

You volunteered at the last department meeting because the managing editor was selected—and he's a nut! He actually encourages smoking (and drinking, you're told) at home. His kid is a real troublemaker at the high school, according to your son. Anyway, you don't know what the best policy should be. You are open to hearing ideas, but that editor does not speak for all staff in the company!

EAP Coordinator

Finally, the opportunity to really make some changes around here! You know you were appointed to this group because you are strongly anti-smoking. Perhaps you can use this as a chance to have meaningful programs to eliminate drinking among staff, too. It's been accepted as part of the territory around here for too long! A comprehensive approach is required: clearly spelled out policies with consequences for breaking rules having both a punishment and a counseling component. A full-scale educational program—taught by you—will be important, as well, targeted at the entry and middle levels, where so many staff start to smoke and drink. A community component will be needed, too. Staff will need to model desired behaviors, so a smoking cessation program (with the American Cancer Society) should be established. You have lots of ideas about how to make this work—when do you get started?!

PORTNOY'S COMPLAINT (REVISITED): A ROLE PLAY IN MORALE BUILDING

Scenario

Elliot Portnoy has been with the company for twenty years. He has his share of accomplishments, to be sure, but he has gained greatest notoriety for his unwillingness to take on new responsibilities. Elliot is perceived as a foot dragger, a low-risk person, and so forth. The other members of his department range from being grateful to him for setting such a low standard and disgust at management for not firing him. Recently, a new Quality Management Initiative has been introduced by the president. Each department is to develop its own quality standards for submission to a QMI task force that will monitor efforts, reward successes (they have a generous budget), and report noncompliance to the president. There will be monthly QMI "Outstanding Department" awards and paid time off for outstanding contributions to the effort.

But Elliot Portnoy has a complaint. "We've had lots of these so-called innovations through the years," he says. "Why should you or I get too excited about something that is merely a new stress, a new pressure? I think we shouldn't fix what isn't broken around here."

You, as one of the people trying to facilitate the development of the new QMI standards in this department, are concerned about how widespread Portnoy's complaint is felt. You've heard that several people view this meeting as a waste of time, just preventing them from getting their work done. Yet, there are others who have gone out of their way to thank you for coming to get their team together and moving. You believe this QMI is great stuff—your department is excited about it, why not everyone else?

This scenario is a loosely structured situation for facilitators to consider. Roles may include management reps, QMI task force members, staff who seek higher standards, and those wishing to maintain status quo. Of course, someone should play Portnoy. Facilitators should recognize their own possible biases here: Are we able to regard Portnoy's complaint with respect, although we support the change he resists?

SUNNYSIDE SOCIAL SERVICES: A CONFLICT IN COMMUNITY DECISION MAKING (Adapted from a role play by CDR Associates, Boulder, CO)

Scenario

Sunnyside Social Services (SSS) is a well-respected agency that has provided services for children and adults with disabilities since 1954. With group homes throughout the state, SSS offers opportunities for persons with mental retardation, autism, and mental illness to become better integrated into the community, rather than face otherwise institutional lives. Through creative approaches to work and curriculum, clients are able to contribute to the communities in which they live. Staff seek employment opportunities for clients and provide job training and supervision with cooperating firms. The result is that SSS has gained a national reputation for its innovative programs and the ability of clients to acquire independent living skills.

A newly proposed group home will house eight to twelve men, ages eighteen to sixty-five. Although family and friends may visit, they may not stay at SSS more than two days, and guest rooms are limited. The site is a former hotel in Waterville, a small town of 4000 people, located near the town's compact business district. The site overlooks Lake Waterville, a popular recreation spot for both summer and winter sports.

A neighborhood group has been formed, "Concerned Citizens of Waterville" (CCW), that is strongly opposed to the location of this group home in Waterville. CCW's chairperson, Pat Leak, has lived in Waterville for many years and has many family members who live in the community. Pat sees the group home as a threat to the good family life of the town, bringing in people who pose a danger to safety. The SSS Director, Bobby Goldberg, has taken a calm, low-key approach to addressing the Concerned Citizens and has requested a meeting to air differences and find solutions.

(You have been asked by the town to facilitate a meeting to try to resolve differences. The mayor would prefer a consensus recommendation regarding the group home. For now, the issue has split the town into two camps whose rhetoric will likely escalate into violence. CCW has threatened to block the SSS home, while SSS is known to have gone to court elsewhere to force communities to accept its clients. The hotel has been on the market for some time, so another buyer is not likely to emerge in the near term. This concerns the chamber of commerce, which has been trying to attract a buyer who would further develop the motel's recreational potential.

The meeting involves Pat Leak, Bobby Goldberg, a chamber of commerce representative, the social worker from SSS who will head the group home, a Department of Human Services representative, a school board member, and a representative from the Waterville mayor's office.

Pat Leak

You are the head of Concerned Citizens of Waterville, the group opposing the home. You feel that these retarded people have no business in a small town, that they might get out and threaten children, and so on. You have lots of friends and family in this town; if the mayor doesn't back you on this, you'll lead a recall effort. This Goldberg is just another New York Jew bringing liberal values to your town . . . a carpetbagger.

Bobby Goldberg

You've seen this nonsense before, as head of SSS since 1980. Throughout the state, small towns are full of people like Leak. Even so, you have found it most fruitful to negotiate, listen, and calmly find solutions. This location is perfect, with great recreational and employment opportunities for clients. Besides, you have a staff person to head the effort from this area. You will work to stay calm, and try to avoid a costly legal battle. You just want to get out so you can return to the city without getting stuck here in the sticks for too long!

Chamber of Commerce Rep

You don't want Waterville to be put on the map by this conflict; it would ruin a business environment that is already suffering from competition from gambling. Leak has lots of friends—including you—but this could blow up in their faces. Why couldn't there be a nice motel operator who could come in and do something positive with this site? Why couldn't SSS find another town for this group home where "these people" could be happy and away from us?

School Board

You are quite concerned about the costs of special education programs in our schools. Any efforts to mainstream are to be opposed.

DHS Rep

You want this site established quickly. You have a backlog of clients who are qualified for such placement, and SSS does good work. You've driven up from Capital City for this meeting and want to get back quickly.

SSS Social Worker

You grew up around Waterville and went to school with many members of CCW. They are good people who are being misled by Pat Leak, a hothead who has bugged you for years. You wish this thing could disappear so the group could get on with renovating the hotel and starting the program. Your spouse is eager to move back here and you'd like to stop your one-hour commute. But Goldberg might not be tough enough here or understand that these people are set in their ways. If they don't agree, go to court.

Appendix C

Sample Set of Meeting Notes from the Facilitator

To: ABC Agency Staff
From: Facilitator Frank
Re: Tentative Understandings Reached
Date: 9/5/97

I appreciated the candor and positive energy with which people approached our initial meeting. Although people came to the meeting with a number of concerns, we made great progress in identifying these issues and developing strategies for addressing them. While this meeting was just the beginning of our work together, it represents some positive initial steps that should result in real long-term progress.

The following notes reflect tentative understandings reached regarding expectations you may hold for one another at this time. Please review these notes for clarity and accuracy, as well as omissions of other ideas agreed upon by the group. Some items may be redundant or otherwise unnecessary to express, as well. You may either send comments to me directly or bring them to our meeting on the 11th. Thanks, again, for your efforts to be honest with one another and your dedication to improving the overall program in your department.

We dedicate ourselves to meeting the following expectations:

1. That we dedicate ourselves to the client as the core of our work, including: (a) providing technical knowledge; and (b) providing additional support and referral resources, as needed.
2. That we need to focus on "we" and set aside "me" in this process.

3. That we focus on the present and the future, rather than the past, in this process.
4. That we recognize one another's dedication and contributions beyond the title. This includes: (a) educating one another regarding additional projects and contributions made by each staff member; and (b) recognizing accomplishments and improvement made over the past few years.
5. That we work to agree on common goals for our clients — and methods to get there.
6. That we develop a quality program that others will recognize as such, and of which all of us will be proud.
7. That we will work together and not "end run" each other. We agree not to make derogatory comments regarding each other to clients, colleagues, or others.
8. That we will work to meet the skills expected of the Standard Training *and* additional academic skills appropriate to an Advanced Professional Certificate.
9. That we will exercise patience and respect for one another as we attempt to make improvements in the program.
10. That we will demonstrate a positive attitude toward one another and our program. We will bring renewed energy to meet these challenges.
11. That we will dedicate ourselves to manage our projects well, for that is at the heart of our enterprise.
12. That we will use the move of the department as an opportunity to forge a better program and improved program identity.
13. That if we have specific issues or concerns, we need to communicate them directly with one another.
14. That we shall treat each other as equals. We will attempt to move beyond the factions of the past to a collective "we."
15. That we recognize Max as a dedicated, hard-working director, deserving our respect. We would benefit greatly from his continued leadership of the department.
16. That we will work to stay current and relevant in the field, updating our knowledge of policy and procedures, research, etc. so we may better serve our clients. We need to inform one another of work we are doing in this effort and share information together.

The group expressed a desire to focus on topical issues that need resolution next time. Some possible topics for this discussion:

Overall Goals of the Program
Project Sequencing
Project Content
Strategies Appropriate to Meet Goals
Internship Program
Additional Responsibilities
Communication With Top Management Regarding Concerns

These are some of the topics I have understood to be difficult for you to discuss and resolve by consensus. I'd appreciate your considering their appropriateness for our next meeting. If possible, select one for that discussion. Please feel free to consider other topics, as well.

Tentative Agenda for the 11th:

Check in
Review of Tentative Understanding of Expectations
Topical Issue (See above list for ideas)
Next Steps/ Timeline for Addressing Key Issues
Communication of the Results of These Discussions: What should be shared with top
    management? Other departments? Others with a need to know? How will this
    occur?
Evaluation of Next Steps

Please review these notes and the tentative agenda for next time. I'd appreciate comments written to my e-mail at *facilfrank@mtgs.org* or your comments by phone at 999-555-1212 no later than the 4th. Thanks, again, for your dedication and interest.

Glossary of Terms

Accommodating: a style of dealing with conflict in which the needs of others overwhelm one's own, in an effort to be diplomatic; characterized by submissive communication; also known as smoothing.

Active listening: the process of seeking to understand another person's point of view, demonstrating a desire to understand the meaning of that person's communication without judgment.

Adjourning: the process of ending a meeting or ending a group's work together.

Affinity grouping: an idea-generating strategy for group problem solving, in which ideas are written down on small sheets of paper, then pooled for evaluation.

Affirming environment: a positive, respectful atmosphere in which to communicate.

Agenda: an intentional ordering of items for discussion, related to the purpose of the meeting.

Assertive communication: the sharing of one's needs and concerns, while respecting the needs of other persons involved.

Avoiding: a conflict style in which disagreements and concerns go unexpressed, often making the circumvented conflict worse.

BATNA: Best Alternative To a Negotiated Agreement.

Behavioral responses: actions in reaction to conflict, such as yelling, walking out, withdrawal, or negotiating.

Blocking: a way of stopping consensus; functions like a veto in group decision making; parliamentary filibusters and reconsiderations are the most formal and subversive examples of blocking.

Brainstorming: a process for generating ideas in a non-judgmental environment; within a group, all members offer thoughts and suggestions as they come to mind, without giving negative feedback or criticism to others' ideas; ideally, an open forum, which enhances creative thinking by building on others' suggestions.

Cadre: from military origins; a group or team, usually with a common background or goal, often to train others in a particular skill.

Caucus: a private meeting outside of a larger group; analogous to a legal sidebar.

Check-in: opportunity at the start of a meeting for participants to share how they are feeling; helps eliminate distractions later in the meeting.

Closed response: a response from a listener that denies a speaker a right to his/her feelings by demonstrating the listener's unwillingness to accept and understand.

Cognitive responses: thoughts and ideas about a conflict, often present as inner voices.

Collaborating: the pooling of individual needs and goals towards a common goal; produces a better solution than any individual party could achieve alone; a conflict style.

Competing: a conflict style in which one's own needs overwhelm the needs of others; often characterized by aggressive communication; tends to result in conflict escalation.

Compromising: a conflict style involving tradeoffs, resulting in some sense of satisfaction, but no real exploration of the underlying needs of the disputing parties.

Conflict styles: personal manners of dealing with conflict.

Consensus: a situation in which all members of a group find an outcome or decision to be acceptable.

Council: a Native American tradition in which participants meet to voice personal, and often passionate, responses to issues and to listen with reverence to others' thoughts on the same issues; primarily concerned with achieving a clear, respectful understanding together; a model for communication as the underpinning of the democratic meeting.

Decision items: on a meeting agenda, items which require judgments and decisions, following discussion.

Democracy: a form of government in which power is invested in a group of people, characterized by an equality of rights and the freedom to express opinions.

Discussion items: on a meeting agenda, items which require judgments and decisions, following discussion.

Emotional responses: feelings during a conflict, such as anger, fear, confusion, or elation.

Empathy: the ability to put oneself in another person's position and understand that point of view.

Facilitator: one who makes a process easy; a person empowered by a group to a guardian of a process, e.g., a meeting.

Filibuster: a way of forcing or blocking a group decision, usually by holding the floor and talking nonstop, thereby using up all the available discussion time; often used in parliamentary or legislative proceedings.

Forming: the initial phase of group development in which the group's members are chosen and the purpose for their work together is determined.

Future Problem Solving Model: a strategy for problem solving which uses scenarios likely to occur in the future to help problem solvers focus on long-term, as well as short-term, solutions.

Ground rules: the rules of conduct that govern the interactions of group members.

IDEAL: a simplified version of the classic linear problem-solving model; stands for Identify the problem, Develop alternative possible solutions, Evaluate solutions, Analyze the preferred solution, and Live and learn.

"I"-message: a technique for expressing one's feelings without evaluating or blaming others; "I"-messages connect a feeling statement with the specific behavior of another person.

Impasse: a point at which parties feel they are no longer able to find effective solutions; often a normal phase of the conflict resolution process.

Information items: on a meeting agenda, items which are brief, timely and offer relevant information; characterized by one-way communication, versus discussion.

MLATNA: Most Likely Alternative To a Negotiated Agreeement.

Mediator: an impartial third party who facilitates the resolution of conflict between two or more parties.

Mind Mapping: a nonlinear problem-solving strategy which usually connects seemingly disparate issues with lines radiating from a common concern, following the mind's associative route and allowing for tangents.

Multi-party disputes: conflicts involving two or more people or factions.

Nominal group technique: a strategy for developing options in problem solving, wherein participants privately generate solutions and share them "round robin."

Norming: the second phase of group development in which the group develops its standards and procedures for effective group functioning.

Open response: a response from a listener that acknowledges a speaker's right to his/her feelings.

Open-ended question: a question that cannot be answered with a simple "yes" or "no" response and might be interpreted to suggest a variety of creative responses or stimulate brainstorming.

Opening statement: in a facilitated meeting, the introduction given by the facilitator to set the tone for the meeting, establish ground rules, and clarify the process.

Participatory management: a strategy for business administration in which all levels of employees are included in the decision-making process and encouraged to feel like stakeholders in corporate outcomes.

Performing: a phase of group development in which all members are functioning as a true team to meet a common goal.

Physical responses: bodily reactions to conflict, such as muscle tension, sweating, and dry mouth.

Polling: the act of canvassing a group to obtain its members' opinions about a specific issue or to determine how they are likely to vote in a decision-making process.

Pre-negotiation: the intervention of a concerned third party to encourage participation in the negotiation or discussion process; can take place prior to a meeting or between meetings.

Problem solving: an intentional and systematic process by which effective responses are sought for difficult situations.

Procedural concerns: issues that relate to process in problem solving.

Psychological concerns: issues that relate to the emotional well-being of group members.

Reconsideration: a usually subversive technique for stalling discussion, in which a group is asked to consider a decision again or vote on an action again in hopes of a new outcome; often used in parliamentary proceedings.

Restating: an active listening technique in which the listener restates by repeating or rephrasing a speaker's basic idea or facts to show that the listener hears and understands.

Robert's Rules of Order: a set of formal rules governing parliamentary procedure, adopted by some organizations as the standard for meeting procedure.

Self-directed work teams: work groups that function outside the traditional corporate hierarchy by conducting primarily internal agenda setting, decision making, reporting, and evaluation.

Stakeholder: one who has a vested interest in a situation or outcome.

Storming: a phase in group development in which conflict or impasse is present.

Substantive concerns: the meat of a discussion; the issue that most view as the basis of a problem to be solved.

Team: any group of people who need each other to accomplish a result.

Team-based management: an alternative to the traditional hierarchical model of centralized management, where employees belong and report to teams, who are largely independent and laterally equivalent to other teams.

Technocratic decision making: decision making based on knowledge of technical or scientific information.

WATNA: Worst Alternative To a Negotiated Agreement.

Win-win problem solving: a collaborative approach to finding solutions, based on understanding all parties' underlying needs and developing alternatives that agree with everyone (vs. competitive win-lose problem solving, where one party wins and another loses).

Bibliography

Ackoff, Russell. *The Art of Problem Solving*. New York: John Wiley and Sons, 1978.

Alexander, Mark. "The Team Effectiveness Critique." *The 1985 Annual Developing Human Resources* 14: 101–5.

Alpert, Rebecca, and Jacob Straub. *Exploring Judaism: A Reconstructionist Approach*. New York: The Reconstructionist Press, 1985.

Auvine, Brian, Betsy Densmore, M. Extrom, M. Scott Poole, and M. Shanklin. *A Manual for Group Facilitators*. Madison, WI: Center for Conflict Resolution, 1977.

Avery, Michel, B. Steibel, Brian Auvine, and Lonnie Weiss. *Building United Judgment: A Handbook for Consensus Decision Making*. Madison, WI: Center for Conflict Resolution, 1981.

Axelrod, Robert. *The Evolution of Cooperation*. New York: Basic Books, 1984.

Bartoo, Glenn. *Decision by Consensus; A Study of the Quaker Method*. Chicago: Progressive Publishing, 1978.

Beer, Jennifer, ed. *Mediator's Handbook—Peacemaking in Your Neighborhood*. Concordville, PA: Friends Suburban Project, 1982.

Blanchard, Kenneth, and Spencer Johnson. *The One Minute Manager*. New York: Berkley Books, 1981.

Block, Peter. *The Empowered Manager*. San Francisco: Jossey-Bass Publishing, 1989.

Bolton, Robert. *People Skills: How to Assert Yourself, Listen to Others and Resolve Conflicts*. New York: Simon and Schuster, 1978.

Bondurant, Joan. *Conquest of Violence*. Princeton, NJ: Princeton University Press, 1958.

Bransford, John, and Barry Stein. *The Ideal Problem Solver*. New York: W. H. Freeman and Co., 1984.

Bridges, William. *Managing Transitions*. Reading, MA: Addison-Wesley Publishing Co., 1991.

Brown, David. "Piecing Together the Evidence." *Washington Post*, 19 May 1992.

Brown, George Isaac. *Human Teaching for Human Learning*. New York: Viking Press, 1971.

Bush, Robert Baruch, and Joe Folger. *The Promise of Mediation.* San Francisco: Jossey-Bass Publishing, 1994.

Buzan, Tony. *Use Both Sides of Your Brain.* New York: Plume Publishing, 1991.

———. *The Mind Map Book.* New York: Plume Publishing, 1996.

Cartwright, D., and A. Zander, eds. *Group Dynamics: Research and Theory.* New York: Harper and Row, 1968.

Center for Conflict Resolution. Archives 1974–1988. State of Wisconsin Historical Society, Madison, WI.

Covey, Stephen R. *Principle-Centered Leadership.* New York: Simon and Schuster, 1990a.

———. *The Seven Habits of Highly Effective People.* New York: Simon and Schuster, 1990b.

Crum, Thomas. *The Magic of Conflict.* New York: Simon and Schuster, 1978.

Davis, M., E. R. Eshelman, and M. McKay. *The Relaxation and Stress Reduction Workbook.* Oakland, CA: New Harbinger Publications, 1988.

Delbecq, Andre, Andrew Van de Van, and David Gustafson. *Group Techniques for Program Planning: A Guide to Nominal and Delphi Process.* New York: Scott, Foresman and Co., 1975.

Deutsch, Morton. *The Resolution of Conflict.* New Haven, CT: Yale University Press, 1973.

Dewey, John. *Democracy and Education.* New York: Macmillan, 1916.

The Empire Strikes Back. Lucasfilms, Ltd. and Twentieth Century Fox, Corp., 1980.

Faber, Adele, and Elaine Mazlish. *Siblings Without Rivalry.* New York: Avon Books, 1987.

Filley, Alan. *Interpersonal Conflict Resolution.* New York: Scott, Foresman and Co., 1975.

Fisher, Roger, and Scott Brown. *Getting Together: Building Relationships as We Negotiate.* Boston: Houghton Mifflin, 1981.

Fisher, Roger, and William Ury. *Getting to Yes: Negotiating Agreement Without Giving In.* New York: Penguin Books, 1981.

Fluegelman, Andres, ed. *The New Games Book.* San Francisco: New Games Foundation, 1976.

Folberg, Jay, and Alison Taylor. *Mediation.* San Franciso: Jossey-Bass Publishing, 1984.

Folger, Joseph, and M. Scott Poole. *Working Through Conflict.* Glenview, IL: Scott, Foresman and Co., 1984

Follett, Mary Parker. *Creative Experience.* New York: Longmans, Green and Co., 1924.

Freire, Paolo. *Pedagogy in Process: The Letters to Guinea-Bissau.* New York: Seabury Press, 1978.

———. *Pedagogy of the Oppressed.* Herder and Herder, 1971.

Gandhi, Mohandas. *Non-Violent Resistance.* New York: Schocken Books, 1951.

———. *My Experiments with Truth.* Boston: Beacon Press, 1957.

Gastil, John. *Democracy in Small Groups.* Philadelphia: New Society Publishers, 1993.

Geschka, Horst, Ute von Reibnitz, and Kjetil Storvik. *Idea Generation Methods: Creative Solutions to Business and Technical Problems.* Battelle Technical Inputs to Planning Review No. 5. Columbus, OH: Battelle Press, 1981.

Goldsmith, Emanuel, Mel Scult, and Robert Seltzer, eds. *The American Judaism of Mordecai M. Kaplan.* New York: New York University Press, 1990.

Havelock, R. G., and A. M. Huberman. *Solving Educational Problems: The Theory and Reality of Innovation in Developing Countries.* Geneva, Switzerland: UNESCO, 1977.

Hayes, J. R. *The Complete Problem Solver.* Philadelphia: Franklin Institute Press, 1981.

Heitler, Susan. *From Conflict to Resolution.* New York: W. W. Norton and Company, 1990.

Hersey, Paul, and Kenneth Blanchard. *Management of Organizational Behavior.* Englewood

Cliffs, NJ: Prentice Hall, 1988.

Holt, John. *How Children Fail.* New York: Dell Publishing, 1964.

———. *How Children Learn.* New York: Dell Publishing, 1967.

———. *Freedom and Beyond.* New York: Dell Publishing, 1972.

———. *Instead of Education.* New York: Dell Publishing Co., 1974.

Illich, Ivan. *Deschooling Society.* New York: Harper and Row, 1970.

Janis, Irving, and Leon Mann. *Decision Making.* New York: The Free Press, 1977.

Karp, Henry B. "Team Building from a Gestalt Perspective." *The 1980 Annual Handbook for Group Facilitators* (San Diego, CA: University Associates, 1980: 157–160.

Kormanski, Chuck, and Andrew Mozenter. "A New Model for Team Building: Technology for Today and Tomorrow." *The 1987 Annual Developing Human Resources* 16: 255–268.

Kozol, Jonathon. *Death at an Early Age.* New York: Bantam Books: 1967.

———. *Free Schools.* New York: Bantam Books, 1972

Kreidler, William. *Elementary Perspectives 1: Teaching Concepts of Peace and Conflict.* Cambridge, MA: Educators for Social Responsibility, 1990.

LaBorde, Genie. *Influencing with Integrity.* Palo Alto, CA: Syntony Publishers, 1987.

Lewin, Kurt. *Resolving Social Conflict.* New York: Harper and Bros., 1948.

———. *Field Theory in Social Science.* New York: Harper and Bros., 1951.

Lippitt, Gordon. *A Handbook for Visual Problem Solving.* Bethesda, MD: Development Publications, 1983.

Mayer, Bernard. "The Dynamics of Power in Mediation and Negotiation." *Mediation Quarterly,* no.16 (1987): 75–86.

McKay, Matthew, Martha Davis, and Patrick Fanning. *Thoughts and Feelings: The Art of Cognitive Stress Intervention.* Oakland, CA: New Harbinger Publications, 1981.

Moore, Christopher. *The Mediation Process.* San Francisco: Jossey-Bass Publishing, 1986.

Osborn, Alexander. *Applied Imagination: Principles and Procedures of Creative Problem Solving.* New York: Scribner's, 1963.

Pfeiffer, J. William, ed. *A Handbook of Structured Experiences for Human Relations Training.* San Diego, CA: University Associates, annual, 1972–1997.

Pilati, David. *Organizational Conflict and the Use of Independent Mediation.* Milwaukee, WI: Pilati and Associates, 1984.

Prutzman, Priscilla, Lee Stern, M. Leonard Burger, and Gretchen Bodenhamer. *The Friendly Classroom for a Small Planet.* Nyack, NY: Children's Creative Response to Conflict Programs, 1987.

Rapoport, Analol. *Fights, Games and Debates.* Ann Arbor, MI: University of Michigan Press, 1960.

———. *Cooperation.* Ann Arbor, MI: University of Michigan Press, 1964.

Reilly, Anthony. "Individual Needs and Organizational Goals: An Experiential Lecture." *1974 Annual Handbook for Group Facilitators:* 215–220.

Return of the Jedi. Los Angeles: Lucasfilms, Ltd. and Twentieth Century Fox Corp., 1983.

Rosen, H. Robert, and Lisa Berger. *The Healthy Company.* Los Angeles: Jeremy P. Tarcher, Inc., 1991.

Satir, Virginia. *Peoplemaking.* Mountain View, CA: Science and Behavior Books, 1972.

———. *The New Peoplemaking.* Mountain View, CA: Science and Behavior Books, 1988.

Senge, Peter. *The Fifth Discipline.* Garden City, NY: Doubleday, 1990.

Senge, Peter, C. Roberts, R. Ross, and A. Kleiner. *The Fifth Discipline Fieldbook: Strategies and Tools for Building a Learning Organization.* New York: Doubleday Books, 1994.

Shaw, Marvin E. *Group Dynamics: The Psychology of Small Group Behavior.* New York:

McGraw-Hill, 1976.

Singer, Linda. *Settling Disputes.* Boulder, CO: Westview Press, 1990.

Star Wars. Los Angeles: Lucasfilms, Ltd. and Twentieth Century Fox Corp., 1977.

Taft, Susan Hoefflinger. "Use of the Collaborative Ethic and Contingency Theories in Conflict Management." *The 1987 Annual Developing Human Resources* 16: 187–196.

Teachable Moments: A Newsletter for Teaching Peace. Available from the Stanley Foundation, 216 Sycamore Street, Muscatine, IA, 52761.

Thomas, Kenneth, and Ralph Killman. *Conflict Mode Instrument.* Tuxedo, NY: XICOM, Inc., 1979.

Trueblood, D. Elton. *The People Called Quakers.* Richmond, IN: Friends United Press, 1966.

Ury, William. *Getting Past No: Negotiating with Difficult People.* New York: Bantam Books, 1991.

Ury, William, Jeanne M. Brett, and Scott B. Goldberg. *Getting Disputes Resolved.* San Francisco: Jossey-Bass Publishing, 1988.

Varney, Glenn. *Building Productive Teams.* San Francisco: Jossey-Bass Publishing, 1989.

Von Oech, Roger. *A Whack on the Side of the Head.* New York: Warner Books, 1983.

Weeks, Dudley. *The Eight Essential Steps to Conflict Resolution.* New York: Tarcher Books, 1992.

Weisbord, Marvin, and Sandra Janoff. *Future Search: An Action Guide to Finding Common Ground in Organizations and Communities.* San Francisco, CA: Berrett-Koehler Publishers, 1995.

Woodcock, George. *Mohandas Gandhi.* New York: Viking Press, 1971.

Zimmerman, Jack, and Virginia Coyle "Council: Reviving the Art of Listening," *Utne Reader* (March/April 1991): 79–85.

Index

Active listening. *See* Listening
Adjourning, 37, 131, 159–61, 164–65
Affirming environment, 8, 50, 110
Agendas, 3, 43–44; in case studies,
118, 119–20, 133; decision items
on, 29, 33–34; discussion items on,
28–29, 33; examples of, 39–40,
45–46, 104; information items on,
28, 33; modifying, 41, 106, 121;
sequencing items on, 29–30; setting,
22, 28–31, 40, 162; time allotments,
30–31; timing meetings and, 30–31;
types of items on, 28–29
Alexander, Mark, 126
American civil rights movement, 172.
See also Nonviolence movement
Amnesty International, 172. *See also*
Nonviolence movement
Assertiveness, 14–16, 127
Axelrod, Robert, 79

BATNA (Best Alternative To a
Negotiated Agreement), 83, 88, 90,
107 n.3. *See also* Conflict
resolution
Blocking, 112. *See also* Consensus;
Decision making

Buzan, Tony, 54. *See also* Mind
Mapping

"Campus Scenario: 2010," 61, 64. *See
also* Problem solving
Caucus, 35–36, 88, 90
Center for Conflict Resolution, 2,
121–24, 169–70
Check-in, 27, 45, 46, 114, 115, 121
Check-out, 45, 46, 114, 127
Chicago Bulls, 130
Closure, 37–38, 41, 42
Collaborative Initiative, 121
Common Ground Network for Life and
Choice, 101–3
Conflict: budget, 76, 77; cycle, 72–75;
defined, 71; responses to, 72–73.
See also Conflict resolution
Conflict resolution, 40, 71–107;
activities in, 92–95; BATNA, 83,
88, 90, 107; case studies in, 95–106;
"Global Deadlines" activity, 94–95;
impasse and, 86–90; MLATNA, 83,
88, 90; multi-party disputes, 81,
90–92; "My Conflict" activity,
92–94; using PEACE/6 in, 82–85;
styles, 76–78, 154; teams and, 126;

triangle of needs in, 81; WATNA,
  83, 88, 90
Consensus: activities using, 94–95;
  blocking, 112; building, 37,
  110–11; case studies in, 41, 115–24;
  defined, 36; facilitating, 109–24;
  polling, 111–12, 119
Council, 11
Creative Education Foundation, 57.
  See also Future Problem Solving
  Model

Decision items, 29; examples of, 46; in
  sample agenda form, 46
Decision making, 41, 42, 43, 53,
  112–14, 127; advisory opinions,
  112–13; consensus, 109–24;
  evaluation, 114–115; voting, 113.
  See also Consensus
Democracy, 5, 44
Democratic educational reform,
  170–71. *See also* Dewey, John;
  Freire, Paolo; Holt, John; Kozol,
  Jonathan
Dewey, John, 170–71. *See also*
  Democratic educational reform
Discussion items, 28–29; examples of
  45–46; in sample agenda form, 46

Employee Involvement (EI) program,
  170. *See also* Participatory
  management
Evaluation, 37–38, 97, 114–15, 127,
  130

Facilitated meeting process, 21–48;
  agenda setting, 28–31, 40; between
  meetings, 38–39; building
  consensus, 36–37; case studies in,
  39–46; closing and evaluation,
  37–38; meeting and greeting,
  22–23, 40; negotiating through
  impasse, 34–36; opening statement
  and ground rules, 23–28, 40; pre-
  negotiation, 21–22, 39–40; problem
  solving, 33–34, 40; sharing ideas
  and concerns, 31–33, 40. *See also*
  Agendas; Conflict resolution;
  Consensus; Evaluation; Ground

rules; Impasse; Pre-negotiation;
  Problem solving
Facilitator: biases, 32, 98; as
  communicator, 11–12, 13–14;
  defined, 1–2; external, 40, 41,
  43–44, 95–101, 103–6, 115–21,
  132–33, 134–35; internal, 41,
  132–33, 133–34; neutrality of, 2,
  12–14, 35, 88, 91, 92; role in
  clarifying goals and agendas, 3, 34,
  42; role between meetings, 38–39;
  role in building consensus, 36–37,
  109–124; role in conflictive
  situations, 71–78, 80–92, 95–106;
  role in managing transitions, 43;
  role in multi-party disputes, 90–92;
  role in negotiating for process,
  14–15, 43; role in negotiating
  through impasse, 34–36, 86–90;
  role in problem solving, 33–34, 42,
  49–70; role in stages of group
  development, 145–165; role in team
  development, 125–142; role in
  value-based disputes, 101–103;
  sharing the role of, 4, 46; summary
  of responsibilities, 5. *See also*
  Agendas; Conflict resolution;
  Consensus; Facilitated meeting
  process; Groups; Impasse; Problem
  solving; Teams
Field theory, 146
Follett, Mary Parker, 168. *See also*
  Quakerism
Ford Motor Company, 170. *See also*
  Participatory management
Forming, 147–50. *See also* Groups,
  stages of development
Fox, George, 167. *See also* Quakerism
Freedom Riders, 172. *See also*
  Nonviolence movement
Freire, Paolo, 47, 170, 171. *See also*
  Democratic educational reform
Future Problem Solvers, 57. *See also*
  Future Problem Solving Model;
  Problem solving
Future Problem Solving Model (FPS),
  57–58, 65–66, 111; Future Problem
  Solvers, 57; Future Search, 55. *See*
  also Problem solving

Future Search, 55. *See also* Future Problem Solving Model; Problem solving

Gandhi, Mohandas, 171–72. *See also* Nonviolence movement
"Global Deadlines" activity, 94–95. *See also* Conflict resolution
"Goldstein's Delicatessen" activity, 60–61. *See also* Problem solving
Ground rules, 23–27, 110; activity, 26–27; in case studies, 40, 43, 102, 104, 115, 119, 133; in conflict resolution, 88, 90; consensus and, 36; establishing, 23–25; examples of, 25; in sample agenda form, 46. *See also* Facilitated meeting process
Groups: adjourning, 159–61, 164–65; forming, 147–50; milestones of development for, 161–65; norming, 150–53; performing, 157–58; stages of development, 145–65; storming, 154–56, 163–64

The Harvard Negotiation Project, 107 n.3
Healthy organizations, 127–29. *See also* Teams
Holt, John, 170, 171, 173. *See also* Democratic educational reform
How Children Fail, 171. *See also* Holt, John
How Children Learn, 171. *See also* Holt, John

IDEAL, 52–54, 70, 111. *See also* Problem solving
"I"-Messages, 15–16. *See also* Listening
Impasse, 96, 163; defined, 34; negotiating through, 34–36; strategies for managing, 35–36, 86–90. *See also* Conflict resolution
Information items, 28; examples of 45–46; in sample agenda form, 46. *See also* Agendas
Interaction theory, 146. *See also* Groups

Jackson, Phil, 130

Jacksteidt, Mary, 102. *See also* Common Ground Network for Life and Choice
Judaism, 169. *See also* Reconstructionist Judaism

Kaplan, Rabbi Mordecai, 169. *See also* Reconstructionist Judaism
Kaufmann, Adrienne, 102. *See also* Common Ground Network for Life and Choice
King, Dr. Martin Luther, Jr., 172. *See also* Nonviolence movement
Kozol, Jonathan, 173 n. *See also* Democratic educational reform

Listening, 3, 82, 111; active listening, 3, 11–12, 13, 31–33, 35, 40, 88, 96, 110; "Active Listening Triads" activity, 17–18, "Spend a Buck" activity 18–19

Meeting and greeting, 22–23; example of 40. *See also* Facilitated meeting process
Meeting process. *See* Facilitated meeting process
Mind Mapping, 54, 57, 66–67, 111; examples of, 56, 68. *See also* Problem solving
MLATNA (Most Likely Alternative To a Negotiated Agreement), 83, 88, 90. *See also* Conflict resolution
Montessori, Maria, 171. *See also* Democratic educational reform
Multi-party disputes, 81, 90–92. *See also* Conflict resolution
"My Conflict" activity, 92–94. *See also* Conflict resolution
My Experiments with Truth, 172. *See also* Gandhi, Mohandas

NAACP, 172. *See also* Nonviolence movement
Neutrality, 2, 12–14, 35, 88, 91, 92
Nonviolence movement, 171–72; American civil rights movement, 172; Amnesty International, 172; Freedom Riders, 172; Gandhi, Mohandas, 171–72; King, Dr.

Martin Luther, Jr., 172; NAACP,
172; Plowshares International, 172;
Search for Common Ground, 101,
102, 172; Southern Poverty Law
Center, 172
Non-Violent Resistance, 172. *See also*
Gandhi, Mohandas
Norming, 150–53. *See also* Groups,
stages of development

"One Hundred Carats" activity, 58–59.
See also Problem solving
Opening statement, 23, 27–28, 40, 90,
92, 96. *See also* Facilitated meeting
process
Osborne, Alexander, 57. *See also*
Future Problem Solving Model
"Outcomes Identification Exercise,"
65, 66, 104, 140–42. *See also*
Teams

Parnes, Sidney, 57. *See also* Future
Problem Solving Model
Participative Management (PM), 170.
See also Participatory Management
Participatory management, 169–70;
Employee Involvement program,
170; Ford Motor Company, 170;
Participative Management, 170
PEACE/6, 82–85, 111. *See also*
Conflict resolution
*Pedagogy in Process: The Letters to
Guinea Bissau*, 47. *See also* Freire,
Paolo
Pedagogy of the Oppressed, 171. See
also Freire, Paolo
Performing, 157–58. *See also* Groups,
stages of development
Phelan, Alice, 138
Plowshares International, 172. *See
also* Nonviolence movement
Polling, 111–12, 119. *See also*
Consensus
Pre-negotiation, 21–22, 90, 92, 134;
examples of, 39, 41, 96, 99, 133.
See also Facilitated meeting process
"The Prisoner's Dilemma," 78–80
Problem solving, 33–34, 40, 49–70,
111, 127; activities, 58–65;
"Campus Scenario: 2010," 61, 64;

case studies in, 65–70; definition,
33, 49; Future Problem Solving
Model, 57–58, 65–66, 111; Future
Search, 55; "Goldstein's
Delicatessen" activity, 60–61;
IDEAL, 52–54, 70, 111; Mind
Mapping, 54–57, 66–67, 111; "One
Hundred Carats" activity, 58–59;
preconditions for, 49–52;
"Riverside, USA" scenario, 61,
62–63, 65; scenarios for Future
Problem Solving, 61–65; strategies
for, 52–58; "The World's Fastest
Paper Airplane" activity, 59–60
Procedural needs/concerns, 80–81, 97
Psychoanalytic orientation, 146
Psychological needs/concerns, 80–81,
97

Quaker meeting, 24, 167
Quakerism, 167–68, 169. *See also*
Follett, Mary Parker; Fox, George;
Quaker meeting

Rapoport, Anatol, 79
Reconstructionist Judaism, 167, 169
"Riverside USA" scenario, 61, 62–63,
65. *See also* Problem solving
Robert's Rules of Order, 3, 24
Rosen, Robert H., and Lisa Berger,
127, 129, 131, 170

Scenarios for Future Problem Solving,
61–64. *See also* Problem solving
Search for Common Ground, 101, 102,
172. *See also* Nonviolence
movement
Self-Directed Work Teams (SDWTs),
109–10
Situational leadership theory, 147
Society for the Advancement of
Judaism (SAJ), 169
Sociometric orientation, 146
Southern Poverty Law Center, 172.
See also Nonviolence movement
"Spend a Buck" activity, 18 – 19. *See
also* Listening
Stanley Foundation, 94
Star Wars, 89
Storming, 154–56, 163–64. *See also*

Groups, stages of development
Substantive needs/concerns, 80–81
Systems theory, 146

Teachable Moments newsletter, 94
Team Effectiveness Assessment Model
    (TEAM), 126, 135–38. *See also*
    Teams
Team Visioning Exercise, 129, 138–40.
    See also Teams
Team-Based Management, 7, 44
Teams: activities for, 135–42; agendas
    and, 45–46; building blocks, 132;
    case studies in, 132–35; definition,
    125; facilitating, 44–46, 125–43;
    factors contributing to effectiveness
    of, 126–27; healthy organizations,
    127–29; "Outcomes Identification
    Exercise," 65, 66, 104, 140–42;
    strategies for achieving healthy,
    129–31; Team Effectiveness
    Assessment Model (TEAM), 126,
    135–38; Team Visioning Exercise,
    129, 138–40
"Tit for Tat," 79–80

Value-based disputes, 101–3

WATNA (Worst Alternative To a
    Negotiated Agreement), 83, 88, 90.
    See also Conflict resolution
Win-win problem solving, 76
"The World's Fastest Paper Airplane"
    activity, 59–60

About the Author

HARRY WEBNE-BEHRMAN is Senior Partner of Collaborative Initiative, Inc., a consulting firm in Madison, Wisconsin. With more than 20 years of experience as facilitator, educator, and mediator, he has worked with hundreds of businesses, public agencies, schools and community groups to facilitate the resolution of complex problems and disputes. Webne-Behrman is well published in the journals of his field and is a past president of the Wisconsin Association of Mediators.

ISBN 1-56720-067-2

90000>

EAN

9 781567 200676

HARDCOVER BAR CODE